Two Queens
in One Isle

ALISON PLOWDEN was born in India and was formerly a script writer and editor for the BBC. Her television credits include *Mistress of Hardwick*, for which she won a Writers Guild Award. She is the author of many successful historical books including *The House of Tudor*, acclaimed by the great historian A.L. Rowse as 'Simply excellent on every count . . . impossible to fault in scholarship or writing'. This has recently been re-published by Sutton, where it joins others of her works, including *The Young Elizabeth, Tudor Women, The Stuart Princesses,* and *Women all on Fire: The Women of the English Civil War.* Alison Plowden lives near Wantage in Oxfordshire.

Praise for Alison Plowden

'The expert and scholar . . . ought to give Miss Plowden the fullest marks for remarkable accuracy'
Jasper Ridley
Glasgow Herald

'a vastly interesting account'
The Times

'Miss Plowden brings to the whole period perceptive judgment and wide sympathy'
Irish Times

'it would be difficult to praise too highly Alison Plowden's *Danger to Elizabeth* . . . her extraordinarily fine book'
Church Times

'Enchanting, scholarly and superbly written, warmly recommended'
Charity Blackstock
Books and Bookmen

'the sustained concentration on the subject and the balanced intellectual control of the elements involved make it the work of a scholar'
Stephen Wade
Catholic Herald

'Professors have something to learn from perceptive women in penetrating the very feminine psychology of Elizabeth I'
A.L. Rowse
Sunday Telegraph

'She writes with verve, brevity and often wit . . . a most entertaining book which, at the same time, is accurate and judicious'
Paul Johnson
Evening News

'an absorbing portrait of possibly the greatest tease in history'
Publishers' Weekly, USA

'a model of clarity'
G.M. Wilson
Times Literary Supplement

TWO QUEENS IN ONE ISLE

THE DEADLY RELATIONSHIP BETWEEN
ELIZABETH I &
MARY QUEEN OF SCOTS

ALISON PLOWDEN

SUTTON PUBLISHING

First published in 1984 by The Harvester Press Limited

This edition first published in 1999 by
Sutton Publishing Limited · Phoenix Mill · Stroud · Gloucestershire

Reprinted in 1999 (twice), 2000

A catalogue record for this book is available from the British Library

ISBN 0 7509 2168 4

Cover illustrations: (top) detail from the Ditchley portrait of Elizabeth I, by
Marcus van Gheeraerts the Younger, 1592; (bottom) Mary Queen of Scots, after
Nicholas Hilliard, c. 1610 (both by courtesy of the National Portrait Gallery,
London)

Printed and bound in Great Britain by
Biddles Limited, Guildford, Surrey.

'Nothing should be left undone
to perfect the amity betwixt the
two Queens in one isle.'

Francis, Duke of Guise

Contents

Acknowledgements

The author would like to thank Dr Bruce Lenman of the Department of Modern History, University of St Andrews for his help in suggesting sources for this book, and also Sir A. Goldberg, Regius Professor of Medicine, University of Glasgow for his kindness in sparing the time to discuss the question of Mary Queen of Scots and porphyria.

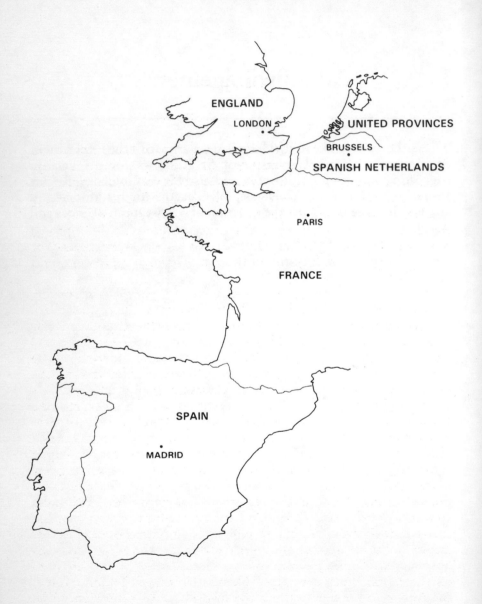

Prologue

On Thursday, 28 April 1603 the royal suburb of Westminster was packed solid with 'multitudes of all sorts of people' crowding the streets, leaning out of windows, standing on rooftops and gutters, clinging precariously to every point of vantage to watch the passing of a great funeral procession. The citizens of London—or as many as could squeeze themselves into the limited space available—had come to say goodbye to the Queen who had been reigning over England for longer than the vast majority of those present that April day could remember.

More than a thousand men and women, all in black mourning hoods and cloaks, from the humblest servants of the royal scullery and woodyard to the great officers of State, the trumpeters and sergeants-at-arms, the heralds and pursuivants, the Gentlemen and Children of the Chapel Royal, the Lord Mayor and Aldermen of the City, the judges and principal law officers of the crown, the Gentlemen Pensioners, the foreign ambassadors, Privy Councillors and lords and ladies of the Court, marched in solemn order from the Palace of Westminster to the nearby Abbey Church of St Peter to do honour to Queen Elizabeth of famous memory in an impressive display of funereal pomp and pageantry. When the purple draped coffin came in sight, drawn on an open chariot by four black trapped horses and surmounted by a lifesize waxen effigy of the Queen, dressed in her Parliament robes, with a crown on her head and a sceptre in her hand, a great sigh went up from the spectators, and such a general 'groaning and weeping as the like hath not been seen or known in the memory of man. Neither', wrote John Stow, 'doth any history mention any people, time or state, to make like lamentation for the death of their sovereign.' They laid Elizabeth Tudor to rest in the Abbey, in the north aisle of the chapel built by King Henry VII, her grandfather, and the officers of the household ceremonially broke their staves and cast them into the open grave.

A little over nine years later, in October 1612, another royal coffin was carried in procession through the London streets, when 'the corpse of Queen Mary, late Queen of Scotland, was translated from Peterborough unto St Peter's Church in Westminster.' The cortege was met at Clerkenwell, at about six o'clock on the evening of Thursday, 8 October by a deputation headed by the Archbishop of Canterbury, the Lord Chancellor and the Lord Privy Seal and escorted to Westminster, with 'plenty of torchlights' flaring in the autumn dusk. It does not appear to have attracted much public interest.

Later that same night the body of Mary Stewart, once Queen of Scotland and Queen Dowager of France, was re-buried on the south side of the Henry VII Chapel, to be closer at last in death to her cousin Elizabeth than she ever came in life. And there they lie, those two sister queens and 'tender cousins', beneath the handsome monuments piously erected by Mary's son, James I and VI, in the chapel of their common ancestor, the first Tudor king—all the bitterness and tragedy, all the passions roused by their deadly rivalry transmuted by time into dust and marble.

I

The Thistle and the Rose

I t all began with a peace treaty and a marriage: on 24 January 1502,
to be exact, when the English royal family gathered at Richmond
Palace to witness the solemn betrothal of Henry VII's eldest
daughter Margaret to James IV of Scotland. The King and Queen
were accompanied by two of their other children, ten-year-old Henry
and six-year-old Mary, and by the Queen's sister Katherine
Courtenay. Also present, as befitted so important an occasion, were
the Archbishops of Canterbury and York, the Spanish and Venetian
ambassadors with their suites, and 'likewise the members of the Privy
Council and a great number of the nobles of England' together with
their ladies. The Scottish delegation was headed by the Archbishop
of Glasgow and Patrick Hepburn, Earl of Bothwell, the bridegroom's
procurator or proxy.

After attending High Mass and listening to an eloquent sermon
preached by the Bishop of Chichester, 'the whole illustrious
company' crowded into the Queen's Great Chamber for the
betrothal ceremony itself. According to established practice, the
Archbishop of Glasgow began by asking all the parties to the
marriage contract whether they knew of any impediments or
objections. King Henry, speaking for his daughter, then asked
whether it was indeed 'the very will, mind and full intent' of the King
of Scotland that the Earl of Bothwell should, in his name, 'assure' the
princess.

Satisfactory answers having been given to all these questions, the
Archbishop turned to Margaret herself to enquire if she was content
'of her own free will, and without compulsion' to wed his master, and
received the very proper reply: 'If it pleases my lord and father the
King, and my lady and mother the Queen, I am content.' The twelve-
year-old bride knelt for her parents' blessing and it was time to
exchange the vows.

The Earl of Bothwell repeated that he had been given sufficient power and authority to contract matrimony *per verba de presenti* on behalf of his sovereign lord, and solemnly plighted King James's faith and troth. Now it was the princess's turn. Standing handfasted with Bothwell, a resplendent figure in cloth of gold, she spoke her piece with perfect self-possession: 'I, Margaret, first begotten daughter of the right excellent, right high and mighty Prince and Princess, Henry, by the grace of God King of England, and Elizabeth, Queen of the same, wittingly and of deliberate mind, having twelve years complete in age in the month of November last past, contract matrimony with the right excellent, right high and mighty Prince James, King of Scotland . . . and take the said James, King of Scotland, unto and for my husband and spouse, and all other forsake during his and mine lives natural; and thereto I plight and give to him . . . my faith and troth.'

The royal trumpeters, concealed in the rafters of the Great Chamber, sounded a fanfare and the musicians struck up in their 'best and most joyfullest manner.' Although the marriage still had to be sanctified by the Church and it had been agreed that the bride should remain with her parents for another eighteen months, betrothal *per verba de presenti*—that is, with the promises made in the present tense—represented a legally binding contract, and at the banquet which followed young Margaret took equal precedence with her mother as a married woman and a queen. The festivities went on for three days, with tournaments, 'disguisings', morris dancing and more banquets. Bonfires were lit in the streets of London, the church bells rang out, a solemn Te Deum was sung at St Paul's Cathedral and twelve hogsheads of free wine were provided for the citizens.

The elaborate celebrations which marked Princess Margaret Tudor's *fiancels*—the lavish indigestible meals, the pageantry, the jousting and dancing and public rejoicing—also marked the successful culmination of nearly seven years of patient diplomacy, during which her father had striven to secure a lasting peace with his next-door neighbours. For centuries Anglo-Scottish relations had been at worst actively hostile, at best in a state of uneasy truce, and a treaty which would safeguard England's vulnerable northern frontier, loosen Scotland's longstanding French connections, as well as putting an end to the perennial nuisance of cross-Border raiding and cattle-stealing, must be a valuable diplomatic achievement. All the same, in spite of the obvious advantages gained by this conversion of the

Truce of Ayton into a 'perpetual peace', and the fact that it was common practice to seal such an alliance with a royal marriage, some of King Henry's councillors had had their reservations.

Naturally enough, no one envisaged the sensational consequences which would result from the union of the Thistle and the Rose during the second half of the 16th century; but certain punctilious individuals, trying to look into the impenetrable future, did feel in duty bound to point out that if, by any awful chance, 'the heritage and succession of the realm of England' should pass to Margaret, as the King's elder daughter, 'the kingdom of England would fall to the King of Scotland, which might prejudice the monarchy of England.' Henry, himself a sufficiently cautious and far-sighted political operator, replied that if, God forbid, such a thing were to happen, 'Scotland would be but an accession to England and not England to Scotland, for that the greater would draw the less.' This, as Francis Bacon was to remark, 'passed as an oracle' and silenced the opposition.

In the long run, of course, history proved the King a true oracle, but at the time when the Scottish marriage was under discussion he had two apparently healthy sons to carry on his line and could reasonably have felt that the possibility of 'the succession of the realm' passing to Margaret or her children was remote enough to be disregarded. The difficulties faced by even the most prescient of 16th century statesmen were, however, grimly illustrated three months after the betrothal ceremony at Richmond by the sudden death of the heir to the throne, Arthur, Prince of Wales, at the age of fifteen. Of the seven children so far born to the first Henry Tudor and his wife, Elizabeth of York, only four had survived infancy. In an age of high infant mortality this was not a bad average, but when the Queen died in her eighth childbed in February 1503 the stark fact remained that the future of the House of Tudor now depended on the life of a single boy.

The King never fully recovered from the grief and shock of his double bereavement, but life and politics had to go on and that summer saw him setting out from London to escort his daughter on the first stage of her journey north. It was not thought worthy of any particular comment that Margaret, still five months short of her fourteenth birthday, was about to embark on married life with a man of nearly thirty, whom she had never seen and who was known to be keeping a mistress. All daughters of royal houses were conditioned from babyhood to make marriages of dynastic or diplomatic convenience, and in some ways it seemed as if Margaret Tudor might be getting an unusually good bargain.

James IV was the sixth Stewart king—a dynasty descended from Marjorie, daughter of Robert the Bruce, and her husband Walter, Hereditary High Steward of Scotland—and five years earlier Don Pedro de Ayala, ambassador of the Catholic Kings of Spain, had given an enthusiastic report of his qualities. Good-looking and good company, he was 'of noble stature, neither tall nor short, and as handsome in complexion and shape as a man can be.' He was also pious, intelligent, well-read and a talented linguist, fluent in Latin, French, German, Italian and Spanish. As well as his own Scottish dialect, he spoke Gaelic, 'the language of the savages who live in some parts of Scotland and on the islands' which, according to de Ayala, was 'as different from Scotch as Biscayan is from Castilian.'

'Neither prodigal nor avaricious, but liberal when occasion requires', James was a hard worker with a reputation for being a humane prince, for dispensing even-handed justice and for keeping his word. During his stay in Scotland, the Spanish envoy had himself taken part in one of the numerous Border forays and had been particularly impressed by the King's reckless personal courage. 'I have seen him undertake the most dangerous things in the last wars', he wrote. 'On such occasions he does not take the least care of himself. He is not a good captain, because he begins to fight before he has given his orders. He said to me that his subjects serve him with their persons and goods, in just and unjust quarrels, exactly as he likes, and that, therefore, he does not think it right to begin any warlike undertaking without being himself the first in danger.'

Warlike undertakings apart, just being King of Scotland was a chancy business. None of James's immediate predecessors had died in their beds, and consequently the Stewarts had been plagued by a succession of long minorities, resulting in the transferance of a disproportionate amount of wealth and power into the hands of their nobility—a notoriously factious, greedy and unlikeable body of men. James himself, in his early teens, had been seized by a group of rebellious lords headed by the Home and Hepburn families, and made the figurehead of a rising which ended in his father's murder.

Although not directly implicated in the crime, it has been suggested that his disregard for his own safety, his exaggerated, sometimes morbid piety and frenetic restlessness were caused by a haunting sense of guilt. Certainly these characteristics appear symptomatic of an inner disquiet and perhaps of a general underlying instability but, at the same time, James was undoubtedly a highly gifted individual. His intellectual interests ranged from medicine to music and he was an accomplished all-round athlete. Even more importantly in his circumstances, he had proved himself a strong and competent king, able to impose his authority, superficially at least, on the rough, tough, lawless society he ruled.

Scotland was a poor country and the monarchy chronically short of cash, but when Margaret and her retinue crossed the Border at the beginning of August 1503, James spared no expense in giving her a stylish welcome. National pride demanded that the English should see a civilised people who knew how to honour a royal bride, not poor relations to be despised and patronised.

The King of Scots' shoulder-length red hair and long full beard made him a striking figure in any company, and from the couple's first meeting at Dalkeith on 3 August it was he who dominated the scene with effortless gaiety and charm. The state entry into Edinburgh was brilliantly stage-managed with all the proper trimmings of cloth of gold, velvet and satin richly bejewelled, pageants and tableaux and cheering crowds, and throughout the hectic social round of feasting, dancing, jousting and ceremonial church-going which followed the wedding in St Giles Cathedral, James missed no opportunity of kissing his bride in public and showing her every distinguishing courtesy. Everything, in fact, went off splendidly and the English escort returned home laden with gifts and 'giving great praise, not only to the valour and manhood of the Scottishmen, but also to their good manners, and the hearty entertainment which they received of them.' James had spent a good deal of time conferring privately with the Earl of Surrey, King Henry's lieutenant in the north, and it really looked as if the ancient enmity between the two countries might be over at last.

On a more personal level, the marriage of the Thistle and Rose turned out no more and no less successfully than most marriages of its kind. The new Queen of Scots was a commonplace young woman of no particular brains or beauty, her somewhat stolid exterior concealing a stubborn, headstrong character, a 'great twang' of the Tudor, or rather the Plantagenet temper, a well-developed sense of her own importance and a sharp eye for a grievance. She shared none of James's interests or aspirations and made no attempt to identify herself with his people, but once she had recovered from her first paralysing homesickness and become acclimatised to her new surroundings, she played her part conscientiously enough. As for James, although he soon re-established relations with his current mistress, he proved a good husband by the standards of the day, treating his wife with generosity and consideration, and showing genuine concern over her difficult childbirths, for in this vital department the marriage was definitely unsatisfactory. The virility of the King of Scots was not in question—he had already fathered a sturdy brood of bastard children by a succession of obliging ladies—but his efforts to beget a legitimate heir met with repeated disappointment. Margaret was seriously ill after each of her confinements and of her first four babies only one survived.

By the time this infant, a boy christened James, was born in April 1512 the Anglo-Scottish peace no longer looked so healthy. Old Henry Tudor had died three years earlier and the new King of England, an ebullient, impetuous teenager, his head stuffed with romantic dreams of war and conquest, wasted no time in trumpeting defiance at the French in a remarkable scene which had only needed a tun of tennis balls to give it the authentic medieval flavour. Henry VIII, it seemed, saw himself as another Harry V, only too ready to assume the port of Mars and re-enact the rugged deeds of his ancestors on the vasty fields of France. This inevitably put a severe strain on Scottish good-neighbourliness, for the Auld Alliance was still very much in being—James's lavish entertainment of a grand French embassy in 1508 had made that ostentatiously clear—and if young Henry really intended to re-fight the Hundred Years' War, the King of Scotland was going to find it difficult to remain neutral.

As it turned out, young Henry was reluctantly obliged to curb his impatience for military adventure until the shifting pattern of events abroad gave him the opportunity to join a league of European powers alarmed by France's empire-building activities in northern Italy. By 1512, however, he had all the excuse he needed to sally forth and prove his manhood and James was under strong pressure both from the French and his own subjects, long deprived of their favourite bloodsport, to resurrect the time-honoured custom of invading through England's back door while she was engaged across the Channel. For a time he hesitated, but in the end a touching appeal to his chivalry from the Queen of France outweighed the more practical representations of his own wife and in August 1513, while his brother-in-law was happily occupied playing soldiers in Picardy, he led an army some 20,000 strong across the River Tweed.

The result was an overwhelming defeat for the Scots at Flodden in the wild Border country a few miles south-east of Coldstream. James himself, as usual in the thick of the fighting, was killed 'within a spear's length' of the English commander—the same Earl of Surrey who had been a guest at his wedding ten years before—and with him died twenty-four earls and barons, two bishops, two abbots and about a third of his army. The slaughter of Flodden has become a part of Scottish folklore, but by far the most serious loss in real terms was that of a vigorous, popular adult king. The shattered corpse of the brave and beautiful James IV was carried off the field by the victors, a seventeen-month-old baby succeeded as James V and once again Scotland faced the prospect of a long royal minority.

James IV had appointed his widow as 'tutrix' or guardian of their son and from the English point of view, Margaret, who could be relied on always to put the Tudor interest first, had every qualification for the position of regent. The Scots were understandably less enthusiastic, nor were they reassured by the King of England's ominously proprietorial attitude towards his little nephew. Henry, who was apparently considering reviving the ancient English claim to suzerainty over Scotland, had sent instructions to Lord Dacre, Warden of the East Marches, to 'endeavour what he can to have the young King of Scots placed in the hands of the King of England, who is his natural guardian.'

But with the expense of a French war on his hands, the King of England lacked the means to follow up the advantage gained at Flodden, and the following summer Margaret lost her precarious ascendancy over a sullen and suspicious Scottish Council by her impulsive second marriage to the young Earl of Angus, titular head of the powerful house of Douglas. Whether the Queen had married 'for her plesour', as most people believed at the time, or simply because she felt the need of a protector, her choice could hardly have been more unfortunate. The Scottish Council, quite beside itself with annoyance over the underhand behaviour of the Douglases, lost no time in depriving the new countess of her regency, cutting off her income and forcing her to surrender the Great Seal. In September 1515 she and Angus were driven out of the country, and on 7 October Margaret gave birth to a daughter at Harbottle Castle in Northumberland.

Meanwhile, the governorship of Scotland had passed into the hands of John Stewart, Duke of Albany, cousin and heir presumptive to the young king. John Stewart had lived all his life in France—his father had been exiled for plotting against James III—and was himself half-French with a French wife. The English, as might be expected, had done their best to keep him out, but by this time England and France had made peace—a peace in which Scotland had been included without consultation—and when Albany landed at Dumbarton in May 1515, he brought conciliatory instructions.

Apart from a short, inconclusive but destructive little war in the early 1520's, consequent on another outbreak of Anglo-French hostilities, Anglo-Scottish relations reverted to a state of *detente*. As the rawness of the emotions engendered by Flodden began to fade, the Scots had been having second thoughts about the wisdom of attacking a powerful neighbour at the behest of a still more powerful but frequently unsupportive ally, and in 1522 Albany was unable to persuade them to cross the Tweed again in force. More thoughtful Scots were also beginning to reflect on the interesting possibilities opened up by the fact that since the King of England's Spanish wife, Catherine of Aragon, had given him only one living child—and that child a daughter —the King of Scots was next door to being his uncle's heir.

The end of the twenties saw several significant new developments. In June 1528 young James V, whose childhood had been uncomfortably spent as a hostage in the hands of one or other of the rival Scottish factions, finally escaped from his gaolers and took control of the government. A tough, intelligent, good-looking boy, with his father's surface charm and high spirits, as well as his father's underlying streak of instability, James had no great liking for the English, but he was far too busy securing his own position and restoring some kind of order at home to have either the time or resources to consider renewing the war. In 1528 Henry VIII was also heavily pre-occupied with domestic affairs, for the previous spring he had taken the first steps in his celebrated divorce case, thus setting in motion a train of events which was to have far-reaching effects on the future course of English and Scottish history. It was another three years before Henry finally saw, or was shown, a radical solution both of his marital predicament and the financial problems now besetting him. In essence it was very simple. If the Pope would not give him his freedom, then he must manage without the Pope. If he were to assume supreme religious power in his own realm, the clergy would become subordinate to the Crown and could be made to do its bidding, the appearances of law could be maintained and the revenues which Rome drew from the church in England diverted to the exchequer.

The Lutheran wind of change blowing out of Germany had so far affected only a tiny minority of Englishmen, but the enormous wealth, privilege and suspected corruption of the Roman establishment made it a natural target for the antagonism of an increasingly literate and articulate urban middle class, and the King and his new councillor and hatchet man, Thomas Cromwell, experienced no difficulty in exploiting the anti-clerical prejudice of the House of Commons for their own ends. By the spring of 1532 the clergy, already badly shaken by the fall of the great Cardinal Wolsey (the first casualty of the battle for the divorce) and lacking any effective leadership, had surrendered their ancient, jealously-guarded independence from the temporal government; for all practical purposes the nationalisation of the English church was an accomplished fact and the way was open at last for the King to marry Mistress Anne Boleyn, the lady who had been his constant companion for the past six years. It was not a popular choice among his subjects, who showed a regrettable tendency to refer to the Queen elect as a goggle-eyed whore or 'that naughty pake Nan Bullen', and when Anne rode in triumph through the City to her coronation in the summer of 1533 she is said to have grumbled that she saw too many caps on heads and heard too few 'God save yous'. But to the King this scarcely mattered, for his new wife was now visibly pregnant and he was confidently expecting the birth of a prince.

To ensure that the coming infant was born in wedlock—at least to his own satisfaction—Henry had spent the past few months ruthlessly manipulating the accepted laws of God and man. The previous January he and Anne had been married under conditions of great secrecy, 'very early before day' in the presence of only three witnesses. At the end of March Thomas Cranmer was consecrated as Archbishop of Canterbury and a few weeks later humbly petitioned to be allowed to hold a court of enquiry into the King's 'great cause of matrimony'. The result of this enquiry, to no one's surprise, was a solemn archiepiscopal pronouncement that the King's first marriage was null and void, his second good and lawful.

In August the Court moved from Windsor to Greenwich, where Henry had himself been born, and there, between three and four o'clock on the afternoon of Sunday 7 September, Anne gave birth to 'a fair daughter'. It was a bitter and grievous disappointment to both parents. In his quest for a male heir Henry had turned the world upside down, made powerful enemies abroad and alienated many influential people at home, and all he had got for his pains was another useless girl. There was nothing to be done, of course, but put the best possible face on it. A Te Deum for the Queen's safe delivery was sung in St Paul's Cathedral and the newest member of the Tudor family was christened with all due pomp and ceremony at the Friars Church at Greenwich. Archbishop Cranmer stood godfather and when the baby had been brought to the font and baptised by the Bishop of London, Garter King of Arms prayed sonorously that God of his infinite goodness would send prosperous life and long to the high and mighty Princess of England, Elizabeth.

Six months later the Pope at long last gave his ruling on the King of England's divorce, and gave it in Queen Catherine's favour. Almost simultaneously Parliament at Westminster passed the Act of Succession, recognising the validity of Henry's second marriage and entailing the Crown on the children of Anne Boleyn. During the winter session the Act of Supremacy, declaring the King to be officially, explicitly and unconditionally 'the only supreme head in earth of the Church of England', came before the Commons, and as from February 1535 it would be high treason for any of the lieges 'maliciously' to deny this revolutionary addition to the royal style.

Events in England were naturally being watched with close attention in Scotland, and the subsequent dismantling of the monasteries and transfer of church assets to secular hands equally naturally aroused some wistful feelings north of the Border. But James was not to be tempted into following his uncle's example and in 1532 had affirmed his resolution to defend 'the authority, liberty and freedom of the seat of Rome and the holy kirk'. This was due in part to the Scottish king's personal preference for orthodoxy, in part to an inbred distrust of England and fear of being swallowed alive if he threw in his lot with her, and in part to the fact that the Pope, appalled at the prospect of losing both the island kingdoms, had already offered him sufficiently generous concessions to make it financially worth his while to stay inside the fold. Indeed, as the political conflict between schismatic England and orthodox Europe developed, James found himself in the fortunate position of being courted by both sides. Literally courted as it happened, for, despite his reputation for indiscriminate sexual athleticism and a numerous family of bastard children, he was still a highly eligible bachelor. A wide variety of young ladies were offered for his choice, but James had long set his heart on a French bride—though he did for a time seriously consider marrying his former mistress Margaret Erskine, who had already given him a sturdy son. In the end, however, politics won and in September 1536 the King of Scots set sail for France where he received a friendly welcome from the royal family. The old bond between the two countries was renewed again 'to endure and stand for ever', and the following January James married the sixteen-year-old Princess Madeleine in Notre Dame amid scenes of unexampled splendour.

James was thoroughly enjoying himself in France, finding the high standard of luxury and entertainment provided at the French court very much to his taste, and it was May before he finally tore himself away. The bridal couple landed at Leith on the 19th, but the delicate Madeleine did not survive transplanting and six weeks later James was a widower.

If the Scottish king's first attempt at matrimony had ended tragically, the English King was being almost equally unlucky. He had been sadly disappointed in Anne Boleyn. Not only had she failed to produce the longed-for son and heir, but her bitter tongue and habit of making jealous scenes still further reduced her value as queen and helpmeet. Not even Henry could expect to make a third marriage with two wives living but when, in January 1536, the indomitable Catherine of Aragon died at last in her dreary exile at Kimbolton, he felt free to make a fresh start. Early in May Anne was arrested and arraigned before a commission of peers on a charge of treason against the King's own person. These proceedings, needless to say, were no more than a formality, and on the morning of Friday, 19 May she was beheaded within the precincts of the Tower of London 'when she had reigned as Queen three years lacking fourteen days, from her coronation to her death.' But Henry was not content with merely killing the woman he had once sworn to love unchangeably. Two days before her execution, 'at a solemn court kept at Lambeth by the Lord Archbishop of Canterbury and the doctors of the law, the King was divorced from his wife Queen Anne . . . and so she was discharged and was never lawful Queen of England.'

The dissolution of the King's second marriage necessitated a second Act of Succession, passed in the summer of 1536, by which

Parliament once again ratified a decision by Thomas Cranmer on Henry's matrimonial affairs and once again bastardised and disabled his heiress. The two-and-a-half-year-old Elizabeth thus joined Queen Catherine's daughter Mary in social limbo, and up in Scotland Margaret Tudor temporarily regained her position as her brother's heir presumptive.

It was not until October of the following year that persistence was finally rewarded and Henry's third wife was delivered of a son at Hampton Court Palace. The nation went hysterical with joy over the birth of Prince Edward, so that the death of Queen Jane Seymour from puerperal sepsis passed almost unnoticed in the general uproar; but the King was now a widower again, and both he and his nephew were looking out for a suitable bride. Both had turned to France in the first instance and for a time both were in active pursuit of the same lady. To Henry's considerable annoyance it was the King of Scots who won the prize and in May 1538 married Marie de Guise, the widowed Duchesse de Longueville, while the King of England was obliged to make do with an obscure German princess, the poor despised Anne of Cleves.

James undoubtedly got the better bargain. Mary of Guise, a daughter of the ancient Carlovingian house of Lorraine, came to Scotland with some reluctance—she had only recently lost a loved husband and would be leaving her little boy and affectionate, close-knit family for what was still widely regarded in Europe as *terra incognita*—but she came with a praiseworthy determination to make a success of her new life. A tall, handsome girl of twenty-two, built on generous lines, who had already proved her ability to bear children, she possessed other valuable qualities of courage, intelligence, good sense and good humour, all of which were to be needed in the years that lay ahead.

As a Frenchwoman, the new Queen's first concern was naturally to foster the French alliance, but she also took the trouble to make friends with her difficult English mother-in-law and publicly expressed a desire to use her influence in helping to maintain the peace with England. Unfortunately, though, her arrival had co-incided with a general deterioration of Anglo-Scottish relations. Henry was growing increasingly alarmed by James's stubborn Francophilia and irritated by his equally stubborn refusal to break with Rome.

By the end of the thirties the international situation, too, looked threatening. European diplomacy was becoming more and more dominated by the rivalry between the two great power blocs of France and the so-called Holy Roman Empire of the Hapsburg family who, by a series of fortunate dynastic accidents, now ruled over Spain, the Netherlands, Austria and a whole patchwork of German states, as well as parts of northern Italy. As long as these two giants remained at one another's throats England was able to use her strategic position on the map to play off one against the other; but in the summer of 1538 the King of France and the Emperor Charles V signed a ten year truce, and in December of the same year the Pope finally summoned up the resolution to publish a bull excommunicating the schismatic King of England. Thus the dread of isolation, of becoming a target for attack by the orthodox Catholic powers combining under the banner of a papal crusade which was to influence English foreign policy for the rest of the century, first became an issue at a time of domestic unrest ominously linked with the names of certain surviving members of the old royal house.

Henry reacted with characteristic violence. He had already stamped hard on the domestic unrest. Now he carried out a purge of all those Plantagenet cousins he could lay his hands on and put the south coast and the Border on full military alert. He was, however, still prepared to employ his own brand of diplomacy and in February 1540 sent Ralph Sadler, one of his most promising young men, on a mission to Edinburgh in another effort to detach James from the papacy and, in particular, from his chief minister, Cardinal David Beaton, Archbishop of St Andrews and champion of both the French and Roman interests.

Sadler received a civil welcome from the King of Scots, who assured him repeatedly that he was only too ready to live in peace with England and knew that his 'good-father', the King of France, felt the same. But James was unimpressed by a rather clumsy attempt to blacken Cardinal Beaton's character, and not even portentous hints of possible expectations from his uncle's will could persuade him to consider cutting himself off from the mainstream of the European church.

Sadler had seen James at his most urbane and charming, but those around him were beginning to notice some disturbing personality changes. Always highly-strung and mercurial, he was becoming increasingly neurotic and unpredictable, subject to sudden outbursts of ferocity and moods of deep depression. So it was particularly unfortunate that in the spring of 1541 he should have had to face an overwhelming personal and dynastic tragedy. In May 1540 Mary of Guise had given birth to a son who, apart from a brief digestive upset in the autumn, appeared to be thriving. The Queen was pregnant again almost at once and the following April bore another son at Stirling Castle. The new baby was christened Robert and everything seemed to be going smoothly. Then Prince James was taken ill at his nursery at St Andrews with one of the sudden, terrifying illnesses of childhood and before his father could reach him he was dead. Almost immediately a messenger arrived from Stirling—Prince Robert had also sickened and within a matter of hours he, too, was dead.

To the stricken parents and that part of the nation which took notice of such things, the scale of the disaster which had befallen the House of Stewart was stupefying and James was still in a state of shock when the King of England extracted, or thought he had extracted, a promise that his nephew would meet him for a conference at York. The crisis of 1539 had now receded. France and the Empire were once again on the brink of war and consequently once again competing for an English alliance, but Henry continued to be uneasy about Scotland. As long as James remained inside the French and papal camps, the northern frontier would never be secure and added to this was the awkward fact of James's proximity to the English throne. Henry was no longer a young man and despite his very best endeavours—he was now married for the fifth time—there had been no more sons. Prince Edward was still only three years old and, as events in Scotland had so recently demonstrated, infant life was always notoriously uncertain. The King had therefore made up his mind to see what his personal powers of persuasion could achieve and, accompanied by his current wife and the whole unwieldy apparatus of the court, set out on the long journey north.

On 18 September he reached York, where elaborate preparations had been put in hand for the forthcoming summit meeting, and waited for ten days in vain for James to keep his appointment. It was given out that the Scottish council had refused to allow their king to venture his person on English soil, but to Henry it was a calculated public insult. He had spent a lot of valuable time and trouble wooing his nephew and now his patience was exhausted. He returned to London in a rage, busily mulling over suitable plans for revenge.

That bad-tempered winter was to see the death of Margaret Tudor but although her disappearance from the scene snapped a link with the past, it made no material difference to the crisis building in the north. Margaret's unfortunate tendency to allow her private passions to influence her public life had long since destroyed any political credibility she might have possessed and, besides, she and her brother had been on bad terms for some time. Henry had always strongly disapproved of his sister's determination to divorce her unsatisfactory second husband, and Margaret never quite forgave Henry for taking Angus's side in their long, bitter and immensely complicated matrimonial dispute. Her daughter and the King's niece, Lady Margaret Douglas, had been brought up at the English court, while Angus himself, banished by James who loathed his step-father and the whole Douglas tribe, had also taken up residence in England, waiting hopefully for better times to return.

By the summer of 1542, Henry, who was contemplating further foreign adventures, was ready to take pre-emptive action against the Scots at a time when he knew they could expect no help from France. The defeat of a party of English raiders at Haddon Rig near Kelso in August was declared an act of aggression, and in October the Duke of Norfolk set out from Berwick on a deliberate show of force, leaving a trail of devastation behind him. Retaliation was expected, but the Scottish warlords seemed in a strangely unbelligerent frame of mind. James had by this time lost the confidence of most of his nobility, who accused him of misgovernance and, significantly, of being 'ane better preistis king, nor he was thaires', and although 'the kingis mynd was verrie ardent on battell on Inglis ground' the army refused to pursue the retreating Norfolk across the Tweed.

Angry, confused and humiliated, James turned to Cardinal Beaton and to his 'familiar servant' Oliver Sinclair of Pitcairns, and on 21 November left Edinburgh for the west with an army variously estimated at between 12,000 and 20,000 strong. The outcome was the battle of Solway Moss fought on the marshy ground near the river Esk, where the Scots, whose hearts were never in the business, were utterly routed. Casualties were minimal, but a large number of prisoners, especially 'great lords and barons of Scotland', fell into enemy hands, and this was disgrace as well as defeat.

Despite his reported thirst for battle, James had not been present on the field and when the news was brought to him 'he grew wondrous dollorous and pensive'. According to the History of Robert Lindsay of Pitscottie, the King now began to examine his conscience and to see that the 'shamfull chance quhilk he had sustained at that jorney' was largely the result of his own folly in listening to the 'evill counsall and fals flattrie' of his bishops and courtiers, 'quhairthrow he tuik sick melancholie and displeasour, that no comfort nor consolatioun in no wayes, by no manes witt, might appease his present grieff, nor bring him to rest.'

Exactly what was ailing James during the last months of his life remains a matter for conjecture, but there seems no doubt that he was suffering from a complete physical as well as mental breakdown. He roused himself to return to Edinburgh and then went on to Linlithgow, where his wife was awaiting the imminent birth of their third child. But not even the hope of another son could put any heart into him and he is said to have spoken constantly of his approaching death. On 6 December he retreated to Falkland, a pretty palace which in happier times he had rebuilt in the French Renaissance style, and there, some forty-eight hours later, they told him that Mary of Guise had been brought to bed of 'a fair daughter'. To the King of Scots this was as bitter a disappointment as that felt by King Henry when Elizabeth was born—indeed, to James it appears to have been the final straw. In the well known story related by Robert Lindsay, he muttered, in a reference to Marjorie Bruce, ancestress of the Stewart dynasty, ' "it came with ane lass and it will pass with ane lass": and so he commendit himselff to the Almightie God, and spak little from thenforth, but turned his back to his lordis and his face to the wall.'

James was thirty-three years old when he died on 14 December and his six-day-old daughter Mary succeeded him as Queen of Scotland. Thus, from the first week of her life, the child born in the dismal aftermath of Solway Moss became a figure of international importance.

To no one was the infant queen of more immediate interest than her great-uncle Henry, and while the Scots bickered over who should rule their unhappy country during what looked like being the longest royal minority yet, the King of England was planning a master-stroke of dynastic diplomacy which would solve the intractable problem of his northern frontier once and for all. A marriage between Edward Prince of Wales and Mary Queen of Scots had everything to recommend it from the English point of view. This time the sexes of the Thistle and the Rose, so conveniently reversed, could only work to England's advantage. This time there would be no question about which country would be absorbed by the other.

Clearly it was necessary to move fast, while the Scots were still off-balance. The Earl of Angus and the prisoners taken at Solway Moss were sped on their way home with enough English gold in their saddle-bags to ensure their support (or so it was hoped), and in March 1543 Ralph Sadler, now Sir Ralph, Henry's expert on Scottish affairs, took the road north to take charge of negotiations in Edinburgh. He found Cardinal Beaton and the clerical party in eclipse and James Hamilton, Earl of Arran, installed as Governor.

The Hamiltons, descended from a daughter of the second James Stewart, were one of the first families in Scotland. Since the death of the Duke of Albany, Arran had become heir presumptive with an undoubted claim to the regency, but although he was believed to favour an English-style Reformation, he had the reputation of being a thoroughly slippery customer, 'facile and inconstant' in everything save the advancement of himself and his own kin—which made him a typical enough example of the Scottish peerage.

On 22 March Ralph Sadler was received by the Queen Mother at Linlithgow and favoured with an intimate glimpse of the object of his mission. There had been rumours that the Queen of Scots was a sickly baby, but Mary of Guise, so Sadler informed his master, 'caused me to go with her to the chamber where the child was, and shewed her unto me, and also caused the nurse to unwrap her out of her clothes, that I might see her naked. I assure your majesty, it is as goodly a child as I have seen of her age, and as like to live, with the grace of God.'

This was satisfactory, but the Queen Mother warned Sadler that the stories of her daughter's fragility were being put about by Arran, 'the second person of this realm' who 'looketh to be king of the same', and it had to be remembered that Arran also had a young son who might, in some quarters, be considered a very suitable bridegroom for the little queen. In the circumstances, it would be a wise precaution to offer him a consolation prize and Sadler was therefore instructed to inform the Governor that King Henry had a daughter called the Lady Elizabeth, 'endowed with virtues and qualities agreeable to her estate, and means, if he (the Governor) sincerely goes through with all things, to condescend to her marriage with his son . . . and to bring up and nourish his said son as a son-in-law in this court.'

But the Master of Hamilton was not destined to be nourished at the English court, and neither was Mary Queen of Scots. The negotiations for the marriage contract continued and the Governor continued to feed Sadler with fair words and promises, but Henry's bullying demands that the little Queen should be handed over to him immediately, or, at the least, surrounded by a household of his choosing, had aroused every latent Scottish suspicion of English intentions; while Sadler, floundering in a morass of double-talk, deceit, jealousy and intrigue, was becoming increasingly disenchanted with the Scots. 'Such malicious and despiteful people, I think, live not in the world' he wrote in a moment of exasperation.

Eventually a compromise was reached, and in the treaty signed at Greenwich on 1 July it was agreed that, although Henry might send a suitable English husband and wife to superintend her education, Mary should remain in the custody of a committee of Scottish barons until she had completed her tenth year, and that a proxy marriage should take place before she left for England. Scottish laws, liberties and national identity were guaranteed, and if the Queen became a childless widow she was to return to Scotland without any impediment or obstacle. This went a long way towards meeting the Scots, but the damage had already been done and by August the forceful Cardinal Beaton and the pro-French party, aided by liberal subsidies of French gold, were regaining their former ascendancy. Arran ratified the treaty, but he could see as well as anyone which way the wind was blowing and early in September, to King Henry's unspeakable disgust, slipped unobtrusively out of Holyrood Palace to join the Cardinal at Stirling, where he 'received absolution, renounced the profession of Jesus Christ his holy Evangel, and violated his oath that before he had made for observation of the contract and league with England.'

Before the end of the year the Scottish Parliament had found a pretext for repudiating the Treaty of Greenwich and was busy refurbishing the old ties with France. The King of England was back where he had been before Solway Moss and a rare opportunity for achieving religious and political union had vanished in a fog of mutual distrust, greed, opportunism and plain bloody-mindedness.

II

France and Scotland Are Now One Country

Elizabeth Tudor was nine years old when her Scottish cousin was born. Anne Boleyn's child had grown into a slim, sharp-featured, red-haired girl, well made and healthy but showing no particular promise of beauty and, as the bastard of a notorious adulteress, she had so far attracted little notice in a world where interest in the daughters of a royal house was measured in terms of their potential value on the international marriage market.

The former 'high and mighty Princess of England' had never deliberately been made to suffer as a result of her mother's disgrace. True, there had been a period of administrative confusion immediately following Anne's execution when the Lady Mistress of the nursery household had complained volubly about lack of information and supplies but Elizabeth, bastardised and disinherited though she might be, remained the King's acknowledged daughter and was treated as such. Her father seems to have been fond of her in his own purely selfish fashion, and she took her place as a member of the family on special occasions such as Prince Edward's christening and the official reception for Anne of Cleves in January 1540. Most of her childhood, however, was spent in one or other of the royal manors scattered around the Home Counties, usually sharing an establishment with her elder sister or the little brother, now the centre of everyone's attention, and her upbringing had been left almost entirely in the hands of her devoted governess, Katherine Ashley, who had first entered her service as a waiting gentlewoman back in the summer of 1536.

An important milestone in Elizabeth's life was reached in July 1543 when, in a quiet ceremony at Hampton Court, her father married his sixth and last wife. The widowed Lady Latimer of Snape Hall, born Katherine Parr, daughter of an old-established Northamptonshire family, was a mature, sensible, pious lady, experienced in the art of managing elderly husbands and with longstanding connections with the Tudors—her mother had been one of Queen Catherine of Aragon's ladies. Katherine Parr was already on friendly terms with Catherine's daughter and quickly established a warm motherly relationship with Edward, but it was Elizabeth who became her special protégée. Certainly she was the first and only influential figure to take a constructive interest in the child of Henry's 'great folly' who, at this time, appeared to have few, if any prospects other than an arranged marriage to some useful supporter—such as the Master of Hamilton—whose family would be prepared to overlook her unfortunate maternity in exchange for an alliance with the English royal house.

There is no record that Elizabeth was ever told, officially or otherwise, about the proposed Hamilton match. Most probably she was not, but she may well have heard whispers in the household. She would, though, undoubtedly have heard all about her brother's proposed match with the Queen of Scotland. 'I would she and her nurse were in my lord prince's house' one Englishman had remarked within a fortnight of Mary's birth, and the hoped-for imminent arrival of the baby queen would have been a topic of excited speculation among all the women. Elizabeth would also have heard about Mary's subsequent removal to the great fortress of Stirling Castle and her coronation in the chapel there when she was nine months old, about the wicked perfidy of the Scots and the steps which the King's grace was taking to punish them. These were both drastic and vindictive, Edward Seymour, Earl of Hertford, being sent north in May 1544 with orders to 'put all to fyre and swoorde, burne Edinborough towne . . . beate down and over throwe the castle, sack Holyrood house, and as many townes and villaiges about Edinborough as ye may conveniently, sack Leith and burne and subverte it and all the rest, putting man, woman and childe to fyre and swoorde without exception where any resistence shalbe made agaynst you . . .'

Although Edinburgh Castle proved too strong for him, Hertford carried out his instructions to the letter, but Henry achieved nothing by his celebrated action for breach of promise save a strengthening of Scottish determination to keep their little Queen out of the clutches of her predatory great-uncle whatever the cost. In fact, the only wedding which the King of England did manage to arrange that summer was between his niece Margaret Douglas and Matthew, Earl of Lennox, representing a collateral branch of the Stewart family, closely related to and deadly rivals of the Hamiltons.

Henry was now preparing to cross the Channel to engage in another French war which, despite his increasing age and girth and his 'sorre legge', he meant to superintend in person. Before he left a third, precautionary, Act of Succession had reached the Statute Book. This confirmed the King's right to dispose of the crown by will, granted to him in 1536, but made it clear that should Edward fail to leave an heir, and failing any children by Henry's latest marriage, the throne would pass first to Mary and then Elizabeth and their 'lawfully begotten' heirs, subject to conditions to be laid down by the King in his will. Neither of the princesses was re-legitimised by the new Act and their constitutional position and their future remained doubtful, to say the least, when their father died in January 1547.

The King's will, a controversial and much discussed document, confirmed the provisions made for the succession in the 1544 Act, but if none of his own children left heirs, then the throne was to pass to the children of his younger sister Mary and their heirs. The claims of his elder sister's descendants, Mary Queen of Scots and Margaret Douglas, were arbitrarily ignored—a piece of Henrician perversity which was to be a contributory cause of grief, bitterness and confusion in the years to come.

Meanwhile, the new regime headed by the Earl of Hertford, uncle of the nine-year-old King Edward and now advanced to the dignity of Duke of Somerset and title of Lord Protector of the Realm, had embarked on a programme of religious reform leading to the adoption of Archbishop Cranmer's Book of Common Prayer. Somerset's preoccupation with reform and his professedly sympathetic attitude towards economic hardship among the poor at home, earned him the soubriquet of 'the Good Duke', but there was nothing in the least sympathetic about his attitude towards Scotland. There the policy of aggression and intimidation continued unabated, with the two-fold aim of forcing the Scottish government to recognise its obligations under the Treaty of Greenwich and to follow England along the path to godliness.

The 'Rough Wooing', however, was still proving conspicuously unsuccessful. In fact, the only good news to come out of Scotland from the English point of view had been the murder of Cardinal Beaton at St Andrews Castle in May 1546 by a band of local lairds who had their own reasons for disliking His Eminence. The

Castilians, as they became known, occupied St Andrews for over a year, but although they were generally held to be pro-English and although the Governor was unable to dislodge them (he was handicapped by the fact that the Castilians were holding his son hostage), they made little long-term difference to the situation.

With the elimination of the Cardinal, Scottish politics dissolved into a duel between the Governor and the Queen Mother. Arran was weak, shifty and irresolute, Mary of Guise strong-willed, patient and shrewd, but she suffered from the serious double disability of being a woman and a foreigner. Then, in March 1547, things began at last to go her way. François I, King of France, died at the end of the month and his son, Henri II, less obsessed by Italian conquest, was readier to look north and consider ways and means of exploiting the Scottish alliance. Mary of Guise also had influential relations in France whom it would be well to conciliate and, as a first step, the new King dispatched an expedition to recapture St Andrews. The principal Castilians were taken prisoner and the lesser fry, including a young renegade priest by the name of John Knox, sent to serve time in the galleys.

By August Protector Somerset was preparing another onslaught, carefully timed to destroy the harvest, in yet another attempt to bring Scotland to its senses and, if at all possible, 'get possession of the young Queen'. The result of this campaign was the Battle of Pinkie and yet another shattering military defeat for the Scots, but the young Queen, who had been hurried away for safety to the island of Inchmahone in the Lake of Menteith, remained in Scottish hands.

Clearly, though, matters could not go on like this. Cardinal Beaton may not have been a very nice man, but he had been an astute and experienced political operator, who occasionally put the national interest first and had been able to impose some semblance of unity on the government. Without him, Scotland was rapidly becoming a disaster area, lapsing into leaderless, lawless, hopeless chaos. The English had now established a base in the town of Haddington, commanding the south-eastern approaches to Edinburgh, and it seemed only too probable that, sooner rather than later, treachery, corruption, brute force, or a mixture of all three, would result in the successful kidnapping of the little Queen and a complete English takeover. Help had to be sought from somewhere, and that could only mean from France.

Shortly after Pinkie an emergency conference had been held at Stirling to discuss the advisability of sending young Mary overseas, and at a Privy Council meeting in November it was reluctantly agreed that a marriage should be arranged for her with Henri's three-year-old son François. Few of those around the council table were happy about the idea, gloomily prophesying 'cruell warres betwixt us and Ingland' and also that 'France would desire us and our realme to be ane province or pertinent unto thame, as thair awin subjectis.' No one, though, in that grim, crisis-ridden winter of 1547 could see any alternative. Arran's consent was bought with the promise of a French dukedom for himself and a rich French bride for his son, and in May 1548 a French army landed at Leith ready to begin the siege of Haddington.

In return, the Scottish Parliament, assembled in the abbey outside the town, had to consent that Mary should be sent to France without delay and in due time 'conjunit in matrimonie' with the Dauphin, 'to the perpetuall honour plesour and proffeit of baith the Realmes.' For his part, the French king undertook to respect Scottish independence but, at the same time, 'to keip manteine and defend this Realme . . . as he does his awin realme of France.' This, of course, would mean a permanent French presence in Scotland but, in the circumstances, the terms of the Treaty of Haddington were pronounced 'verray ressonabill' and on 7 August, exactly a month after the date of its conclusion, the Queen of Scots sailed from the Clyde on board a French galley. England's Rough Wooing had been frustrated and all hope of uniting the two British kingdoms gone for another generation.

When five-year-old Mary Stewart left Scotland for the first time, Elizabeth Tudor was approaching her fifteenth birthday. After King Henry's death it had been decided that the princess should be left in her stepmother's care until she had finished her education. At the time, this seemed a sensible and suitable arrangement. The Queen Dowager was the obvious person to take charge of the King's sister and the home she made for herself at the pleasant suburban palace overlooking the Thames at Chelsea was soon to include Lady Jane Grey, eldest of the late King's English great-nieces, as well as Elizabeth, thus perpetuating the time-honoured custom of using a royal lady's household as a boarding school for high-born young girls. Katherine Parr was already well-known as a patron of scholars and an earnest disciple of advanced Protestant theology, so that Chelsea

Palace became a recognised centre of learning and godliness, where the minds of some potentially very influential wives and mothers were being moulded.

Unhappily for everyone concerned, the peace of this feminine mini-Utopia was to be disturbed by the boisterous loud-voiced advent of the Queen's new husband, Thomas, Baron Seymour of Sudeley, younger brother of the Lord Protector and recently created Lord High Admiral. Thomas Seymour was a fine figure of a man with plenty of breezy surface charm who took no interest in scholarship or advanced Protestant thought. A consuming interest in his own advancement left very little room for anything else. Obsessively jealous of his brother's pre-eminence, he spent most of his time uselessly scheming to obtain the guardianship of the young King, while devoting his leisure moments to a semi-playful pursuit of the Lady Elizabeth.

Matters came to a head one day in the spring of 1548 when the Queen surprised her husband and her stepdaughter locked in an embrace which did not look in the least playful. There was no scandal, but in the week following the Whitsun holiday the princess and her entourage left on an extended visit to Sir Anthony and Lady Denny, old and trusted friends of the royal family. Katherine Parr was then in the sixth month of an uncomfortable first pregnancy and when news of her death in childbirth reached the Dennys' house at Cheshunt early in September Mrs Ashley began unwisely to dream of wedding bells.

But during those autumn months, while the Admiral openly consulted her steward about the state of her finances, her governess sang his praises and my lord sent friendly messages at every opportunity, Elizabeth remained unresponsive. Henry VIII might have failed in a father's first duty by leaving his young daughter unbetrothed and unprotected against adventurers like Thomas Seymour, but even at fifteen Elizabeth Tudor could look after herself. In the privacy of the household she could not always conceal the warmth of her feelings for the Admiral—he was just the kind of bold handsome fellow who would attract her to the end of her life—but in public her discretion was absolute.

This was just as well, for in January 1549 Thomas Seymour was committed to the Tower, evidence of his numerous 'disloyal practices' having become too blatant to be condoned any longer. On the day after his arrest the government's investigators descended on the old Bishop's Palace at Hatfield where the princess was now living, and over the next few weeks Elizabeth was subjected to a gruelling ordeal by interrogation. She was told it was being said that she was with child by the Lord Admiral and invited grimly 'to consider her honour and the peril that might ensue.' But Elizabeth flatly denied that there had ever been anything remotely treasonable or even underhand about her behaviour, and no trick of the interrogator's trade could trap her into any damaging admissions.

The Lord Admiral's enterprising career ended at the place of execution on Tower Hill on 20 March and the Lady Elizabeth was somewhat grudgingly exonerated. Her own good sense, courage and self-control had saved her from disgrace, or worse, but she had received a timely lesson in the art of survival. Elizabeth learned early that the world was a hard and unforgiving place and it was a lesson she never forgot. 'Her mind has no womanly weakness', her tutor Roger Ascham wrote of her early the following year, 'her perseverance is equal to that of a man, and her memory long keeps what it quickly picks up.'

In spite of everything, the princess had not abandoned her studies, both of the classics and modern languages—especially French and Italian, which, according to Ascham, she spoke as fluently as English. Now she had another task before her, that of repairing the harm done to her public image by the recent scandal. Here she was helped by external events. 1549 had been a disastrous year from the Lord Protector's point of view and that autumn a *coup d'état*, efficiently stage-managed by John Dudley, Earl of Warwick, toppled him from his precarious throne. Warwick bore the Princess Elizabeth no personal ill-will and in December she paid a visit to court where, reported the Imperial ambassador, she was welcomed with great pomp and triumph and was continually with the King. Her future, though, remained as uncertain as ever. Rumours of possible marriages for her are scattered through the diplomatic despatches of the time but Elizabeth, now well into her seventeenth year, was still an eligible spinster, spending most of her time on one or other of her country estates, cultivating a reputation for modesty and virtue, and steering clear of politics.

The mid-century political landscape as seen from London had a very unappealing look about it. Warwick, the new strong man, had inherited a formidable legacy of domestic problems from his defeated rival, while in the field of foreign affairs England was reaping the sour

fruit of Henry VIII's aggressive policies towards France and
Scotland. The Queen of Scots was now securely established at the
French court under the watchful eye of her maternal grandmother
and powerful Guise uncles. In Scotland itself the Earl of Arran—or
Duke of Châtelherault as he had recently become—might still be
clinging to his titular Governorship, but Mary of Guise and the
French resident ambassador Henri d'Oysel between them ruled in
Edinburgh and French troops garrisoned the main strongpoints of
the south-east, so that the French king could reasonably boast that
Scotland and France were now one country.

England, brought close to bankruptcy by the military adventures
of the past few years and in the grip of a deepening economic
recession, was powerless to reverse this regrettable state of affairs
which meant that her hereditary enemy could walk through her back
door virtually at will. Not that Henri II was currently contemplating
anything so crude. He had no need to. With the Queen of Scotland in
his custody and her mother so loyally looking after his interests on
the ground, French hegemony over the northern half of the British
Isles seemed comfortably assured. Nor did the King forget that,
Henry VIII's will regardless, by every accepted law of inheritance
only two lives separated young Mary Stewart from the English
throne. But that was for the future. In the meantime England
urgently needed friends abroad.

The Earl of Warwick had chosen to throw in his lot with the more
extreme elements of the Protestant party at home and as a result his
religious policies were rapidly bringing him into collision with the
Holy Roman Emperor. Warwick, therefore, had little option but to
cultivate the French, and the price of friendship was naturally high.
In the treaty signed at Angers in July 1551 England had to accept the
annulment of the Treaty of Greenwich and formally relinquish any
further claim to Mary Stewart as a bride for Edward VI. It was agreed
instead, amid an elaborately insincere exchange of diplomatic
civilities, that Edward and the French king's daughter Elisabeth
should make a match of it, and in October the Scottish Queen
Dowager was given an hospitable reception at the English court.

Mary of Guise had just spent thirteen months in her homeland,
enjoying a reunion with her family and especially with her daughter,
who had celebrated her eighth birthday during her mother's visit.
After allowing for the usual measure of flattery, optimism and family
bias in the contemporary reports, it is clear that the Queen of Scots

was developing into an exceptionally attractive and promising child—a 'most perfect child' declared her prospective father-in-law after their first meeting. She was tall for her age, with a clear, glowing complexion, deep-set brown eyes and fair, almost ash-blonde hair. Graceful in her movements, bright, healthy, pretty and showing an engaging readiness to please and be pleased, she was a daughter of whom any mother could be justly proud.

Her education was proceeding along conventional lines and although Mary Stewart possessed none of the formidable academic brilliance of Elizabeth Tudor, she had plenty of natural quickness which enabled her easily to acquire all the accomplishments considered proper to her rank. French was now her first language, but she learnt Latin as a matter of course, together with some Italian and Spanish. She enjoyed and was good at music and dancing and all forms of outdoor exercise, was already becoming a skilful needlewoman and later even learnt to knit. According to her grandmother she performed her religious duties with exemplary devotion, hearing Mass every day and waiting eagerly to make her first communion.

While Mary of Guise could be more than satisfied with her daughter's progress, she must also have been reassured to see at first-hand the anxious care being lavished on this so precious and important little girl. Mary divided her time between her Guise relations and the court, but wherever she happened to be—at Meudon or the Hotel de Guise with her grandmother and uncles, or at Saint-Germain, Fontainebleau or the palace of Blois with the royal children—she was always cocooned in that atmosphere of opulent, ultra-civilised luxury which only the French seemed to know how to create and rigorously guarded from any contaminating outside influence. Everyone, from the King downwards, sang the praises of the Queen of Scotland, so that it became a matter of obligation to extol her virtue and charm, her grace and goodness and physical perfection. Whether so much cosseting and uncritical adulation were altogether good for her is open to doubt; that, though, was not the concern of the French propaganda machine. The eight-year-old Mary Stewart represented a very valuable weapon in the government's (and the Guise family's) political armoury, and naturally they made the most of it.

The only cloud on the horizon during the early fifties was the sickly constitution of the Dauphin. Young François looked ominously frail and stunted beside his bonny, bouncing fiancée, whom he followed about like an adoring shadow. Nevertheless, when mother and daughter said goodbye for the second and last time in the autumn of 1551, the elder Mary could congratulate herself on having made the right decision in parting from her beloved child, who was obviously well and happy, safe from danger and, so far as one could be certain of anything in an uncertain world, had a brilliant future before her.

The Dowager returned uncomplainingly to her lonely, careworn life in Scotland by way of England, where she was sumptuously entertained by King Edward, who had just attained the dignity of his fifteenth year. Members of the royal family summoned to attend the state banquet at Westminster included the Countess of Lennox, once Lady Margaret Douglas, Henry VIII's other niece Frances, Duchess of Suffolk and her daughter Lady Jane Grey, but the King's half-sisters were conspicuously absent from the festivities. The staunchly Catholic Mary Tudor was currently at loggerheads with her brother's government over her refusal to accept the new Protestant prayer book, but Elizabeth on her last appearance at court had been 'most honourably received by the Council . . . in order to show the people how much glory belongs to her who has embraced the new religion and is become a very great lady.' The great lady's failure to meet Mary of Guise may have been connected with the fact that the French, with Mary Stewart's claim in mind, were already insinuating that as a bastard, she had no right to a place in the succession. This was a piece of political kite-flying, but in the present pro-French climate Elizabeth would naturally be reluctant to risk a public slight and she stayed at home, pointedly ignoring the new interest in French fashions aroused among the ladies. When she did come up to town again the following March, she demanded and got the loan of St James's Palace for herself and her suite, riding through London 'with a great company of lords and knights and gentlemen, and after her a great number of ladies and gentlewomen to the number of two hundred on horseback . . . and so she was received into the Court goodly.'

At the court she found that John Dudley, now created Duke of Northumberland, had consolidated his position as Lord Protector in all but name. His numerous brood of sons filled the Privy Chamber and the Lords of the Council waited on him daily to learn his pleasure. A man of powerful personality and commanding presence, he was, inevitably, disliked but no one seemed at all anxious to offer him a challenge. In any case the situation was already changing, for that autumn Edward developed tuberculosis and by the spring of 1553 England's first Protestant king was dying.

In spite of strict censorship and a flow of reassuring official bulletins, the capital seethed with rumour. Northumberland could expect nothing good from Mary Tudor and few people believed he would surrender without a struggle. His French allies, too, had a particular interest in keeping Mary from her inheritance. Catherine of Aragon's daughter was also first cousin to the Emperor Charles V, and her accession would automatically take England back into the Imperialist camp. Whitsun saw the arrival in London of M de l'Aubespine, a secretary often employed by the King of France on high level diplomatic missions, and, despite the secrecy surrounding his visit, it was reliably reported that he had come to offer his master's services to the Duke of Northumberland in the event of King Edward's death.

Northumberland's plans in the event of King Edward's all too obviously approaching death were well advanced by this time, and Edward himself was busy working on his Devise for the Succession which excluded both his half-sisters on the grounds that they were not only illegitimate, but liable to marry foreign princes who would gain control of the government and thus 'tend to the utter subversion of the commonwealth.' Instead, the King proposed to bequeath his crown to his Protestant cousin Jane Grey (newly married to the Duke of Northumberland's son Guildford) and her heirs.

Although the legality of Edward's Devise would bear very little scrutiny, to Northumberland and to the French this mattered a great deal less than its swift and successful execution. Northumberland was principally and understandably concerned with his own short-term survival, but once he had done the King of France's dirty work by removing Henry VIII's daughters from the scene, he would be at the mercy of Henri II, who was looking forward to using his accomplice in crime as a convenient satrap until the moment arrived to enforce Mary Stewart's claim to occupy the English throne.

Edward VI died on 6 July and three days later the hapless Jane Grey was informed of the change in her circumstances. On paper Northumberland's mastery of the situation looked complete. Mary Tudor was a woman of thirty-seven, in poor health and without money, influence or any visible means of support. No one believed she stood a chance—least of all the Emperor—but even as the heralds were proclaiming Queen Jane before an ominously silent crowd at the Cross in Cheapside, events had begun to slip out of the Duke's control. Mary, forewarned of his intentions and moving with unexpected speed and decision, had already reached the comparative safety of the Howard stronghold in East Anglia, and already disquieting reports were coming in that groups of substantial gentlemen with their tenantry, not to mention 'innumerable companies of the common people', were rallying to her side. The common people had had more than enough of Dudley arrogance and Dudley greed. They were not prepared to stand aside while King Harry's daughter was cheated of her rights, and within a fortnight they had swept the great Duke of Northumberland out of sight, confounding all the expectations of the European powers by a spontaneous demonstration of loyalty and affection for the true Tudor line.

One of the first people to congratulate the new Queen was her sister Elizabeth. But although Elizabeth had plenty of reason to be thankful for the failure of Northumberland's *coup*, she was now entering on a period of danger and anxiety the memory of which would leave a permanent scar. Her relations with her half-sister had never been close and were bound to be fraught with tension. Mary had suffered bitter personal unhappiness and public humiliation at the time of her parents' divorce and, as the Imperial ambassador observed, still resented 'the injuries inflicted on Queen Catherine, her lady mother, by the machinations of Anne Boleyn, mother of Elizabeth.' A more obvious and immediate cause of dissension was, of course, religion. Although the Protestant heiress soon found it expedient to accompany the Catholic Queen to Mass, she managed to make it pretty plain that she was doing so out of policy, thus confirming Mary's suspicions that Anne Boleyn's daughter was a hypocrite as well as a heretic and a bastard. The Imperial ambassador also regarded her as thoroughly untrustworthy. Simon Renard, who was rapidly becoming Mary's confidential adviser, warned her repeatedly and unnecessarily not to trust her sister, as she was 'clever and sly' and might easily prove disloyal. By the end of November the two were barely on speaking terms and the French ambassador told the Queen Dowager in Scotland that 'Madame Elizabeth is very discontented and has asked permission to withdraw from this Court.'

Elizabeth was not alone in her discontent and her withdrawal from court coincided closely with the inception of a conspiracy designed to prevent the Queen's projected marriage with the Emperor's son, Philip of Spain, which, it was widely believed, would result in England's enslavement by foreigners and papists. By the end of January 1554 this mounting wave of panic and prejudice had erupted into one of the most serious domestic confrontations of the Tudor century, and during the first week of February Sir Thomas Wyatt and his Kentishmen very nearly succeeded in taking control of the capital. They failed, due partly to Queen Mary's own gallantry and refusal to be intimidated by violence, but dissatisfaction with her policies remained and even in failure Wyatt's Rebellion did much to equate Protestantism with patriotism in the public mind.

Throughout the crisis Elizabeth had remained in the country, suffering, so she assured her sister, from such a cold and headache as she had never felt before. The princess's name had never been publicly invoked by Wyatt, but it was an open secret that the rebels' ultimate aim had been to depose the Queen, marry Elizabeth to young Edward Courtenay, last surviving male representative of the old Plantagenet royal line, and place them jointly on the throne. Certainly this was what the French, in their anxiety to stop the Spanish marriage at all costs, had been hoping to achieve and the French ambassador appears to have taken the princess's co-operation for granted, though it seems unimaginable that she had ever honoured Antoine de Noailles with her confidence. Elizabeth was far too shrewd not to have seen through his false-friend approach and knew as well as anyone that all France's long-term cross-Channel interests were bound up in the person of the Queen of Scots.

Just how much she had known about the ramifications of the conspiracy is still anybody's guess. She had written no letters, made no promises and the subsequent enquiry failed to uncover any evidence which could be used to incriminate her. At the same time, it was obvious that the Protestant heiress would continue to be a natural focus for discontent and the decision to send her to the Tower, taken after much heated argument, was, in part, a political gesture by the Catholic hard-liners on the Council and in part because none of the lords could be persuaded to accept responsibility for her safe-keeping.

Elizabeth herself believed, no doubt quite sincerely, that she was in imminent danger of death. Nor is there much reason to doubt that

Mary would have sacrificed her sister had she been in a strong enough position to do so. But when, in the second week of April, Thomas Wyatt on the scaffold publicly exonerated the princess of all complicity in his treason, the joyful reaction of the Londoners made it plain that there was no longer any question of bringing her to trial, much less of putting her to death. So, on 19 May, after an incarceration of some two and a half months, Elizabeth, inscrutable as ever, was transferred to the suitably remote royal hunting lodge at Woodstock under the escort of Henry Bedingfield, one of those true-blue, old-fashioned Catholic gentlemen who had gone to Queen Mary's aid the previous summer.

She was to remain there, still officially in disgrace, for nearly a year, during which time the Queen married the Prince of Spain and, in November, realised another, even dearer ambition by seeing England solemnly absolved from the sin of schism and welcomed back into the bosom of the Roman church. Greatest joy of all, Mary announced that she was pregnant and in April 1555 moved out to Hampton Court, ready 'to take her chamber.'

All the great ladies of the realm had come, as was their right, to support the Queen through her ordeal, but by the end of the month there was one great lady in the palace whose presence can have given the mother-to-be little comfort. Elizabeth had been brought up from Woodstock and reluctantly 'forgiven' by her sister at King Philip's insistence, for if Mary were to die in childbed, Elizabeth's right to succeed would have to be supported by Spain. Hypocrite, heretic and bastard though she might be, she would still be an infinitely preferable alternative to Mary Stewart from the Hapsburg point of view.

It was a restless, uneasy summer. Few people seriously believed that Mary Tudor, now in her fortieth year, would be able to bear a healthy child. But if she did—and she had already once triumphed over seemingly impossible odds—then the European scene would be transformed, perhaps permanently, and the Hapsburg family would have absorbed the strategic island of England as efficiently and cheaply as in the previous generation they had absorbed Spain, and the rich Burgundian inheritance of the Netherlands in the generation before that. As Simon Renard remarked, 'everything in this kingdom depends on the Queen's safe deliverance.'

The empty cradle waited while the doctors and midwives nervously revised and re-revised their calculations, until at last the pathetic self-deception had to be brought to an end and Philip, irritated and humiliated, seized the opportunity to escape. But before he left for a more congenial climate, he took the precaution of telling the Queen that he wanted Elizabeth to be treated with consideration and, according to the French, followed this up by writing to Mary from Flanders 'commending the princess to her care.'

Over the next three years the Imperial family continued to worry intermittently about Elizabeth's future, and several rather half-hearted attempts were made to find her a suitable husband. In 1556 the King of France heard of a plan to marry her to Archduke Ferdinand of Austria, which prompted the French ambassador in Brussels to threaten that his master would give Mary Stewart to Lord Courtenay rather than allow the Hapsburgs to increase their influence in England. Edward Courtenay's death from fever or, as was whispered, poison two months later removed this particular danger, as well as putting an end to another smouldering home-based conspiracy to marry him to Elizabeth.

Philip paid a short visit to London in the summer of 1557, amid more speculation that he intended to take the princess over to Flanders to be married, but in fact the purpose of his coming was to embroil the English in the latest round of the perennial Franco-Hapsburg conflict, the result of which was to hasten preparations for the Franco-Scottish wedding. Mary Stewart would be fifteen in December and the Dauphin fourteen and of marriageable age the following January; the Guise family were anxious to see their young kinswoman settled—there was always the danger, even at this late stage, that the King of France might decide to bestow his son elsewhere—and so, on 19 April 1558, the couple were betrothed *per verba de presenti* in the great hall of the Louvre.

In the marriage contract Mary bound herself by her royal word faithfully to observe and keep all the ancient laws, liberties and privileges of Scotland, and recognised the right of the next heirs—that is, the House of Hamilton—to succeed her if she were to die without issue. But, unknown to the Scottish Commissioners who had come over for the ceremony, she had already signed certain other documents repudiating in advance any agreements she might make with the Scottish Estates, and making over the kingdom of Scotland (as well, incidentally, as her rights to the kingdom of England) unconditionally to the crown of France in the event of her death 'without heirs begotten of her body.'

Of course it would be quite unfair to blame the Queen of Scots for initiating this deliberate and cynical act of treachery, but at the same time her apparently unquestioning compliance was not a good omen for the future. She was, after all, fully old enough to understand the significance of what she was signing away, and even at fifteen queens had responsibilities as well as rights. It was in her failure ever really to grasp this simple fact that so much of Mary Stewart's tragedy was rooted.

The wedding of the Dauphin and the Queen of Scotland took place in the cathedral of Notre Dame four days after their formal betrothal. The beauty of the bride was universally conceded to have been breathtaking, and the event was celebrated amid all the pomp of church and state with a display of wealth and pageantry so lavish, so magnificent, so sumptuous as to be almost beyond the powers of description of those whose task was to record it. It was, without question, the wedding of the century, but it aroused little interest and less enthusiasm on the other side of the Channel, where sad Mary Tudor was now terminally ill.

England's fortunes, both at home and abroad, had seldom been at a lower ebb. The religious persecution, which earned the Queen her unenviable nickname, was casting a shadow of gloom and disgust over the whole country and the recent loss of Calais—last outpost of a once-great continental empire—in the French war had added national humiliation to the national malaise of a sullen, resentful population, an incompetent, factious government and a steadily worsening economic situation. The sense of great changes impending rumbled in the air like distant thunder and every man's mind was 'travailed with a strange confusion of conceits, all things being immoderately either dreaded or desired.' The English people had suffered more than a decade of bad housekeeping, uncertainty, violence and internal dissension. Above all they wanted peace and stability, and the sort of leadership which would enable them to get on with their lives undistracted by fear of interference from abroad or civil strife at home. The predominantly and vocally Protestant Londoners were looking forward without reservation to the accession of 'their' Elizabeth, but at the same time there was understandable anxiety in some quarters as to whether 'the succeeding Prince'—still very much an unknown quantity outside her own immediate circle—would be capable of providing that leadership.

The succeeding Prince was twenty-five years old on 7 September

1558, and although she could never begin to compete with her Scottish cousin's fabled beauty, she was by no means bad-looking. Of about average height, probably five foot three or four, with a slender, wiry, upright figure, she had 'fine eyes', hair 'reddish rather than yellow', the pale skin which often goes with red hair and which she accentuated with cosmetics (the commentator who described her complexion as 'olivastra' must have seen her in a bad light or on a bad day), and beautiful hands. As she grew older she became thin to the point of emaciation, her teeth decayed and she took to hiding her greying hair under a series of amazing orange wigs, but in her prime Elizabeth Tudor was a handsome creature, vital, elegant and stylish.

While opinions may have differed over the details of her physical appearance, there was never any question about her mental qualities. Endowed with great natural intelligence and taught by adversity and experience, 'two most effectual and powerful masters' as William Camden put it, she was, even in her twenties, a woman of mature political sense. As early as 1557 Giovanni Michiel, the retiring Venetian ambassador, spoke respectfully of the excellence of her mind and the wonderful intellect and understanding she had shown when facing danger and suspicion; while Roger Ascham, who was still reading with her on a regular basis, continued to write to his friends abroad praising not only the academic prowess of his star pupil, but her wide knowledge of things in general and her 'wise and accurate judgement.'

The Venetians had also noticed with interest that, in spite of being born 'of such a mother', the princess was far from regarding herself as in any way of inferior degree to Queen Mary. Nor, it seemed, did she consider herself as illegitimate, since her parents' marriage had been blessed by the Archbishop of Canterbury. 'She prides herself on her father and glories in him' reported Giovanni Michiel; 'everybody saying that she also resembles him more than the Queen does.' No doubt this gave Elizabeth particular satisfaction, in view of the Queen's publicly expressed scepticism that she was even King Henry's bastard.

By mid-October the news of his wife's condition reaching Philip in Flanders had become sufficiently serious for him to send his special envoy, Count de Feria, over to England 'to serve the Queen during her illness.' But when de Feria reached London on 9 November, he found Mary in a coma and the Spaniard wasted no time in joining the stream of courtiers and place-seekers already thronging the Hatfield road.

Mary Tudor died at six o'clock on the morning of Thursday, 17 November, 1558 and that afternoon the citizens of London rang the church bells 'and at night did make bonfires and set tables in the streets, and did eat and drink and make merry for the new Queen Elizabeth.' The transition to the new reign had been accomplished without a hitch.

In spite of Mary's steady reluctance to recognise her sister's claim, Elizabeth had long been generally accepted as the heir presumptive, and after the disastrous outcome of the French war no Englishman, however Catholic, was likely to contemplate inviting Mary Stewart across the Channel. Nor was there any other easy alternative to whom the Catholics might have rallied. The change-over had also been smoothed by the statesmanlike behaviour of Nicholas Heath, Lord Chancellor and Archbishop of York.

Parliament was then in session, and on the morning of 17 November Heath sent for the Speaker and 'the knights and burgesses of the nether house' to come immediately to the Lords. After announcing the news of Mary's death, he went on to tell them that Almighty God 'hath left unto us a true, lawful and right inheritrice to the crown of this realm, which is the Lady Elizabeth, of whose lawful right and title we need not to doubt. Wherefore the lords of this house have determined with your assents and consents, to pass from hence into the Palace, and there to proclaim the said Lady Elizabeth Queen of this realm without further tract of time.'

There were no dissenting voices and, by his prompt action, the Chancellor had not only secured Elizabeth's solemn recognition by parliament before it was automatically dissolved on the death of the reigning monarch; but, as a leading Catholic himself, had helped to ensure the loyalty of his party for the new sovereign.

Ten days later the new sovereign, wearing purple velvet with a scarf about her neck, rode in procession through London with the trumpets blowing before her and 'all the heralds in array', while the city literally exploded with joy all around her. England's Elizabeth had come into her own and an entirely new and disturbing element had entered the European political scene.

III

Queen of France, England and Scotland

In November 1558 England and Spain were still technically at war with France and Scotland. Hostilities, however, had now ended and peace talks were already in progress at Cercamp, a Flemish village near the French border. The two great powers, having fought one another to a standstill during the past fifty years, were both on the edge of bankruptcy and anxious to reach a settlement. But for England the negotiations were over-shadowed by the fact that the French king was currently 'bestriding the realm, having one foot in Calais and the other in Scotland', and also by his parade of 'the Scottish queen's feigned title to the crown of England.' According to Lord Cobham, reporting home from Brussels in December, the French 'did not let to say that Her Highness is not lawful Queen of England and that they have already sent to Rome to disprove her right.' A few weeks later, Sir Edward Carne was writing from Rome itself that 'the ambassador of the French laboreth the Pope to declare the Queen illegitimate and the Scottish Queen successor to Queen Mary.'

For the English envoys abroad this was a touchy subject. In the eyes of Rome and the rest of orthodox Catholic Europe, indeed of anyone who honestly doubted Henry VIII's and Parliament's competence to manipulate the natural laws of inheritance, Elizabeth Tudor *was* illegitimate (come to that, she was still illegitimate by Act of Parliament). The Scottish Queen therefore possessed an undeniable claim to be regarded as Queen Mary's successor. Queen Elizabeth, understandably, would admit no discussion of these legal niceties. Advised by the new Lord Keeper, Nicholas Bacon, she took her stand firmly on the 1544 Act of Succession and on the principle that 'the Crown once worn quite taketh away all defects whatsoever.' Her first Parliament, meeting in January 1559, passed a short bill confirming her title and as far as Westminster was concerned the matter was closed.

The French, though, continued to make political capital out of Mary Stewart's dynastic position. Henri II had his daughter-in-law proclaimed as Queen of England and Mary and her husband began to quarter the English royal arms with those of France. The young Queen-Dauphiness was styled as Queen of England and Scotland in official documents, and when the question of the restitution of Calais was raised at Cercamp, the French commissioners wondered aloud to whom Calais should be restored, for was not the Queen of Scotland true Queen of England?

All this, of course, irritated the English profoundly and it was to be remembered and held against the Queen of Scotland in years to come. But in those early months of 1556 the French were simply taking advantage of their unusually good cards in the diplomatic poker-game. Elizabeth, after all, following the precedent of her ancestors, was still styling herself Queen of England and France. Nicholas Wotton, a member of the English negotiating team, might reflect gloomily on his country's present weakness, on French perfidy and the 'commodity they now have to invade us by land on Scotland-side'; but Henri II was in no position just then to consider mounting a full-scale attack on England which, apart from anything else, would have been to invite a rapid resumption of the Hapsburg war. Queen Elizabeth might have little or no hope of recovering Calais, but she could also rely on her former brother-in-law to obstruct any serious French aggression, either in Rome or on Scotland-side.

Philip had succeeded his father the previous September and, although the Electors of Germany had conferred the Holy Roman Emperorship on his uncle Ferdinand of Austria, Philip, at thirty one, had become King of Spain, Lord of the Netherlands and of a temporal empire stretching from Naples to Peru. He was, on paper at least, the most powerful monarch in Christendom, but he continued to cling to his special relationship with the small, inhospitable off-shore island where he had spent such an unsatisfactory year as Mary Tudor's husband, and it is only necessary to glance at a map of Europe to see why. If England and Ireland were to follow Scotland into the French sphere of influence, the balance of power would tilt decisively in France's favour and Philip would be faced with a solid block of hostile territory lying across the narrow seas and capable at any time of cutting his maritime lifeline to the Netherlands.

The King of Spain wanted the English alliance badly enough to make a rather lukewarm proposal of marriage to his deceased wife's sister, but he was emphatically not prepared to help her regain Calais by force—as little as the King of France did he want to risk hotting up the war again just then. Elizabeth was therefore obliged to accept a face-saving formula which would leave the town in French hands for the next eight years, and by April 1559 the contending powers had come to terms in the Treaty of Cateau-Cambrésis. A month later England was once again a Protestant country, although here again the Queen had had to accept a compromise.

The settlement of the religious question, so vital to national unity, had occupied the attention of Elizabeth's first Parliament to the virtual exclusion of everything else. The Franco-Scottish menace, England's vulnerability to attack—'the Queen poor, the realm exhausted . . . want of good captains and soldiers . . . divisions among ourselves'—added to the need to conciliate at least one of the Catholic powers—all seemed to indicate extreme caution over this highly sensitive issue. Elizabeth herself, whose own religious convictions were conservative, would pretty certainly have been content with a return to royal supremacy and a liberalised version of the national Catholicism established by her father, based on the 1549 Prayer Book. But it quickly became clear that such pusillanimity would not do for the militant Protestants. Although still very much in a minority, the militants had gained enormously in dignity and status as a result of Mary's ill-judged policy of repression and now formed a well-organised, vociferous pressure group—represented in the House of Commons by an influential 'choir' of members, openly impatient of playing politics with the Word of God. On the other hand, in the Lords, the government was having to contend with the intransigence of the surviving Catholic bishops, which meant that the Elizabethan church would have to rely for its hierarchy on the younger generation of clerics. A significant number of these had taken refuge in such Protestant havens as Frankfurt, Strasbourg and Geneva during the Marian reaction and were now returning home determined to assist at the building of a new Jerusalem.

The Queen and Council had begun by resisting radical pressure, but the signing of the Cateau-Cambrésis treaty, together with the urgent need for a religious settlement acceptable to the Protestants of London and the south-east who had supported Elizabeth in her darkest days and still provided her principal power base, led to a change of mind. When Parliament reassembled after the Easter recess new proposals were put before the Commons, and an order of service

based on the second Edwardian Prayer Book—that which explicitly
denied the Real Presence in the eucharist and completed the process
of transforming the sacrifice of the Mass into an act of communion or
commemoration—was finally agreed upon. Neither side was
particularly pleased with the newly established Church of England,
enshrined in the twin Acts of Supremacy and Uniformity of
Common Prayer, which received the Royal Assent on 8 May. The
radicals were disappointed by the Queen's lack of godly zeal while
Elizabeth had been pushed further than she had wanted to go and
knew she was taking a gamble on international Catholic reaction. But
despite the increasingly shrill tirades of Count de Feria, who did not
hesitate to tell his master that England had fallen into the hands of a
woman who was a daughter of the devil and told his friends that the
only way to deal with the English was 'sword in hand', no Spanish or
papal thunderbolts followed the Elizabethan Settlement. There had,
of course, never been any question of a second Spanish marriage, but
the Queen, already displaying her skill at the game of playing both
ends against the middle and making full use of the priceless asset of
her single status, had allowed Philip to propose his archducal cousins,
Ferdinand and Charles of Austria, in his stead and was giving the
Hapsburg family just enough encouragement to keep them hopeful
—and friendly.

One way and another, Elizabeth and her Secretary of State
William Cecil could feel justifiably proud of their first six months.
England was at peace with her neighbours, the population at large
had accepted the latest set of religious changes with apparent
satisfaction and the native Catholics, leaderless and demoralised
as they were, seemed resigned if not reconciled. Then, early in July,
came news from Paris which threatened to upset the delicate new
equilibrium of the European apple-cart. Henri II, a vigorous man in
the prime of life, had been seriously injured in an accident in the
tiltyard. Ten days later he was dead—an unforeseeable twist of fate
which brought Mary Stewart to the French throne beside her young
husband, a queen twice over at sixteen-and-a-half and, according to
the English ambassador Nicholas Throckmorton, already boasting
that she would soon be Queen of England too. 'The Queen of
Scotland' wrote Throckmorton on 13 July, 'is a great doer here, and
taketh all upon her.'

In the circumstances, the style to be adopted by the new King and
Queen of France was a matter of considerable concern to the English

government. At his father's funeral François II was proclaimed as King of France only, but Nicholas Throckmorton heard that a great seal had been sent to Scotland engraved with the arms of England, France and Scotland quartered, and bearing the inscription *Franciscus et Maria, Dei Gratia, Franciae, Scotiae, Angliae, et Hiberniae Rex et Regina*. 'The same arms', added Throckmorton, 'are also graven upon the French Queen's plate'—something he could personally confirm since on a recent visit to the court he and his colleague, Sir Peter Mewtas, had been obliged to eat their dinner off it. Again, at the coronation, which took place at Rheims in September, the arms of England, France and Scotland quartered were prominently and provocatively displayed over the town gates.

François' coronation, too, was notable for a massive presence of the Guise family. As early as 13 July Throckmorton had reported that 'the House of Guise ruleth and doth all about the French King.' The principal appointments in the Queen's household were filled by her grandmother and aunts, while the government of France was now firmly grasped in the hands of her two senior uncles, the Cardinal of Lorraine and the Duke of Guise—a formidable and predatory pair whose sole ambition, as every member of the English diplomatic corps knew in his bones, was 'to seek all the means possible to increase the power and authority of their niece.' As the summer wore on, Nicholas Throckmorton's despatches became full of gloomy warnings about aggressive Guise intentions. 'Almost they care not who knoweth, that they mind to prosecute the French Queen's title to England' he wrote on 24 September, and on the 30th: 'the common bruit of all men touching the French Queen's title to England is a certain confirmation of their meaning towards your Majesty.'

In fact, the Guise ascendancy was by no means as secure as it looked, being based on the fragile foundation of a mentally retarded, physically underdeveloped teenage boy, and a teenage girl who was no longer so sturdy as she had been in childhood. Mary had suffered from a series of fevers and gastric upsets during her adolescence and was quite seriously ill again in 1559 with fainting fits, breathlessness and bilious attacks. The Guises urgently needed some great-nephews to secure the future, but so far there was no sign of their niece obliging them in this direction. There was, indeed, considerable doubt as to whether her marriage had even been fully consummated. Nor was the family's authority unchallenged in France. The rival

House of Bourbon, represented by the King of Navarre and his pugnacious younger brother the Prince of Condé, bitterly resented Guisard encroachment and was prepared to resist it by any means. But far the most immediate threat to the House of Guise and France's international position lay in the developing crisis in Scotland which was also, incidentally, about to present the Queen of England with the first major test of her resolution and statecraft.

Trouble had been brewing in the north for the past eighteen months or so and the hard-pressed Mary of Guise, who in 1554 had finally ousted Châtelherault and assumed the title of regent, was reaching the end of her resources. The Queen Regent had tried honestly to give Scotland good and stable government while fulfilling her trust as guardian of her daughter's and her family's interests. Unfortunately, the Scots, increasingly discontented with their near colonial status, were not at all grateful for the benefits of French rule and balked at paying the taxes associated with stable government. But, as always in the mid-16th century context, the real battle for power was fought out over religious issues. The regent herself, though a good Catholic, was a politician first, and during the pro-Spanish regime of Queen Mary Tudor had been obliged to appease the Scottish Protestant party with a wide measure of toleration. The accession of Elizabeth, followed by the Protestant resurgence in England, brought this to an end, but the Scottish Protestants were now too strongly entrenched to be easily suppressed. The Scottish robber barons, seeing the corrupt and moribund Catholic church as a plum over-ripe for the picking, had already banded together under the title of Lords of the Congregation of Jesus, and flashpoint came with the timely return of John Knox in May 1559.

By the middle of June reports were reaching London that the nobility, with few exceptions, were united in their determination 'to proceed to set forth God's word', and by the end of the month they had asked for English help. 'Open defiance is now given to all who maintain idolatry' wrote William Kirkcaldy of Grange to William Cecil on the 23rd. He went on to warn the English Secretary of State that the regent was appealing for reinforcements from France and added 'if you suffer this, you will prepare a way for your own destruction . . . I beg speedy answer, for if this occasion is lost, ye may thirst for, yet not find another.'

Cecil scarcely needed telling that this might well be a unique opportunity to drive the French out of Scotland once and for all, and neither did Queen Elizabeth. But it was by no means as simple as it sounded. Elizabeth detested the revolutionary Calvinism preached by the Scottish reformers, but even more she detested John Knox, author of the recently published *Blast . . . Against the Monstrous Regiment of Women*. She was not in the least impressed by his attempts to explain that the *Blast* had been directed against the rule of the three Catholic Marys—Tudor, Stewart and Guise—and flatly refused to allow him to set foot in her realm.

Apart from these considerations and her instinctive reluctance to be seen lending aid and comfort to another sovereign's rebels, any interference in Scotland's internal affairs would be an open violation of the Cateau-Cambrésis peace treaty and the Queen was understandably nervous of provoking French reprisals. The Guises might be unwilling to risk another European conflict by a direct attack on England (there was still a force of several thousand unemployed Spanish troops in Flanders), but neither were they likely to stand aside while their Scottish hegemony was threatened and their sister insulted by a rabble of heretics.

There were, though, some things the English government could do, and on 8 August that old Scottish hand Sir Ralph Sadler left for the north, ostensibly to report on the defences of Berwick but carrying with him messages of encouragement and £3,000 painstakingly 'laundered' into French crowns to be distributed secretly among the rebels. The House of Hamilton in particular seemed worthy of encouragement and William Cecil was pondering on possible ways and means by which the Stewarts, as represented by the alien and Catholic Queen of France, might be replaced by 'the next heirs'—that is, of course, the Hamiltons—and the Scottish throne occupied by 'a mere Scotsman in blood.'

Cecil, whose most immediate concern was to prevent France from making Scotland into 'a footstool thereof to look over England as they may', naturally maintained that the Scots themselves would benefit if they were freed from the French entanglement. 'The best wordly felicity Scotland can have', he wrote, 'is either to continue in a perpetual peace with the kingdom of England, or to be made one monarchy with England, as they both make but one isle.' While this undoubtedly made sound political sense, especially in the current international climate, it still did not take account of Scottish pride and prejudice, suspicion of English intentions and fears of being swallowed alive. No feud as ancient as that between England and

Scotland was going to be easily or quickly forgotten. Nevertheless, some of the Lords of the Congregation were now advocating a marriage between the Queen of England and their ex-Governor's son, James Hamilton, Earl of Arran (the same with whom Henry VIII had once offered to match his younger daughter) and who was believed to be 'very well bent in religion'.

No one, as usual, knew what the Queen of England meant to do, but she was certainly taking a close interest in Arran's welfare. Her agents abroad organised his escape from France, where he had been living as a hostage for his father's good behaviour, and smuggled him over to England by way of Geneva and Germany, disguised as a merchant.

All this was kept very quiet, but the new Spanish ambassador, Alvaro de Quadra, heard that Elizabeth had spoken of taking a husband 'who would give the King of France some trouble', and rumours about Arran's arrival were circulating as early as July 1559. He actually reached London towards the end of August and was secreted in Cecil's house in Cannon Row. On the 29th he had a private interview with the Queen at Hampton Court but, despite de Quadra's information that he was to be 'something more than a guest' and that news of a marriage could be expected to break at any moment, Elizabeth did not make him a proposal. Instead, she sent him up to Scotland, apparently hoping he would take over the leadership of the revolt and provide it with a popular figurehead. The Earl, who may already have been showing signs of the mental instability which later degenerated into hopeless insanity, proved a disappointment in this respect but his return did put new heart into the Congregation and had the result of bringing the old Duke of Châtelherault out on the Protestant side, at least for the moment, though little reliance could be placed on a man 'so inconstant, saving in covetousness and greediness, that in three moments he will take five purposes.'

The Lords of the Congregation were now happily and profitably occupied in dismantling the old church. 'All the monasteries are everywhere levelled with the ground: the theatrical dresses, the sacrilegious chalices, the idols, the altars, are consigned to the flames; not a vestige of the ancient superstition and idolatry is left' wrote an English bishop triumphantly. The Congregation was now in undisputed possession of Perth, Dundee, Stirling and St Andrews, and in October formally 'deposed' the Queen Regent.

All the same, as winter drew on, it was becoming painfully obvious that the iconoclastic fervour of the Scottish Protestants did not match their military capabilities, and that they were going to need a great deal more than kind words and surreptitious subsidies before they could hope to dislodge Mary of Guise and her three thousand or so French veterans from the strategic stronghold of the port of Leith —or even contain them there for long. Early in December François and Mary, as 'King and Queen of France, Scotland and England', appointed their uncle René of Lorraine, Marquis d'Elboeuf, to act as their lieutenant general in Scotland, and soon reports were coming in that a French fleet commanded by d'Elboeuf was about to sail from Calais, had perhaps already sailed. Also in December that astute politician William Maitland of Lethington arrived in London on behalf of the Lords of the Congregation to beseech the Queen of England, 'as a prince planted by God next to them within the same land and sea, to afford them her gracious protection against the French intended conquest.'

The Queen of England hesitated, and hesitated again, before committing herself to a policy of open intervention. She was only too well aware that, if things went badly, she could very easily find herself with a victorious Guisard army sitting on the Border, poised ready to sweep down through the still predominantly Catholic English north country into the undefended south, and add another kingdom to Mary Stewart's collection before anyone could stop them. And there was now a distinct possibility that no one would try to stop them. Philip of Spain was about to seal his treaty with France by marrying the French king's sister, and might well be persuaded to come to an arrangement with his new in-laws by which England and Scotland were parcelled out between them.

While Elizabeth stalled—as always, her instinct was to play for time, to let other people make the adventurous decisions and the mistakes—William Cecil had made up his mind that, whatever the risks, England must seize this apparently God-given chance to settle the Scottish problem. By Christmas he had carried the majority of the Council with him and, after resorting to threats of resignation, he finally managed to carry the Queen. Early in January a squadron of fourteen royal ships sailed from Harwich to the Firth of Forth under the command of Sir William Winter with orders to annoy the French and blockade the garrison at Leith. At the same time, any action Sir William took was to appear to come 'of his own head and of himself, as though he had no commission therefore' from the Queen. Winter performed his task with skill and imagination, and has the distinction of being the first in a long line of Elizabethan naval commanders to weigh anchor with instructions of this kind.

It was beyond even Elizabeth's ingenuity to disclaim responsibility for an army, and on 24 March 1560, about a month before her land forces eventually joined up with the Scots under the walls of Leith, she issued a public statement, printed in French and Italian as well as English, to explain that her intervention was being undertaken purely in self-defence against the aggressive intentions of the principal members of the House of Guise who, it was 'evident and notorious', were planning an attack on England by way of Scotland in order to further their niece's pretended right to the English crown. The Queen had no quarrel with the princes of the blood or the estates of France—she wanted only to live at peace with her neighbours— and no desire to encourage the people of Scotland to depart from due obedience to their sovereign, provided 'they may no longer have to fear oppression and conquest.' She was even ready to believe that the young Queen of Scots was not personally responsible for the insolent usurpation of her arms and title, but for her own safety she was determined to insist on the recall of the French soldiers in Scotland, 'it being too perilous to have them for so long a period so near to England.'

By April it was clear enough that while Spain might make some threatening noises, Philip had neither the means nor the will to take any active part with his French allies, and a number of other factors had begun to make it look as if a Protestant God was indeed disposed to help those who helped themselves. Storms in the North Sea had scattered and partially destroyed d'Elboeuf's fleet. The French treasury was empty and it would be months before another expedition could be got together. As well as this, the House of Guise was now having serious trouble at home, both with the disgruntled Bourbon faction and the French Protestant party. A conspiracy to kidnap the King, the so-called Tumult of Amboise, had failed and been bloodily revenged, but it had revealed internal dissensions alarming enough to force the Guises to cut their losses in Scotland, at least temporarily, and they had indicated their willingness to talk even before the death of the Queen Regent, that brave, intelligent and much abused woman, had taken the heart out of the resistance at Leith.

At the end of May William Cecil went north to represent Queen Elizabeth at the conference table at Edinburgh, and during the course of several weeks of hard bargaining succeeded in extracting a series of important concessions from the French commissioners acting on behalf of the Queen of Scots and her husband. It was, for example, agreed that all French troops should be withdrawn immediately, and the fortifications at Leith and Dunbar dismantled. It was also agreed that the government of Scotland should be handed over to a council of nobles for the time of their Queen's absence abroad, while England and France pledged themselves to observe a policy of strict non-intervention. Finally, the French consented to recognise that the realms of England and Ireland did, in fact, belong by right to 'the serene lady and princess Elizabeth' and undertook that the Queen of France would give up her provocative use of the English royal arms. The religious question was tactfully avoided, but when the Scots Parliament met in August they proceeded to adopt a Calvinistic confession of faith with such enthusiasm that one English observer was moved to remark that he had never seen 'so important matters sooner dispatched, or agreed to with better will.'

It was never wise to be too certain of anything in Scottish affairs, but from London it really did look as if the foundations of a durable peace had been laid at last. A Protestant Scotland must inevitably turn away from Catholic Europe towards Protestant England, and whatever Queen Elizabeth's opinion of Calvinism might be, even she would have to admit that John Knox and his brethren made more desirable next door neighbours than a French army.

The text of the treaty signed by their commissioners in Edinburgh got a cold reception from the Scottish Queen and from the government in Paris. There were none of the 'demonstrations of gladness' customary on such occasions and Nicholas Throckmorton warned his mistress that he feared the French meant 'only to gain time and no peace at all.' The ambassador had two interviews with seventeen-year-old Mary Stewart during August in which she made her own feelings pretty clear. She laid great stress on her close kinship with Elizabeth, telling Throckmorton that 'being issued out of the same race I have the same heart she hath, and assuredly can as ill bear injury as she can.' Elizabeth, therefore, should judge her cousin by herself, who would doubtless find it equally hard to put up with the sort of disobedience Mary's subjects had been showing to her. Nevertheless, she was glad about the peace and hoped that, although

they were not able to meet, she and Elizabeth could always use the
mutual kindness proper between cousins and sister queens. She had
heard people say that the Queen of England was both a 'wise and very
fair lady' and talked graciously about arranging an exchange of
portraits. But Mary and François were still quartering the Queen of
England's arms—'here at the Court gate very notoriously' reported
Throckmorton indignantly—and refusing to ratify the Treaty of
Edinburgh as long as their Scottish subjects showed themselves so
undutiful.

All the same, the French troops in Scotland were withdrawn and
the government was now firmly in the hands of the Lords of the
Congregation. The Treaty of Edinburgh, ratified or not, had ended
the first and, in many ways, the deciding round of the contest
between the cousins and sister queens with a victory for Elizabeth
which went a long way towards establishing her international
prestige. So it was particularly unfortunate that she should just then
have been touched by a domestic scandal which reverberated round
Europe.

The 'controversy of lovers' surrounding Elizabeth and its likely
outcome had been occupying the minds of her councillors to the
exclusion of almost everything else ever since her accession, but by
the early autumn of 1560 it was beginning to look horribly as if the
Queen, on whose future as a wife and mother so much depended ('for
without posterity of her highness what hope is left unto us?') was
wasting her time and ruining her good name by having an affair with a
married man.

Elizabeth's predilection for the company of Lord Robert Dudley
—fifth son of the late and unlamented Duke of Northumberland
—had first been commented upon as early as April 1559, when
Count de Feria told King Philip that 'Lord Robert has come so much
into favour that he does whatever he likes with affairs and it is even
being said that her Majesty visits him in his chamber day and night.'
Not long afterwards, an Italian newsmonger in London was
reporting that 'my Lord Dudley is in very great favour and very
intimate with her Majesty', and by the end of the year Lord Robert's
privileged position had become a matter of common gossip.

Elizabeth and Robert Dudley were almost the same age and had
known one another on and off since childhood. They had even been
in gaol together—Robert and three of his brothers were still in the
Tower under suspended sentence of death during Elizabeth's

sojourn as a state prisoner after the Wyatt Rebellion. In November 1558 Robert Dudley had been among the first to pay homage to his new sovereign and was rewarded with the prestigious office of Master of the Horse. He received other valuable tokens of the Queen's regard during the first year of the reign, which quickly earned him the jealousy of many in high places, and by November 1559 the young Duke of Norfolk was saying openly that unless he was very careful, the presumptuous Lord Robert 'would not die in his bed.'

None of her contemporaries ever understood what the Queen, who could have taken her pick of the royal bachelors of Christendom, saw in this upstart younger son of a convicted traitor, and the historian William Camden, who knew them both, could only hazard a guess that the undoubted conjunction and affinity of their minds was caused by some 'hidden conspiracy and consent of the stars.' On a more earthly plane, Robert Dudley possessed a number of attributes calculated to appeal to Elizabeth. He was tall, dark and flamboyantly handsome—a perfect foil for the pale, redheaded Queen. Looks mattered to the Queen and she set high standards, but looks were not everything. Robert was also an accomplished athlete, a good dancer, amusing company, witty, sophisticated and accustomed to moving in the first social and political circles. He was no intellectual, but he had been well-educated and, within his limits, was to prove a useful, conscientious public servant, as well as being a natural impresario with a flair for stage-managing the processions and pageants which played such an important part in the life of the court. But probably what mattered most to Elizabeth was the fact that she and Robert were already old friends, who talked the same language, shared the same jokes, the same background and experience. With Robert as with no one else, she could drop her guard, relax and enjoy her off-duty moments.

Of course there was a strong element of sexuality in this remarkable conjunction of minds, but the answer to the question: were the Queen and her Master of the Horse lovers in the obvious sense? is almost certainly that they were not. Apart from anything else, it would have been virtually impossible to conceal the existence of an illicit relationship from the prying gaze of matchmaking ambassadors, to whom every detail of Elizabeth's private life was of the greatest interest and who were prepared to pay good money for information from the palace servants—even down to the laundresses. Baron Caspar von Breuner, an agent of the Hapsburg family, who spent the greater part of 1559 in London trying unsuccessfully to promote a marriage with the Austrian Archduke Charles, made searching enquiries among the bedchamber women and came to the conclusion that while the Queen showed her affection for Lord Robert more openly than was consistent with her dignity, there was no reason to suppose she had ever been 'forgetful of her honour.' At the same time, von Breuner gave it as his opinion that Elizabeth was becoming so swollen-headed that she imagined she could do as she liked. 'But herein she errs', he wrote severely, 'for if she marry the said my Lord Robert, she will incur so much enmity that she may one evening lay herself down as Queen of England and rise the next morning as plain Mistress Elizabeth.'

The good Baron may well have been right about this, but whatever the Queen's intentions, the awkward fact remained that Lord Robert already had a wife and in June 1560 celebrated the tenth anniversary of his marriage to Amy Robsart, daughter of a wealthy Norfolk squire. Originally, it seems, this had been a love match—a boy and girl romance founded on physical attraction and very little else. By the beginning of 1559 all passion, at least on Robert's side, was long since spent and, with a brilliant new career opening out before him, his unfortunate wife had become an encumbrance, to be kept out of sight and, as far as possible, out of mind. The couple had no settled home and, while Robert remained in constant attendance upon the Queen, Amy spent her time moving round the country staying in the houses of various family friends and connections.

As Lord Robert's star rose at court, interest naturally focussed on Lady Robert and her future—or lack of it. Count de Feria reported that she was suffering from 'a malady in one of her breasts and the Queen is only waiting for her to die to marry Lord Robert.' His successor heard from a reliable source that Lord Robert was planning to hasten the processes of nature by poisoning his wife or, alternatively, that he intended to divorce her.

But Amy was still alive and still married when William Cecil left London to attend the peace talks in Edinburgh. Cecil was away for two months, during which time it has often been said, the Queen's infatuation for Robert Dudley reached some sort of climax. Of course the Secretary's absence meant that she had more free time than usual and was thrown more than usual into Robert's company, but all that actually seems to have happened is that, encouraged by Robert, she had developed a passion for riding and hunting, and was happily improving her horsemanship under his expert tuition.

However, when Cecil returned home at the end of July he was, for the first time, seriously alarmed by the situation. He found Elizabeth in one of her most tiresome moods, refusing to attend to business or, perhaps more accurately, refusing to attend to William Cecil, while Robert was lording it around the palace in a manner which disturbed the Secretary of State profoundly. So profoundly that, on Sunday, 8 September while the court was at Windsor, Cecil told the Spanish ambassador in a burst of calculated indiscretion that 'he clearly foresaw the ruin of the realm through Robert's intimacy with the Queen, who surrendered all affairs to him and meant to marry him.' He did not know how the country would put up with it and, as for himself, he would ask leave to retire, though he thought they would cast him into the Tower first. He begged the ambassador, in God's name, to point out to the Queen the effect of her misconduct and ended by saying that 'Robert was thinking of killing his wife, who was publicly announced to be ill, although she was quite well, and would take very good care they did not poison her.' On the following morning, in a piece of dramatic timing which could scarcely have been improved upon, a sweating messenger arrived at the Castle bearing the stunning news that Amy Dudley was dead—killed not by poison but by 'a fall from a pair of stairs.'

Amy's violent and mysterious death, coming as it did at the end of more than a year of scandal-mongering, created a noisy political storm. Alvaro de Quadra, writing on 11 September, remarked that 'the cry is that they do not want any more women rulers, and this woman may find herself in prison any morning, she and her paramour with her.' Certainly things looked bad for Robert Dudley and the Queen wasted no time in sending him away from court until the matter of his wife's death had been fully investigated by a coroner's jury.

Unfortunately, no record of the inquest proceedings has survived and the only first-hand information about the circumstances surrounding the tragedy is contained in two letters, dated 11 and 13 September, addressed to Robert by his kinsman and employee Thomas Blount. It so happened that on the morning of 9 September, Blount was actually on his way to Cumnor Hall—the house near Abingdon rented in the name of Anthony Forster, Robert's 'treasurer' or steward—where Amy spent the last few months of her life. He had not gone far before he encountered the messenger,

George Bowes, and heard the story from him, but instead of turning back for further instructions, continued on his journey to Cumnor. Nor did he seem in any great hurry to reach his destination, choosing rather to put up for the night at Abingdon where, without revealing his identity, he called for the landlord of the inn to ask 'what news was thereabout.' Mine host was naturally full of 'the great misfortune' which had just befallen only three or four miles from the town—how my Lord Robert Dudley's wife was dead by falling downstairs—but was unable to supply any other details. When Blount suggested that 'some of her people that waited on her' should be able to say what had happened, he was told no, apparently not, for they were all at the fair in Abingdon 'and none left with her.' Her ladyship, it seemed, had risen up very early and 'commanded all her sort to go to the fair and would suffer none to tarry at home.'

This all sounded rather odd, but Thomas Blount would soon be making enquiries on the spot and was more interested that evening in finding out what was being said about Amy's death. What was mine host's own opinion, he asked, and what was 'the judgement of the people?' Some were disposed to say well and some evil, answered mine host cautiously. For himself, he judged it a misfortune because it had taken place in an honest gentleman's house.

Blount needed no telling that public opinion was going to be a vital factor in the case, and the same thought was uppermost in the mind of the newly bereaved widower, who wrote frantically to his 'Cousin Blount' on that same Monday: 'The greatness and suddenness of the misfortune doth so perplex me until I do hear from you how the matter standeth . . . as I can take no rest. And, because I have no way to purge myself of the malicious talk that I know the wicked world will use, but one which is the very plain truth to be known, I do pray you as you have loved me . . . and as now my special trust is in you, that you will use all the devices and means you can possibly for the learning of the truth.'

But truth was to prove an elusive commodity. In his first report from Cumnor, Blount could only tell Lord Robert that the tale he had already heard from Bowes and from the landlord at Abingdon was confirmed by the household, and by Amy's personal maid, Mrs Pirto who, according to Blount, 'doth dearly love her.' Everyone agreed that her ladyship had insisted on sending all her servants out on the day of her death, 'and was so earnest to have them gone to the fair, that with any of her sort that made reason for tarrying at home she was very angry.' This was obviously considered uncharacteristic behaviour and Blount added: 'Certainly, my lord, as little while as I have been here, I have heard divers tales of her that maketh me to judge her to be a strange woman of mind.'

He had talked to the devoted Pirto, who should surely have known her mistress best, and went on: 'In asking Pirto what she might think of this matter, either chance or villainy, she said by her faith she doth judge very chance, and neither done by man or by herself.' Her lady, said Pirto, 'was a good virtuous gentlewoman, and daily would pray upon her knees.' Nevertheless, Pirto did let fall the possibly significant information that she had more than once heard the dead woman pray to God to deliver her from desperation. It was not conclusive, of course—'it passeth the judgement of man to say how it is'—but, all the same, Blount evidently believed that suicide could not be ruled out.

Robert had been insistent that the inquest jury should be chosen from 'the discreetest and most substantial men . . . such as for their knowledge may be able to search thoroughly the bottom of the matter, and for their uprightness will earnestly and sincerely deal therein.' They were to be given every opportunity to view the body and 'to proceed according to law' without respect to any living person. Robert's best defence, of course, was to demonstrate as openly as possible that he had nothing to hide, nothing to fear from the most searching enquiry, and he had taken the additional precaution of sending Amy's kinsmen, Arthur Robsart and John Appleyard, to be present at Cumnor and be 'privy to all the dealing there.'

Thomas Blount was able to vouch for the fact that the coroner's jury was indeed composed of 'as wise and as able men, being but countrymen, as ever I saw' and that these worthies were taking great pains to learn the truth. 'They be very secret' he wrote; 'and yet I do hear that they can find no presumptions of evil. And if I may say to your lordship my conscience, I think some of them may be sorry for it, God forgive me. And, if I judge aright, mine own opinion is much quieted; the more I search of it, the more free it doth appear unto me . . . The circumstances and as many things as I can learn doth persuade me that only misfortune hath done it and nothing else.'

The inquest, as Blount had predicted, presently returned a verdict of misadventure and on 22 September Amy was buried in the church of St Mary the Virgin at Oxford with all the funereal pomp and ceremony due to her position. Offically the incident was closed, but few people were convinced that 'the very plain truth' or anything like it had been uncovered and, for the rest of his life, Robert was to be haunted by the forlorn ghost of Cumnor Place.

Ironically enough, modern medical opinion tends to support the verdict so reluctantly reached by that 16th century jury, for it is now known that in fifty per cent of cases of advanced breast cancer secondary deposits are present in the bones. The effect of such deposits in the spine is to make it so brittle that the slightest stumble, perhaps even the mere act of walking, or hurrying, down a flight of stairs, can result in a spontaneous fracture of the vertebrae. This explanation of the mystery of Amy Dudley's broken neck, put forward by Professor Ian Aird in 1956, is generally accepted today as the most plausible hypothesis (always bearing in mind that we don't even know for certain that she was suffering from breast cancer), but it still does not entirely account for her unusual behaviour on the day of her death. Was she, as Thomas Blount seems to have believed, mentally disturbed and planning to take her own life, or could she have been expecting a visitor? The question marks remain and, while it is only fair to remember that no evidence of foul play has ever been brought to light, it is also hardly surprising that in the autumn of 1560 the notion that so spectacular and convenient a death could have been due to simple 'misadventure' was treated with widespread and freely expressed disbelief.

Nevertheless, by the middle of September Robert was back at court, a free man in every sense of the word, and in diplomatic circles speculation ran riot. Alvaro de Quadra was not sure if the Queen intended to marry her favourite at once, or even if she would marry at all, as he did not think her mind was sufficiently fixed. But, as he told the Duchess of Parma, 'with these people it is always wisest to think the worst.' In France they were not only thinking the worst, they were gleefully anticipating it, and the young Queen of Scots, so it was said, had exclaimed: 'So the Queen of England is to marry her horsekeeper, who has killed his wife to make room for her!'—a remark which pretty well summed up opinion in the European courts.

Among Elizabeth's own representatives abroad there was consternation. Thomas Randolph in Edinburgh wrote that the 'bruits and slanderous reports' being spread by the French and their sympathisers 'so passioneth my heart that no grief ever I felt was like unto it!', while Nicholas Throckmorton in Paris was almost beside himself. 'I wish I were either dead or hence', he lamented on 10 October, 'that I might not hear the dishonourable and naughty reports that are made of the Queen.' The French princes, it seemed, were not hesitating to pass remarks about Elizabeth and 'some others' which made Throckmorton's hair stand on end. 'One laugheth at us, another threateneth, another revileth the Queen. Some let not to say, What religion is this that a subject shall kill his wife, and the Prince not only bear withal but marry with him?' One thing was certain, if these terrible rumours were not scotched, or if they turned out to be true, then England's reputation was gone for ever, war would follow and the utter subversion of Queen and country.

On 15 October de Quadra was able to inform King Philip that Cecil, now back in his accustomed place at the royal right-hand, had told him the Queen had decided *not* to marry Lord Robert, 'as he had learnt direct from her.' This, of course, did nothing to silence the gossip that 'Lord Robert did swyve the Queen', or prevent the circulation of stories that they were already secretly married; and Throckmorton kept up a plaintive jeremiad about the unspeakable consequences for God, religion and the commonwealth if Elizabeth were to 'so foully forget herself' until Cecil was finally obliged to ask him to shut up. Robert was still reported to be in high favour, but as the weeks passed with no further startling developments, the crisis began gradually to subside and before the end of the year international attention had switched to the personal affairs of the Queen of Scots.

The young King of France, whose health had always been a source of concern to his family, had not grown any stronger as he grew up. François suffered, among other things, from a chronic inflammation of the middle ear which suddenly became acute during the second week of November 1560—the result, it was thought, of a chill caught during a cold day's hunting. Although every effort was made to conceal the seriousness of his condition, Throckmorton wrote that 'the King's sickness doth so succeed as men do begin to doubt of his long lasting.' A few days later there was a temporary improvement, but on 2 December the wretched youth 'fell again into his fit, which has ever since so increased upon him, together with the grief or imposthume in his head, that within forty-eight hours he became speechless . . . and the 6th of this present, at eleven of the clock at night, he departed to God, leaving as heavy and dolorous a wife, as of right she had good cause to be.'

Thus Mary Stewart was widowed, four days before her eighteenth birthday, and immediately the balance of the various European power groups shifted into yet another pattern.

IV

Think You I Could Love My Own Winding Sheet?

As a young and lovely widow, 'dispossessed of the Crown of France, with little hope of recovering that of Scotland', Mary Stewart now became an object of compassion. 'She universally inspires great pity', wrote the Venetian ambassador in Paris. She was also inspiring considerable curiosity, for, as Nicholas Throckmorton put it, 'during her husband's life there was no great account made of her, for that, being under the band of marriage and subjection of her husband . . . there was offered no great occasion to know what was in her! Now, for the first time, 'La Royne Marie' was about to emerge as a personality in her own right and although Throckmorton, in the absence of instructions from London, had not joined the other members of the diplomatic corps in paying a visit of condolence to the widow, he had heard enough to enable him to send a glowing report to the Lords of the Council. Since her husband's death, it seemed, Mary had shown that she was 'of great wisdom for her years, modesty, and also of great judgement in the wise handling of herself and her matters, which . . . cannot but turn greatly to her commendation, reputation, honour and great benefit of herself and her country.' She did not think herself too wise, but was content 'to be ruled by good counsel and wise men.' This, in Throckmorton's opinion, was a most desirable virtue in a princess, and the inference that the Queen of England could with advantage take a few lessons in prudence, discretion and 'kingly modesty' from her Scottish cousin is inescapable.

The 'matters' currently exercising the minds of the Queen of Scots and her advisers were, of course, concerned with the question of her future, following the recent dramatic change in her circumstances. Three possible courses of action lay open to Mary Stewart at this crossroads in her life. She could have stayed on in France, the country of her adoption, where she had a loving family and many friends, and where her social and financial position would have been assured; she could go back to Scotland and take the reins of government into her own hands, or she could marry again, choosing a husband whose power would increase her 'estimation and fame'.

There is nothing to indicate that Mary ever seriously considered the first of these options. The French throne had now passed to François II's younger brother Charles, a child of ten, while the power behind the throne passed into the hands of the Queen Mother, that formidable matriarch Catherine de Medici, whose chief preoccupation lay in defending the rights of her remaining Valois sons against any further incursions by the predatory House of Guise, and who was making no particular secret of the fact that she hoped the Queen of Scots would soon be making other arrangements.

No doubt Mary could have ridden out the new regent's hostility had she wished, but she was not interested in playing second fiddle. Like her former mother-in-law, like her cousin Elizabeth, she was interested in power and, although she wrote to the Scottish Council telling them that she intended to come home as soon as she had settled her affairs in France, her real preference was for another continental marriage at least as glorious as her first—indeed speculation about the identity of her second husband had begun over the deathbed of the unhappy François.

The candidates ranged from the Earl of Arran, who had just been finally rejected by Elizabeth, to the King of Sweden, yet another of the Queen of England's unsuccessful suitors, and Philip of Spain's fifteen-year-old son and heir. The fact that Don Carlos was an epileptic, physically degenerate and mentally disturbed, did not apparently disqualify him as a bridegroom for the most exquisite princess in Europe and a possible begetter of future kings of Scotland. Whatever his personal peculiarities, an alliance with the Spanish Infante would give the Queen of Scots all the help she was ever likely to need in dealing with Queen Elizabeth.

The merest hint of so deadly an alliance in the making was enough to raise alarm in English diplomatic circles. Nicholas Throckmorton warned the Council early in January 1561 of the impending arrival of a special emissary from Spain and of much secret conferring already going on between the Spanish ambassador, the Queen of Scots and the Cardinal of Lorraine. The House of Guise, he added, would undoubtedly 'use all means to bring to pass the marriage between the Prince of Spain and the Queen of Scotland.'

Throckmorton had urged that some 'personage of honour' should be sent from London to establish relations with the new French court, and in February Francis Russell, Earl of Bedford, arrived at Fontainebleau on a courtesy visit. After paying his respects to the Queen Mother and the Princes of the blood, he was conducted to the Queen of Scots to convey Elizabeth's formal condolences. Mary, reported Bedford, answered 'with a very sorrowful look and speech that she thanked the Queen for her gentleness in comforting her woe . . . and considering that the Queen now shows the part of a good sister, whereof she has great need, she will endeavour to be even with her in goodwill.'

Bedford and Throckmorton had two more audiences with the widow during the course of the next few days, and again there was plenty of talk about Mary's desire for 'amity' with Elizabeth, seeing 'they were both in one isle, of one language, the nearest kinswomen that each other had, and both queens.' For her part, Mary would use all good offices, to move Elizabeth to think her 'an assured friend', but when Bedford asked her to 'put the same in proof' by ratifying the Treaty of Edinburgh without further ado, she became evasive. She had no counsel, she said, the matter was great for one of her years and she must first discuss it with the nobles of her realm, some of whom, she heard, would soon be coming to visit her. When she had 'communed' with them, she would give the Queen of England 'such an answer as she trusts will please her.' Mary wished that she and Elizabeth could meet, as she was sure they would then be able to settle any outstanding differences much more satisfactorily than through intermediaries, and she challenged Throckmorton with breach of promise—she had sent Elizabeth *her* portrait, but had not yet received one in return.

Bedford's mission was inconclusive, but it had certainly demonstrated that the Queen of Scots was not to be underrated. For all her protestations about her youth and lack of 'counsel', Mary had handled the professionals like a veteran, giving nothing away, yet still contriving to maintain a cordial atmosphere.

Meanwhile, the Scots were contemplating the prospective home-coming of their sovereign lady with mixed feelings. There had been unfeigned relief over the 'taking away' of the French king—'commonly taken for a great benefyte off Godes'—but William Maitland of Lethington did not hesitate to express his misgivings about the future to his friend and confidant William Cecil. Already, it seemed,

factions were forming. The irreconcilables, opposed to a Catholic
Queen on any terms, were so few that 'no accompt was to be made of
them'; but the majority, although agreed that since the Queen of
England had dashed their hopes of an Anglo-Scottish union by
rejecting the Earl of Arran they would have to make the best bargain
they could with their own Queen, were divided among themselves.
The Hamiltons, characteristically, wanted to make marriage with
Arran a pre-condition of Mary's return. The rest, 'no small party
either in number, degree, or power' and less interested in the
advancement of the House of Hamilton, thought it would be better
policy to welcome her home on no other conditions than that 'she
neither bring force nor counsel of strangers, but trust only in her
native subjects.' It should then, they reasoned, be possible to find
ways of persuading her to forget the past, live peaceably and favour
'the Religion'. Maitland was not very optimistic, believing that 'here
wylbe a madde worlde', but much would depend on Mary's attitude
and nothing could be decided until Lord James Stewart, bastard son
of the late King of Scotland by Lady Margaret Erskine, had been to
France and 'fully groped her mynd.'

Lord James, now a man of thirty, was 'one of the precise
Protestants, knowen to be trew and constant, honest and not able to
be corrupted.' In addition to these useful qualifications, it was hoped
that their close relationship 'must move her hyghnes to beare him
some good will, and . . . rather trust him than any other.'

Whether or not Mary trusted her half-brother, it was only too
obvious that he represented the party of power in Scotland. The
previous autumn she had told Nicholas Throckmorton that her
Scottish subjects 'must be taught to know their duties.' Now, as a
childless dowager, unable to count on the support of the French
crown and with no other marriage alliance immediately in view
(negotiations with Spain having bogged down in the hostile intrigues
of Queen Catherine de Medici and King Philip's indecision), she was
no longer in a position to take such a high tone. It looked as if her
future, for the time being at least, must lie in Scotland and her uncle
the Cardinal, a shrewd and pragmatic politician, had advised her 'to
repose most upon them of the reformed religion.' Lord James, her
nearest kinsman and one familiar with all the murky byways of
Scottish affairs, certainly seemed a natural choice of guide and
mentor, and the meeting between brother and sister, which took
place at St Dizier in mid-April, resulted in as satisfactory an

understanding as could be expected in the circumstances. Mary indicated that she was ready to let bygones be bygones, to come home alone and to accept the *status quo* in Scotland, but she refused to change her religion and insisted on being given the proper facilities to practise it. This was conceded. James Stewart, precise and incorruptible Protestant though he might be, was also a politician and had already told his more fanatical fellow countrymen, notably John Knox, that he saw no reason why the Queen should not have her Mass privately in her own chapel, although he warned her not to attempt to meddle in religious matters.

Lord James went home with a generally favourable report. Mary had shown herself both gracious and amenable, and as it began to dawn on the Scots that their young Queen's dynastic potentialities would now work in favour of Scotland rather than France, they cheered up and got ready to give her 'an honourable reception.' Maitland of Lethington had wanted Mary to travel overland through England and meet Queen Elizabeth on the way, hoping to lay the foundations of a personal relationship which would help to 'breed us quietness', but Mary told Nicholas Throckmorton that she intended to go by sea straight to the port of Leith. She was sending M d'Oysel, once her mother's most trusted councillor, to the Queen of England to inform her of her plans and to ask for a safe-conduct in case she should be forced to land on English soil.

This sort of request was normally no more than a matter of routine courtesy between friendly sovereigns, but when d'Oysel reached London early in July he soon found there was going to be nothing routine about it. The first thing Elizabeth wanted to know was whether he had brought any answer concerning the ratification of the Treaty of Edinburgh. D'Oysel was obliged to admit that he had not, whereupon the temperature in the audience chamber dropped to freezing point. There would, it appeared, be no safe-conduct and no welcome for the Queen of Scots in her cousin's realm until she had fulfilled her obligations by ratifying the treaty, as she was in honour bound to do.

This display of uncousinly hostility quite shocked international opinion and gave Mary an opportunity to score, which she promptly exploited. Receiving Throckmorton at Saint Germain on 20 July she declared she was only sorry that she had demeaned herself by asking for a favour she did not need. The English had not been able to prevent her voyage to France thirteen years ago. They could not prevent her from returning now. Mary only wanted to be friends, but it was beginning to look as if the Queen of England was more interested in 'the amity of her disobedient subjects than of their Sovereign.' Elizabeth had called her young and inexperienced. Yet, said Mary, she hoped she knew how to behave uprightly towards her friends and kinsfolk and would never allow *her* passion to betray her into using unbecoming language of another Queen and her nearest kinswoman. She was not without allies, she added pointedly, and Elizabeth would find she was not to be bullied. As for the treaty, that had been made in her husband's lifetime and she could not be held responsible for his failure to ratify it. She might be young, but she was not foolish enough to proceed in such a matter without proper advice and, as she had often told Throckmorton, as soon as she had consulted the Scottish Council, she would send his mistress a reasonable answer. But now, just as she was about to hasten home for that very purpose, it seemed that the Queen of England would not suffer her to pass into her realm.

Throckmorton could only repeat that delay and indirect dealing over the treaty had caused Elizabeth's 'miscontentation'. When he brought up her other grievance—the Queen of Scotland's quartering of the English royal arms—Mary retorted that she had then been under the commandment of her husband and father-in-law and since her widowhood she had neither borne the arms or used the title of England. She herself had never thought or meant anything against her cousin, and brought the interview to a close by begging Throckmorton 'to behave like a good minister, whose part was to make things rather better than worse.'

Slightly stunned by this accomplished flow of oratory, Throckmorton still did not know what Mary meant to do, and the following day he went to see her again to try and find out whether or not the Queen of Scotland 'minded to continue her voyage.' It appeared that she did. If her preparations had not been so far advanced, she told him, Elizabeth's unkindness might have given her pause, 'but now she was determined to adventure the matter whatsoever came of it. She trusted that the wind would be so favourable that she need not come on the coast of England; and if she did, then the Queen, his mistress, would have her in her hands to do her will of her; and if she was so hard-hearted as to desire her end, she might then do her pleasure and make sacrifice of her.' 'In this matter', exclaimed Mary in a final flourish of self-dramatisation, 'God's will be done!'

Just what Elizabeth might have done had Mary been forced 'to come on the coast of England' in 1561 remains an unanswered question. D'Oysel had reported that the Queen told him she would provide to keep Mary from passing home, and William Camden, the near contemporary historian, states in his *Annals* that Lord James Stewart had advised the Queen to provide for her religion and her safety by intercepting and (presumably) somehow disposing of his sister during her journey. Lord James had certainly been in close touch with the English government and had spent two weeks in London on his way back from France in May but, while neither he nor Elizabeth would have been exactly inconsolable if an unfortunate accident had overtaken Mary at sea, it is highly improbable that any fell design was ever openly discussed between them. If Mary had been forced to land on her shores, Elizabeth's first emotion would most likely have been acute embarrassment, and the Queen of Scots would most likely have found herself being hustled over the Border with all possible speed—albeit at a place of the Queen of England's choosing.

Elizabeth's motive in refusing her safe-conduct had been a last minute attempt to keep Mary penned up in France, where she was now relatively innocuous. There's little doubt that the Queen of England had been disagreeably surprised by the political acumen and seductive qualities displayed by her eighteen year-old cousin over the past few months, or that she shared William Maitland's misgivings about the sort of havoc the pretty creature might create among the hot-blooded, volatile Scottish warlords. Who could tell, indeed, how many simple men might be 'carried away with vain hope, and brought abed with fair words'? In the circumstances, therefore, it was natural enough that Elizabeth should have been prepared to go to considerable lengths to secure Mary's ratification of the Treaty of Edinburgh, which could be interpreted to embody a virtual renunciation of her claim to the English throne, before she set foot in Scotland.

But just as Mary's unexpectedly accommodating attitude towards the Scottish Protestants had smoothed her path home, so her calling of the Queen's bluff further strengthened her position, and both Maitland and Throckmorton felt Elizabeth had made a serious mistake in tactics. Throckmorton knew of no 'equipage or force by sea in readiness to impeach the Queen of Scots' passage' and thought that if his mistress did not mean to make good her threat to d'Oysel and close the seaways, 'it would have been better if no such thing had been said, but passage granted.' As it was, she had simply risked antagonising Mary to no purpose, annoyed the French and won herself a good deal of adverse publicity. The Venetian ambassador in Paris commented severely on the inhumanity of the Queen of England 'in refusing to give passage through her dominions to a woman, a widow, unarmed and almost banished from her own home.' Elizabeth was, in fact, obliged to climb down in a conciliatory letter to Mary dated 16 August containing 'friendly and sisterly offers of friendship' and assuring her that there was no truth in the rumours that she had sent her navy to impeach her cousin's passage. She had only two or three small barks at sea operating against the pirates who were preying on the North Sea fishermen.

By the time this letter reached France Mary was no longer there to be conciliated. She had left Saint Germain on 25 July and set out for the coast escorted by a solid phalanx of uncles. Three of them—Claude, Duke of Aumale, François, the Grand Prior, and René, Marquis d'Elboeuf—were to see her safely home to Scotland, but the young Queen had now to say a poignant farewell to those careful guardians of her childhood, the Duke of Guise and the specially beloved Cardinal Charles of Lorraine. She sailed from Calais on 14 August, when Throckmorton's servant saw her 'haling out of that haven . . . about noon, with two galleys and two great ships.' The long journey to Fotheringay had begun.

Despite all the alarms which had preceded it, Mary's passage was smooth and trouble-free. Thomas Randolph, the English ambassador in Edinburgh, told Nicholas Throckmorton that 'she neither met nor saw ship upon the sea, for all the bruit that was of her stay that should have been.' But according to William Cecil, 'the Queen's Majesty's ships, that were upon the seas to cleanse them of pirates, saw her and saluted her galleys; and staying her ships, examined them of pirates and dismissed them gently. One Scottish ship they detain, as vehemently suspected of piracy.'

Mary had left France in tears, but when she stepped ashore at Leith on the morning of Tuesday, 19 August she was composed and cheerful, her spirits undamped even by a thick sea-mist, which the more pessimistic members of her party saw as an omen and John Knox saw as a symbol of the 'sorrow, dolour, darkness and impiety' which the Queen was bringing to Scotland. The pessimists were, however, in a minority and Mary had nothing to complain of in the general enthusiasm of her welcome. Nor did the crowds who came to cheer her on her way, or the nobility who hurried to present themselves at Holyrood, have any reason to be disappointed by their first glimpse of their sovereign lady. One thing at least on which all her contemporaries were agreed is that Mary Stewart was beautiful, but a mere catalogue of her charms—the tall willowy graceful figure, the flawless complexion, the wide pure brow, heavy-lidded soft brown eyes and rich dark gold hair—does not reveal the full secret of her fascination. It was the genuine out-going warmth of her manner, the endearing little acts of kindness, the pretty tricks of speech (despite her long sojourn abroad she had not forgotten her Scots), the glamour of royalty combined with physical beauty, the shining personal charisma, which united to create that 'inchantment whareby men ar bewitched.' Only John Knox remained untouched. 'In communication with her I espied such craft as I have not found in such an age', he told William Cecil some six weeks after her return and in this opinion, if in nothing else, he and the Queen of England were at one.

Fairly or unfairly, it has been said of Mary that she regarded Scotland as no more than a convenient stop-over between the France of her past glories and England, which was to be the scene of a still more glorious future. Certainly she wasted no time in sending William Maitland south to open the campaign to persuade Elizabeth to recognise her status as heir presumptive to the English throne.

The question of the Queen of Scotland's dynastic claims was already exercising the minds of her more important subjects, and early in August Lord James Stewart had ventured to raise this delicate issue with the Queen of England. In common with the majority of his fellow councillors, Lord James was extremely anxious to preserve the English alliance and he dwelt on God's providence which had so miraculously transformed the old enmity of the two nations into reciprocal goodwill. He could see no reason why anything should interfere with the present satisfactory state of affairs, if only 'the heads could so heartily be joined in love as be the members, I mean your Majesty and the Queen my sovereign lady.' To a plain man there seemed 'many natural causes, and straight bonds of amity' between these two tender cousins, both Queens in the flower of their ages, who resembled one another in most excellent and goodly qualities and whose sex should surely preclude any desire to engage in such unfeminine pursuits as war and bloodshed. Lord

James then gingerly approached the 'one root from which any variance can grow.'

'I wish to God', he wrote, 'the Queen my sovereign lady had never by any advice taken in head to pretend interest or acclaim any title to your Majesty's realm, for then I am fully persuaded you would have been and continued as dear friends as you be tender cousins—but now since on her part something hath been thought of it . . . I fear that unless the root may be removed, it shall ever breed unkindness betwixt you. Your Majesty cannot yield, and she may on the other part think of it hard, being so nigh of the blood of England, to be made a stranger from it!' He therefore suggested that, as long as Elizabeth's title, both for herself and for her children, were guaranteed, she might safely acknowledge Mary's place in the succession of the Crown of England. 'Which your Majesty will pardon me, if I take to be next by the law of all nations, as she that is next in lawful descent of the right line of King Henry the Seventh your grandfather.'

This was undeniably true and, on the face of it, Lord James's proposition looked reasonable enough—the most obvious objections being Mary's religion and her great-uncle Henry's will. If the provisions of this debatable document were to be followed, then of course the next heir was Henry VIII's other great-niece Lady Katherine Grey, elder of the two surviving sisters of the unfortunate Lady Jane and now in her early twenties. Elizabeth, however, had never bothered to conceal her poor opinion of Katherine Grey and Katherine herself had not helped matters by making a secret marriage with the young Earl of Hertford, son of the late Lord Protector Somerset. This came to light during the eventful August of 1561, when the bride could no longer conceal her pregnancy, and as a result she was promptly committed to the Tower where she proceeded to compound her offence (and complicate the situation still further) by giving birth to a healthy son.

Despite exhaustive enquiries, no evidence that Katherine had been guilty of anything worse than idiocy ever came to light, but Elizabeth remained unconvinced. As a Protestant and an Englishwoman born, Katherine Grey's claim to recognition commanded an influential body of support and the Queen, who had caught a sulphurous whiff of treason in her cousin's underhand behaviour, could never quite rid herself of the suspicion that there had been more to the affair than met the eye. In the circumstances, though, she was obliged to be content with having the marriage declared invalid, imposing a hefty fine on Lord Hertford for having deflowered a virgin of the blood royal, and keeping the couple in detention.

Katherine's fall from grace and their own Queen's arrival in their midst had emboldened the Scots, so that when William Maitland came to London towards the end of September he brought with him a formal letter 'in the name of the Nobility' which was distinctly minatory in tone, warning that if the Queen of England should 'use any discourtesy towards the Queen their sovereign' the lords would not forget their duty to support her in any just quarrel. Either for the benefit of those members of her Council whom she suspected of having aided and abetted Katherine Grey, or because she realised that now Mary's presence in Scotland was an accomplished fact, some discussion of her place in the succession could no longer be postponed, Elizabeth gave Maitland a friendly reception and in the course of three interviews talked with unusual freedom about her attitude to Mary and the succession in general.

She knew that Mary was 'of the blood of England' and her nearest kinswoman, so that she was bound by nature to love her. And even in the time 'of most offence', she went on, when Mary 'by bearing my arms and acclaiming the title of my crown, had given me just cause to be most angry with her, yet could I never find in my heart to hate her, imputing rather the fault to others than to herself. As for the title of my crown, for my time I think she will not attain it, nor make impediment to my issue, if any shall come of my body. For so long as I live, there shall be no other Queen in England but I.' The Queen refused to meddle in the rights and wrongs of the succession question. It was like the sacrament of the altar. Some thought one thing, some another and 'whose judgement is best, God knows.' If Mary's right was good, Elizabeth would do nothing to prejudice it. 'I for my part', she told Maitland, 'know none better, nor that myself would prefer to her.' Nor could she think of any serious competitor.

At their next meeting, the Queen returned to the same thorny topic. 'I have always abhorred to draw in question the title of the crown', she said feelingly, 'so many disputes have been already touching it in the mouths of men. Some that this marriage was unlawful, some that someone was a bastard, some other, to and fro, as they favour it or mislike it . . . Howsoever it be', declared Elizabeth Tudor, summing up the whole tangle with masterly simplicity, 'so long as I live, I shall be Queen of England. When I am dead, they shall succeed that have most right.' If that person was the Queen of Scots, well and good. If someone else could show a better right, then it was not reasonable to ask Elizabeth to do them 'a manifest injury.'

Maitland had urged that settling the succession on Mary would cement the friendship between them. Elizabeth did not agree. 'Think you that I could love my own winding sheet?' she enquired brutally. And there was another consideration—the weightiest of all. 'I know the inconstancy of the people of England', remarked their Queen, 'how they ever mislike the present government and have their eyes fixed upon the person that is next to succeed, and naturally men be so disposed.' Many a politician since has learnt to his sorrow the truth of that particular piece of Elizabethan wisdom.

The Queen went on to illustrate her point by favouring Maitland with one of her infrequent references to her own early days. 'I have good experience of myself in my sister's time', she said, 'how desirous men were that I should be in (her) place and earnest to set me up. And if I would have consented, I know what enterprises would have been attempted to bring it to pass, and now perhaps the affections of some are altered. As children dream in their sleep of apples, and in the morning when as they wake and find not the apples they weep; so every man that bore me goodwill when I was Lady Elizabeth . . . imagineth with himself that immediately after my coming to the crown every man should be rewarded according to his own fantasy, and now finding the event answer not their expectation it may be that some could be content of new change, in hope to be then in better case.'

At the age of twenty-eight Elizabeth saw things clearly and saw them whole, without bitterness but without illusion. 'No princes' revenues be so great that they are able to satisfy the insatiable cupidity of men', she observed. 'And if we, either for not giving to men at their discretion or yet for any other cause, should miscontent any (of) our subjects, it is to be feared that if they knew a certain successor of our crown they would have recourse thither; and what danger it were, she being a puissant princess and so near our neighbour, ye may judge. I deal plainly with you, albeit my subjects I think love me as becomes them, yet is nowhere so great perfection that all are content.'

Maitland did his utmost to reassure her. He had no doubt, he said, that Mary would be only too pleased to agree to whatever safeguards Elizabeth liked to name, but Elizabeth was unimpressed. She 'still harped on that string: saying "It is hard to bind princes by any security where hope is offered of a kingdom.'' In private conversation she was fully prepared to admit that she regarded Mary as her natural and lawful heir. When Maitland told her he did not think Mary would ever ratify the Treaty of Edinburgh as it stood, she agreed to consider having it reviewed and modifying the clause which bound the Queen of Scots to abstain 'henceforward' from using and bearing the English royal arms and title. She would be content if Mary would undertake not to bear the arms of England or style herself Queen of England during Elizabeth's lifetime or that of her children. Further than that she would not go. She would not agree to make the Queen of Scots her heir 'by order of Parliament', for 'if it were certainly known in the world who should succeed her, she would never think herself in sufficient surety.'

So, for the moment, the matter stood in *re integra*, but the Laird of Lethington left on his homeward journey by no means unhopeful of the outcome. Elizabeth had suggested that before any formal commission was appointed to review the treaty, the two Secretaries —Maitland and Cecil—should prepare the ground by a correspondence to which she and Mary 'should be privy.' Maitland, therefore, hastened to set the ball rolling in a letter to Cecil dated 7 October.

He found in his Queen, he wrote 'a good disposition to quietness, but therewith joined a careful regard to her own estate, and a courage such as will be loath to forego her right.' If only Elizabeth would be 'conformable'—that is, redress the manifest injustice done to Mary by Henry VIII's will—everyone would be happy. After all, Margaret Tudor had married James IV as 'eldest lawful daughter' of King Henry VII and there was nothing to indicate that he had meant to debar her descendants from the English succession; rather the contrary. Elizabeth had complained that the like was never demanded of any Prince 'to declare his heir apparent in his own time', but in this case, where so much doubt and confusion now existed, it would surely be more statesmanlike for the Queen to determine the succession of her crown, rather than 'suffer it thus to hang in suspense.' 'For Princes be as fathers of their country; and what father, seeing clearly that his sons will contend for his inheritance will not rather himself appoint the difference?'

Maitland ended by begging Cecil not to allow any minor difficulties or misunderstandings 'frustrate both realms of so great a benefit as is to be looked for by conjunction of these two Princesses.' He had been credibly informed, he said, by a number of his fellow

countrymen with long memories that if the two kings, Henry VIII
and James V, had succeeded in meeting at York back in September
1541, 'King Henry was determined to limit the succession of his
Crown to their Sovereign his nephew, which may serve as a precedent
to the Queen.' If Henry, irritated by James's failure to keep the
appointment, had chosen to vent his annoyance on his nephew's
posterity, where was the equity in that?

Maitland continued to press Cecil for advice on how best to handle
Elizabeth, but evoked a tepid response from that ultra-cautious
individual who, nervously conscious of his mistress's extreme
touchiness on the subject of the succession, was taking care to keep
his involvement to an irreducible minimum. Lord James Stewart also
wrote to the English Secretary of State and to Robert Dudley,
piously exhorting him to use his well known influence with the
Queen to further the cause of peace between the two realms.

The Duke of Guise added his voice in a conversation with Nicholas
Throckmorton. He and his brother the Cardinal were of one mind,
he said, that 'nothing should be left undone to perfect the amity
betwixt the two Queens in one isle.' They could see no valid reason
why their niece should not be accepted as the next heir to the English
throne. Queen Mary, the Duke pointed out, was now in a state to
accept the guidance of her kinsmen and the Scottish Council, but
being young she would no doubt marry again, and if, as was likely, her
second husband were 'a puissant Prince' who could tell what attitude
he might take 'if the matter be left at large'? On the other hand, once
the succession was settled, Queen Elizabeth, her nobles and subjects,
could be assured that the Queen of Scotland would do nothing,
either in marriage or anything else of importance, without their
approval and her uncles would certainly never advise her otherwise.
Throckmorton could see for himself how reasonably she had behaved
since her return home. She was 'one of the meekest, best natured
Princesses in the world' and if she ever did come to the English
throne, 'this benefit all should have from her—that she would answer
with mind and intent to win all hearts, being void of partialities,
affectionate to no faction, free from inveterate malice and desire to
revenge displeasures and things past.'

While this could hardly be counted as an unbiassed assessment of
her character, no one could deny that Mary's conduct to date had
been a model of discretion, conciliation and prudent statecraft. She
had, as she had warned her half-brother she would, insisted on

freedom of worship for herself, but she had also kept her promise not to interfere with the Protestant kirk and had issued a proclamation forbidding any 'alteration or innovation of the state of religion . . . which her majesty found public and universally standing' on her arrival in her realm. Nor had she shown any signs of trying to encourage the remnants of the Catholic party and had taken John Knox's outspoken animadversions on the harlotry and idolatry of the 'kirk of Rome' in surprisingly good part. In affairs of state she was relying on the advice of James Stewart (soon to become Earl of Moray) and Maitland of Lethington, generally recognised as the two ablest politicians in Scotland, and was deliberately setting herself out to charm, working hard and on the whole very successfully to please her subjects. But her best efforts were reserved for her English cousin.

When Elizabeth indicated that she would prefer negotiations over the Treaty of Edinburgh to be conducted privately, rather than through a commission, Mary took it 'as a plain declaration of your good mind, and token of your natural love to us.' She would have no arbiter but Elizabeth and was ready to place herself unreservedly in the Queen of England's hands, such was her confidence in that lady's 'uprightness in judgement.' As for the treaty, 'we will do all that in reason may be required, or rather enter into a new one, such as may stand without our prejudice, in favour of you and the lawful issue of your body; provided that our interest to that crown, failing yourself and the said issue, may be put in good surety. Whereon the matter being so knit up, and all seed of dissension uprooted, we shall present to the world such an amity as has never been seen.' Mary had written to show the bottom of her mind nakedly, and trusted to be answered in like fashion.

It was, of course, on her sincerity that the whole matter depended. Thomas Randolph, who was in regular contact with the Queen of Scots, simply could not make up his mind whether she was to be trusted or not. 'I receive of her grace at all times very good words', he wrote in October, and Lord James and the Laird of Lethington assured him that 'they are meant as they are spoken.' In November he was reporting that so far as he could tell, 'she meaneth no less than hath been spoken often both by herself and others, to do what she can to unite the two realms in so perfect an amity as the like hath not been seen.' Mary missed no opportunity of declaring her love and admiration for her 'tender cousin' and Maitland told William Cecil repeatedly that her intentions were just and sincere. She trusted the Queen of England as if they were natural sisters and 'loveth her as entirely.'

If it was an act, it was a very good act and Randolph, himself no mean exponent of the art of duplicity, finally came to the conclusion that either Mary's sisterly affection for Elizabeth 'was never greater towards any, or else it is the deepest dissembled and covered that ever was.' Not that this was impossible, for 'whatsoever policy is in all the chief and best practised heads in France, whatsoever craft, falsehood or deceit there is in all the subtle brains of Scotland, is either fresh in this woman's memory, or she can fett it (call it up) with a wet finger.'

But all the policy and craft of France and Scotland had not yet succeeded in extracting anything that looked like a concession from Queen Elizabeth, except that by the end of the year she had begun to show interest in arranging the personal interview which Mary desired so ardently that she would 'stick for no ceremonies' to attain it. By no means everyone shared her eagerness. A royal summit meeting would cost a lot of money, at least £40,000 by one estimate, and presented some formidable logistical problems. The Scottish Catholics were against it, France was doubtful and the Scottish Council would have preferred to wring some sort of prior commitment out of the English. Even Maitland was nervous that if the cousins met and settled nothing, it might do more harm than good; while William Cecil, 'knowing the diversity of both their intents', maintained a strictly neutral stance. The English Council as a whole were not enthusiastic. The Catholic Queen of Scots, with her French Guisard connections and her 'pretended title to the crown', remained an object of deep suspicion in political and ecclesiastical circles south of the Border, where it was widely believed that her motives in wishing to make the journey were selfish ones, 'intended chiefly for her own profit.' It was feared that she would use the opportunity to further her claims to the throne, give hope and courage to the native papists, besides ingratiating herself with all sorts of other undesirables and 'such people as love change.'

In the end it was Mary herself who took the initiative. With the natural self-confidence of one accustomed to personal success she had little doubt of her ability to charm away Queen Elizabeth's misgivings once they were face to face, and in May 1562 she sent Maitland of Lethington back to London to ask for an invitation. In

June she received a friendly letter from Elizabeth which she carried
about ostentatiously tucked into the bosom of her dress, and told
Thomas Randolph that if she could put it closer to her heart she
would.

Maitland had returned from his mission bringing the long awaited
portrait of the English Queen and Mary showed it to Randolph,
asking if it was a good likeness. Randolph replied diplomatically,
hoping her grace would soon be able to judge for herself. 'That', said
Mary, 'is the thing that I have most desired ever since I was in hope
thereof, and she shall well assure herself there shall be no stay in me
. . . and I trust that by that time we have spoken together, our hearts
will be so eased that the greatest grief that ever after shall be between
us, will be when we take leave the one of the other; and let God be my
witness', she added impressively, 'I honour her in my heart and love
her as my dear and natural sister.'

Elizabeth, it seemed, had been a little out of sorts and Mary was
full of anxious enquiries, asking Randolph about her cousin's
'hability' of body when she was in health, of her exercise, diet and
many more questions which he could not answer 'save by report.'
'Well', she said, 'I trust that God will do better unto us both than so
that either of us should be sick, and for my part . . . I would that I
might bear half the pain rather than that should stay our journey.'
And she brought the interview to a close by begging Randolph to
keep her informed of anything he might hear, 'for truly I shall not be
merry until I hear that she be well.'

William Cecil having finally come down off the fence in favour of
the visit and Elizabeth herself showing an unwonted degree of
keenness, preparations were now going ahead with every appearance
of serious intent—despite continued opposition from a majority on
the Privy Council. It was agreed that the two Queens should meet at
Nottingham early in September and although the weather was
frightful—incessant rain making already bad roads almost impassable
—Maitland found Elizabeth 'so earnestly bent to go forward to this
voyage that she will sail whether the wind blow or not.'

Considering Mary's background, it was a supreme irony that the
cancellation of the Nottingham summit should have been caused by
events in France, where Catherine de Medici, in her determination to
prevent the House of Guise from regaining its former hold on the
government, had been encouraging their rivals the Huguenot
leaders—especially the Bourbon family and Gaspard de Coligny,

Admiral of France. Given the rabid animosity between the two factions and their followers, this was a dangerous policy and it led to disaster. In January 1562 the French Protestants were granted religious toleration, amounting to virtual self-government in certain districts, a measure furiously opposed by the Guises. On 1 March a Huguenot congregation in the town of Vassy was massacred on the orders of the Duke of Guise and by April the first of the religious civil wars which were to ravage France for the rest of the century was in full swing. In June there was a temporary truce but on 12 July, six days after the Queen of England had signed the Articles for her meeting with the Queen of Scots, a despatch from Nicholas Throckmorton in Paris brought the news that hostilities had broken out once more. The Huguenots were appealing to Protestant England for help, the Catholics were reported to be turning to Spain and in the circumstances it was obviously out of the question for the Queen to leave London.

Sir Henry Sidney went up to Edinburgh to tell the Scots that the meeting was off and Mary dissolved into floods of disappointed tears, despite assurances that the interview had only been postponed, due to 'lets and hindrances' from foreign parts which were beyond Elizabeth's control, and a promise that it would be re-arranged at some suitable location north of the Trent in the following spring. Maitland, too, was disappointed and begged Cecil not to let his goodwill towards Mary be diminished 'by anything you think amiss in her uncles, at least so long as you shall see her affection towards your sovereign remain always one.'

Unprofitable though it may be, it is hard to resist the temptation to speculate on how an encounter between Elizabeth Tudor and Mary Stewart in the summer of 1562 might have affected the future course of their relationship. Both were then young women, Mary still in her teens, Elizabeth still in her twenties. Both still had some room for manoeuvre, both had something to gain from friendship and, dissimilar though they were in so many ways, as unmarried Queens reigning in a male-dominated society they should have been able to find some common ground. On the other hand, it is in the highest degree unlikely that Elizabeth would have granted the one thing Mary wanted from her—nor was it really in her power to do so. Of the two, she was taking the greater risk of being upstaged by letting the sweet-talking Queen of Scots into her realm, and the surprising thing is that she was apparently so willing to do so. Or was she?

Would she, whatever the state of affairs in foreign parts, have found some convincing pretext for a last minute postponement?

It might have been expected that Mary's sympathies would have been publicly engaged with the struggles of her uncles, but her interests now lay in England and although she expressed anxiety about the troubles in France she remained carefully neutral. Indeed, so far from favouring the Catholic cause, instead of journeying south that summer she went north, going as far as Inverness on a progress which turned into a successful punitive expedition against the unruly Gordon clan led by the Earl of Huntly, Scotland's principal Catholic magnate. The Queen thoroughly enjoyed her adventure in the Highlands. Thomas Randolph reported that he had never seen her in better spirits, adding she only regretted she was not a man 'to know what life it was to lie all night in the fields, or to walk on the causeway with a jack and a knapscalle (helmet), a Glasgow buckler, and a broadsword.'

Queen Elizabeth, meanwhile, had yielded, unwisely as it turned out, to appeals from the Prince of Condé and committed herself to armed intervention on behalf of the Huguenots. In October she wrote to Mary from Hampton Court explaining that she was only acting, as a good neighbour should, to help the King of France suppress the atrocities and disorders of civil war. 'Think of me as honourably as my good will to you merits . . .' she ended. 'My hot fever prevents me writing more.'

Elizabeth's fever proved to be the early stages of a near fatal attack of smallpox. Her letter to Mary was written on 15 October and by that night she was desperately ill. William Cecil, summoned from London at midnight, reached the palace in the small hours of the sixteenth, and as the Queen lay unconscious, perhaps dying, the Council went into emergency session to discuss the horrifying crisis facing the country.

According to the Spanish ambassador, out of the fifteen or sixteen members present, 'there were nearly as many different opinions about the succession to the Crown.' In fact, the Council seems to have been split more or less down the middle. One group, almost certainly led by Cecil, wanted to follow King Henry's will and nominate Lady Katherine Grey; others, 'who found flaws in the will', pressed the claims of Henry Hastings, Earl of Huntingdon, who could boast double descent from Edward III and was known to be a reliable Protestant. The Earls of Bedford and Pembroke supported

Huntingdon, and so—although they were not council members —did the Duke of Norfolk and Lord Robert Dudley. Huntingdon was married to Lord Robert's sister, and Alvaro de Quadra believed Robert would be ready to back his brother-in-law by force of arms. A third and smaller group, headed by the old Marquis of Winchester who had already survived the alarums and excursions of three reigns, urged against too much haste and suggested referring the matter to a committee of jurists, who could examine the rights of the various claimants and advise the Council accordingly. No one, it seemed, within the precincts of Hampton Court, had mentioned the name of Mary Stewart and de Quadra reported that the Catholics, too, were divided—some favouring the Queen of Scotland, others preferring her aunt Margaret Lennox, who had been born in England and was considered to be 'devout and sensible.'

While the Council was still deliberating Elizabeth recovered consciousness and, in her confused and feverish state, begged the anxious throng at her bedside to make Robert Dudley Protector of the Realm with an income of £20,000 a year. She swore, in what she believed might be her last moments, that although she loved and had always loved Lord Robert dearly, 'as God was her witness, nothing improper had ever passed between them', and asked that the groom who slept in his room should be given a pension of £500 a year. 'Everything she asked was promised', wrote de Quadra, 'but will not be fulfilled.'

Only one thing emerged with any certainty out of the terror and turmoil of that dreadful day; if the Queen had died—and she was 'all but gone'—she would have left a vacuum which would rapidly have been filled with political anarchy, with bitter faction fighting and, most probably, with civil war on the French pattern. To the unspeakable relief of everyone concerned, she recovered. She even escaped the dreaded disfigurement of the pox and within an astonishingly short space of time she was up and about again and in full command once more. But the nation had had a fright it would not soon forget and pressure on the Queen to overcome her reluctance to name her heir would now no longer be coming from the Queen of Scots alone.

V

Yonder Long Lad

As a result of the general alarm caused by Elizabeth's illness, Alvaro de Quadra heard that groups of gentlemen were meeting privately, on the excuse of dining together, in order to discuss the forbidden topic of the succession. One such gathering, held at the Earl of Arundel's house and attended by the Duke of Norfolk, lasted until two o'clock in the morning and was believed to have come down in favour of Lady Katherine Grey. When the Queen heard about this she was furious and was said to have wept with rage. She regarded the succession, like her marriage, as a matter which came entirely within the royal prerogative and over which she would tolerate no interference, however well-meant. She summoned Arundel and they appear to have had a first-class row, the Earl telling her that if she wanted to govern the country by passion he could assure her that the nobility would not allow it. The succession was something which affected them all vitally and they had every right to be concerned.

As well as a mutinous nobility, Elizabeth now had to face another Parliament and the fears of the nation, as reflected by its elected representatives, were succinctly expressed in a petition presented to the Queen by the Speaker of the House of Commons on 28 January 1563. They foresaw with awful clarity 'the unspeakable miseries of civil wars, the perilous intermeddlings of foreign princes with seditious, ambitious and factious subjects at home, the waste of noble houses, the slaughter of people, subversion of towns ... unsurety of all men's possessions, lives and estates' if the sovereign were to die without a known heir, and pointed out that 'from the Conquest to this present day the realm was never left as now it is without a certain heir living and known.' The Commons still wanted Elizabeth to marry, of course, and have children of her own, but it was significant that, since the 'great terror and dreadful warning' of her recent sickness, the emphasis of their anxiety had shifted.

Whether she married or not, they wanted the succession to be settled, and settled *now*.

The Lords' petition, delivered a couple of days later, put marriage first and begged 'that it would please your Majesty to dispose yourself to marry, where it shall please you, to whom it shall please you, and as soon as it shall please you.' But their lordships, too, were acutely worried about the succession—understandably so in a society where, as they grimly reminded the Queen, 'upon the death of princes the law dieth'—and earnestly prayed her to give the matter urgent and serious attention.

Replying to the Commons, Elizabeth told them that she knew she was as mortal as the next woman. There was no need to keep on rubbing it in. Nor did she need any prompting to remember the awesome nature of her responsibilities towards God and the nation. She understood the members' anxiety and did not take it amiss, but they could hardly expect an immediate answer on so 'great and weighty a matter'. In any case, they surely knew her well enough by this time to trust her to look after them and to be 'neither careless nor unmindful' of their future welfare. 'And so I assure you all', she concluded, 'that, though after my death you may have many stepdames, yet shall you never have a more natural mother than I mean to be to you all.'

If the Spanish ambassador is to be trusted, the Queen expended less tact on the Lords. According to his report, she told them crossly that the marks they saw on her face were not wrinkles, but the scars of smallpox, 'that although she might be old (she was twenty-nine) God could send her children as he did to St Elizabeth, and they had better consider well what they were asking, as, if she declared a successor, it would cost much blood to England.'

In spite of the depth of feeling on the subject, the Lords and Commons had to wait until the end of the Parliamentary session on Easter Saturday for any further word from their sovereign lady. Then, in the presence of both Houses, the Lord Keeper read a message from the Queen, written in her own hand and containing what might be construed as a conditional promise to get married in the not too distant future. As a 'private woman' Elizabeth still infinitely preferred the single state, 'yet', she went on, 'do I strive with myself to think it not meet for a Prince. And if I can bend my liking to your need, I will not resist such a mind.' About the succession she was not to be drawn, taking refuge behind a baffling smoke-screen of words whose only discernible meaning seemed to be that the Queen did not feel the time was ripe for any announcement. 'But', she ended, 'I hope I shall die in quiet with *nunc dimittis*, which cannot be without I see some glimpse of your following surety after my graved bones.'

This was not much comfort to her audience, and in the spring of 1563 Elizabeth herself was seriously troubled over what to do for the best. Apart from her deeply-rooted personal reluctance to have a named heir, she believed, and she was almost certainly right, that any attempt to 'solve' the problem of the succession would have encouraged rather than disarmed faction and controversy. Her instinct was to do nothing, to go on gambling on her own survival until—as she had told another Parliamentary delegation back in 1559—until such time as Almighty God saw fit to make 'good provision . . . whereby the realm shall not remain destitute of an heir that may be a fit governor, and peradventure more beneficial to the realm than such offspring as may come of me.' But her recent brush with death had undoubtedly shaken her, and she knew that by leaving the future to take care of itself in this apparently heedless fashion, she was taking a finely calculated risk. After all, if the worst came to the worst, her subjects could but lose their lives. She, who was answerable to God for her care of the English people, hazarded to lose both body and soul if she failed in her duty to discharge that 'great burthen.'

As she had already made clear to Maitland of Lethington, Elizabeth did not question Mary Stewart's hereditary rights, but if she were now to overcome her natural repugnance at the thought of setting up her winding sheet before her eyes, she would be inviting confrontation not only from the party which supported Katherine Grey, but also from those who actively opposed Mary's claim. None other than Sir Ralph Sadler, that eminent public servant and authority on Scottish affairs, had spoken out openly on the subject during the recent Parliament. While not presuming to give an opinion on who had the best title to succeed, Sir Ralph, as an Englishman, found in himself 'a great misliking to be subject to a foreign prince. . . . And for the Queen of Scots', he went on, 'though she were indeed next heir in blood to the Queen's Majesty, yet being a stranger by the laws of the realm, as I understand, she cannot inherit in England.'

Ralph Sadler could still vividly remember the abortive negotiations for the marriage between Prince Edward and the infant Mary Stewart of twenty years ago, when a Scottish gentleman had told him that his nation, 'being a stout nation', would never tolerate an Englishman as King of Scotland and that even if the nobility had consented, the common people and the very stones in the streets would have risen in rebellion against it. Now, said Sadler, if these 'proud, beggarly Scots' were so ready to disdain an Englishman as their King, why should the English, well-known for their detestation of 'the regiment of strangers', be expected to sink *their* pride and accept a Scotswoman as their Queen? 'I fear', he ended solemnly, 'lest I may say with the Scot, that though we do all agree unto it, yet our common people and the stones in the street would rebel against it.'

These were fighting words and there is not much doubt that a great many other Englishmen felt the same way, but it was emphatically not the way Elizabeth's mind was working. Elizabeth Tudor did not regard the crown of England as a piece of real estate to be bestowed according to political convenience or prejudice. Her father's will might, as the hardline Protestants urged, have been given statutory force by Act of Parliament, Mary might be a Catholic and born north of the Border, but no arguments—constitutional, religious, political or just plain xenophobic—would persuade the Queen even to discuss the claims of the other contenders in the succession stakes. If any way was to be found out of the present *impasse*, it would have to involve the Queen of Scots.

Mary had been a widow now for more than two years and much, if not everything, would depend on the identity of her second husband. In December 1559 Nicholas Throckmorton had been moved to express the wish 'that the one of these two Queens of the Isle of Britain were transformed into the shape of a man, to make so happy a marriage as thereby there might be an unity of the whole isle'; and Mary herself used to joke with Thomas Randolph that if only she or Elizabeth were a man, they could have married and put an end to all further debate.

In the absence of a transformation scene, the problem remained, large and intractable—the lack of suitable candidates for the post of either English or Scottish consort making it more intractable still. Unlike Elizabeth, Mary had no conscientious objections to matrimony and rumours of projected alliances with the Spanish Infante, with the Hapsburg Archduke Charles, with the French Duc de Nemours, even with the young King of France, continued to crop up in diplomatic correspondence. But somehow Elizabeth did not think the Queen of Scots would marry to disoblige her—at least not as long as she had hopes of cajoling her into changing her mind about the succession. So, if a suitable, really trustworthy husband could be found, then perhaps something might be arranged.

So the Queen of England appeared to be thinking early in 1563, for it was in March, while Parliament was still sitting, that she first broached the matter to Maitland of Lethington. Maitland had come south again, ostensibly to offer his sovereign's services as mediator between the warring factions in France, but more importantly to confer with the Spanish ambassador in London and try to prod the slow-moving King of Spain into renewing his interest in Mary Stewart as a bride for his son.

Elizabeth's plan—that Mary should agree to accept a husband of her choosing in return for an implicit promise of recognition as the English heir presumptive—might indeed have offered a possible solution, or, at any rate, a basis for negotiation. Unfortunately, Elizabeth's choice seemed so preposterous as to put the whole scheme right out of court from the start. Alvaro de Quadra, who had the story from Maitland himself, hastened to pass it on to King Philip in a despatch dated 28 March. The Queen, according to Maitland, had told him that 'if his mistress would take her advice and wished to marry safely and happily she would give her a husband who would ensure both and this was Lord Robert, in whom nature has implanted so many graces that if she wished to marry she would prefer him to all the princes in the world.'

Maitland's long experience in the diplomatic field should have rendered him shockproof, but the thought of that shop-soiled and notorious widower, Robert Dudley, sharing the throne of Scotland caused him to heave almost visibly. However, he managed to respond with a nicely barbed compliment. It was certainly a great proof of the love the Queen of England bore his queen if she was willing to give her a thing she prized so much, but he felt sure that Mary, even if she loved Lord Robert as dearly as Elizabeth did, would not wish to deprive her cousin of the joy and solace she derived from his company. Elizabeth did not take the hint. It was a pity, she mused, that Ambrose Dudley (Robert's elder brother, now restored to the earldom of Warwick) did not possess Robert's charm and good looks, for then she and Mary could each have had one of them. This was too much for Maitland. If the Queen of England could make tasteless jokes on such a serious subject, then so could he. Elizabeth had better marry Robert herself, he said, 'and then when it should please God to call her to himself, she could leave the Queen of Scots heiress both to her kingdom and her husband'—that way Lord Robert could hardly fail to have children by one or other of them.

Maitland found it difficult to believe that Elizabeth could be in earnest, but apparently she was. At any rate, she kept returning to the idea that Mary should marry an Englishman, and before he left London ordered the Scottish Secretary to warn his mistress that if she married the Prince of Spain, or any other member of the Hapsburg family for that matter, the Queen could not avoid becoming her enemy. If, on the other hand, she was prepared to be guided by her cousin, Elizabeth would not fail to act the part of a good friend and sister, and in due course make her her heir.

In August Thomas Randolph was instructed to repeat the warning about entering into any foreign alliance. If pressed to say what marriage *would* please Elizabeth, 'ye may of yourself say that you think, by such indirect speeches as we have used, that none could better content us, than if some person of noble birth within our realm, having also conditions and qualities meet for the same—*yea, perchance such as she would hardly think we could agree unto* (the italics are Elizabeth's own)—might be found out to content her . . . and therewith further her interest, if so she should appear, that she be our next heir.' More broad hints along these lines were dropped during the winter, but it was not until the following spring that Randolph was finally authorised to actually mention the name of the chosen 'person of noble birth.'

Randolph did not relish his task, writing mournfully that 'to persuade the Queen of Scotland to marry any man under the degree of a prince, and that the greatest . . . can neither be honourable to her that is born a queen, and has married a king, nor wisdom for any man her subject to give advice in. Were I able to answer all this', he went on, 'and if her grace would yield to me therein', there was a greater obstacle still. Everyone knew how reluctant Elizabeth would be to part with Robert Dudley, 'and how hardly his mind could be divorced, or drawn from that worthy room where it is placed, let any man see.' How, then, was the Queen of Scots to be induced not merely to accept a husband so far beneath her socially but one whose affections were already so obviously engaged elsewhere?

How indeed? But when, towards the end of March 1564, the dreaded name of Dudley was at length spoken aloud in her presence Mary listened 'with meetly good patience', if with understandable lack of enthusiasm. Was it conformable with Elizabeth's promise to treat her as a sister or daughter to offer to match her with one of her subjects, she enquired. 'What if the Queen my sister should marry herself and have children, what have I then gotten? Who will judge this to be wisely done of me, or who will allow it?'

All the same, the proposal could not be turned down out of hand. Maitland spent a long time closeted with Mary that evening and next day told Randolph that, although his mistress must have time to think it over, 'so would she not so little esteem it, as strait to reject it.' She had therefore suggested that a conference should be arranged at Berwick between the Earl of Bedford and a representative of her own to discuss the matter further. 'This is her grace's answer as near as I can give it', reported Randolph, adding 'I am advised not to be discouraged.'

It had been a depressing year for the Queen of Scotland. The previous spring she had lost one of her most powerful friends when the Duke of Guise had been murdered by a Huguenot assassin. Her patient cultivation of Elizabeth had produced no tangible results— beyond the insulting offer of the infamous horse-keeper—and her own marriage plans were making no progress. She had been noticeably out of sorts during the autumn and Randolph attributed her general malaise to despair of ever securing the class of husband she had set her sights on.

It ought not to have been so difficult. Mary, like Elizabeth, could fairly claim to be 'the best match in her parish' and her marriage should have been a trump card in Scotland's dealings with England. But the hostility of Catherine de Medici, King Philip's lack of interest, Elizabeth's veto on 'the children of France, Spain and Austria', plus the visible reluctance of her own nobility (several of whom were in receipt of pensions from the English exchequer) to risk upsetting the *status quo*, were combining to create what looked like an unbreakable stalemate. Mary had never considered the Earl of Arran as a bridegroom, and in any case he had now definitely crossed the borderline of insanity, 'drowned in dreams' and feeding himself with fantasies.

The Queen's heart, of course, was still set on a Spanish alliance. Married to Don Carlos she would be in a position to snap her fingers at Elizabeth, at John Knox, who was also having the impudence to dictate to her on her choice of husband, and at all those dour, greedy, untrustworthy Scottish lords she had had to be so careful to propitiate. But it seemed as impossible to get a straight answer out of the King of Spain as the Queen of England until at last, in August 1564, Philip informed Guzman de Silva, his new ambassador in London, that the proposal to marry the Queen of Scots to his son must be considered at an end. Philip did not say so, but it was becoming increasingly difficult to conceal the fact that the unhappy Don Carlos, too, had degenerated into hopeless insanity. Certainly all the luck was running against Mary Stewart, and that summer Elizabeth re-opened negotiations with Archduke Charles on her own account, apparently for the express purpose of spoiling her cousin's chances. In the circumstances, it is hardly surprising that those 'inward griefs and grudges' which poisoned relations between the two Queens should by now have been working their way to the surface. An attempt by Randolph to revive the idea of a personal interview met with no encouragement from the Scots, the Dudley proposal still hung in suspense and Anglo-Scottish friendship was further strained by the curious affair of the Earl of Lennox.

Matthew Stewart, Earl of Lennox, had been living in exile in England ever since the mid-1540's, but in June 1563 Elizabeth had written to Mary urging that he should be allowed to come home to set his long-neglected affairs in order. In May 1564 Mary had agreed, but almost immediately Elizabeth had had second thoughts and tried to persuade her to revoke the Earl's passport on the grounds that his return might cause trouble—there was an old feud between the Lennox Stewarts and the Hamiltons. Mary refused and both Maitland and the Earl of Moray wrote firmly to Cecil that if the Queen of England wanted to 'stay' Lord Lennox she must do it herself and not expect their sovereign 'to put her reputation in doubt before the world for breach of promise.'

Lennox was of no great consequence by himself, but his wife Margaret—daughter of Margaret Tudor's second marriage—stood close to the English throne and, more to the point, the couple possessed a hopeful son, Henry Lord Darnley, whose name was already being linked with the Queen of Scots in some quarters. In fact, in 1561, the Countess of Lennox had got into serious trouble with Elizabeth for scheming to promote the match, but now it appeared the family were in high favour. The Queen made no further move to prevent the Earl's journey north, though she would not allow him to take his wife and son, and young Darnley was much in evidence at court. Towards Mary, however, her attitude had become definitely chilly. On 4 September the Spanish ambassador reported that 'instructions are sent to keep a sharp look out on affairs in Scotland as, although the two Queens correspond and keep each other in play until one or the other of them shows her hand, they both go in fear and will give but short grace.'

At the end of the month Mary despatched Sir James Melville to London with a general commission to treat with Queen Elizabeth, Guzman de Silva and her other friends in England, including her aunt Margaret. Melville, a much travelled soldier, courtier and diplomat with a talent for anecdote, found Elizabeth in tetchy mood and more than inclined to take offence over her good sister's unaccountable lack of interest in my lord Robert Dudley. She told Melville that she 'esteemed him as her brother and best friend, whom she would herself have married, had she ever minded to have taken a husband. But being determined to end her life in virginity, she wished that the queen her sister should marry him, as meetest of all other and with whom she could find in her heart to declare the queen second person rather than any other.' This marriage, she explained, 'would best remove out of her mind all fear and suspicion, to be offended by usurpation before her death; being assured that he was so loving and trusty that he would never give his consent nor suffer such thing to be attempted during her time.'

Robert was about to receive his long-coveted peerage, to make the Queen of Scots 'think the more of him', and James Melville, of course, had to witness his investiture as Earl of Leicester and Baron Denbigh 'which was done at Westminster with great solemnity.' The object of all this attention conducted himself with very proper gravity and decorum throughout the ceremony but the Queen, helping to put on his robes, rather spoilt the effect by putting a hand down his neck 'to tickle him smilingly.' She asked Melville what he thought of her new creation and received the tactful reply that 'as he was a worthy subject, so he was happy who had a princess who could discern and reward good service.' 'Yet', said Elizabeth disconcertingly, 'you like better of yonder long lad', pointing to Lord Darnley who, as nearest prince of the blood, was bearing the sword of honour. Melville, uncomfortably conscious of his secret instructions to confer with the 'long lad's' ambitious and doting mamma on how best to get permission for him to join his father in Scotland, was quick to disclaim—no woman of spirit would choose a beardless boy, he protested.

Elizabeth now seemed determined to press ahead with the Dudley marriage project, promising to send commissioners to Berwick as soon as possible. In the meantime, her ill-humour vanished, she made a great fuss of Melville, seeing him every day during his nine day visit, and sometimes as often as three times in one day. 'She appeared to be so affectionate to the queen her good sister', he was to recall in his Memoirs, 'that she had a great desire to see her. And because their desired meeting could not be so hastily brought to pass, she delighted to look upon Her Majesty's picture. She took me to her bed-chamber and opened a little desk, wherein were divers little pictures wrapt within paper, and their names written with her own hand upon the papers. Upon the first that she took up was written, "My Lord's picture". I held the candle, and pressed to see that picture so named. She was loath to let me see it; at length my importunity prevailed for a sight thereof (and found it to be the Earl of Leicester's picture). I desired that I might have it to carry home to my queen; which she refused, alleging that she had but that one picture of his. I said again that she had the original; for he was at the farthest part of the chamber, speaking with secretary Cecil. Then she took out the queen's picture, and kissed it; and I kissed her hand, for the great love I saw she bore to my mistress. She showed me also a fair ruby, as great as a tennis-ball. I desired that she would either send it, or else my Lord of Leicester's picture, as a token unto the queen. She said, if the queen would follow her counsel, that she would in process of time get them both, and all she had; but in the mean time she was resolved for a token to send her with me a diamond.'

Elizabeth questioned Melville about his travels and about the customs and fashions in clothes of the different countries he had visited. She had clothes of every sort, she told him, and proceeded to dazzle him with her wardrobe. 'She asked me which of them became her best. I said, the Italian dress; which pleased her well, for she delighted to show her golden coloured hair, wearing a caul and bonnet as they do in Italy.'

The Queen now began to ask embarrassing questions about whether Mary's hair or her own was best, 'and which of them two was fairest.' Melville tried to wriggle out of it by saying that Elizabeth was the fairest queen in England and Mary in Scotland. But this would not do, and at last he was driven to admit that Elizabeth was 'whiter', although Mary was very lovely. Elizabeth was still not satisfied. 'She enquired which of them was of highest stature. I said our queen. Then, saith she, she is too high and that herself was neither too high nor too low.'

The Queen of England's curiosity seemed insatiable. She wanted to know how Mary passed her time. When she had leisure from the affairs of her country, said Melville primly, she read good books such as 'the histories of diverse countries', and sometimes played on the lute and virginals. Did she play well? asked Elizabeth. Reasonably well, for a queen, was the cautious reply. After this, of course, Melville was taken up into a quiet gallery to eavesdrop on Elizabeth playing 'excellently well' on the virginals. When she discovered she had an audience, she pretended to be angry, 'alleging that she used not to play before men', but she drew Melville into the room, making him kneel on a cushion beside her. 'Then she asked whether my queen or she played best. In that I gave her the praise.'

By this time Sir James was beginning to find his visit rather a strain, but he was not allowed to go until he had seen Elizabeth dance and answered the inevitable question 'whether she or my queen danced best.' Mary danced 'not so high and disposedly' said Melville. At this, their final encounter, Mary remained the principal topic of conversation, Elizabeth wishing again 'that she might see the queen at some convenient place of meeting.' Melville offered jokingly 'to convoy her secretly to Scotland by post, clothed like a page, disguised, that she might see the queen . . . telling her that her chamber might be kept in her absence as though she were sick, and in the meantime none to be privy thereto, except my Lady Stafford and one of the grooms of her chamber. She appeared to like that kind of language, and said "Alas! if I might do it."' According to Melville's account, Elizabeth 'used all the means she could to cause me to persuade the queen of the great love she did bear unto her, and that she was minded to put away all jealousies and suspicions, and in times coming to entertain a straiter friendship to stand between them than ever had been of before.'

If Mary was reluctant to pay the price of friendship by going to the altar with her cousin's 'best friend', it seemed that the bridegroom-elect shared her disinclination for sacrifice. The Earl of Leicester was not at all grateful for the kind plans being made for his future. On the contrary, he regarded them with consternation. He did not want to marry the Queen of Scots and be banished to the barbarous north. He wanted to stay at home and marry the Queen of England, and before James Melville left for home the Earl contrived to get him alone and assure him that the proposal was none of his making. It was all Cecil's doing, intended to discredit him, and he hoped Melville would make his private apologies to Mary for his apparent presumption.

Nevertheless, the solemn charade went on. According to Melville, the Queen of Scots told him shortly after his return that she had no intention of marrying Leicester but she continued to listen politely to Thomas Randolph, indicating her willingness to follow Elizabeth's advice more than any other and 'to please her in all things reasonable.' At the same time, Randolph was reporting that the Earl of Lennox, restored to his Scottish estates, was being made much of in Edinburgh. Rumour had it that his wife and son would soon be coming to join him and Randolph found 'marvellous good liking' of young Lord Darnley. He also heard, 'in all men's mouths', that Mary had already made up her mind to marry him and that Maitland of Lethington was 'wholly bent that way.'

But Darnley remained in England and in November a conference duly took place at Berwick to discuss the Leicester marriage. However, as it seemed the English had nothing new to offer, nothing was achieved. The Scots were determined to see the colour of the Queen of England's money before committing themselves, demanding parliamentary recognition of Mary's rights in the English succession as a pre-condition for further negotiations.

It is quite possible that Mary would have conquered her natural disdain of a husband who came of no great or noble house and whose blood was spotted with treason (not to mention the little matter of suspected wife-murder), if he had come gift-wrapped in guarantees, signed and sealed, about the succession. But neither she nor Moray and Maitland were prepared to put their faith in promises alone, and Elizabeth, who preferred to deal in hints, allusions and tacit understandings, would not oblige.

In the weeks which followed the inconclusive meeting at Berwick letters continued to go to and fro between London and Edinburgh, the Scots begging plaintively for 'frank dealing', indignantly denying that their mistress had designs on her cousin's realm—after all, those who were planning to make an Englishman King of Scotland could also be accused of 'hunting a kingdom'—and pointing out that Mary could not wait indefinitely. In fact, if the Queen of England was determined not to settle her succession, it would cause less offence in the long run to call a halt now. Although, they added hastily, they saw no reason why the alliance should be dissolved whoever the Queen of Scots chose to marry. All they got from Cecil by way of reply was a repetition of previous assurances, admittedly rather more well-defined than before, that Mary's best, if not her only chance of getting what she wanted was to swallow her pride, marry the Earl of Leicester and trust Queen Elizabeth to protect her interests.

This was just what Mary could not bring herself to do. She had suspected from the beginning that she was being hoaxed, and that the Leicester proposal was some kind of elaborate tease intended to make her look foolish before the world and discourage other, more eligible suitors. (She later claimed that the Earl himself had written secretly warning her to this effect.) The Queen of Scots was not alone in her suspicions and many people since have found it just as hard to believe that the Queen of England ever really meant to part with her favourite man—and not merely part with him, but hand him over to another woman, younger, prettier and her most dangerous rival.

Had she ever meant it seriously? With Elizabeth it is never wise to be too sure of anything, and her thought processes could be as convoluted as her prose style. But the original idea, born out of a genuine dilemma, had been worth exploring. It offered certain obvious advantages and had at least demonstrated to parliament and people that she was not wilfully shutting her eyes to the succession problem. Undoubtedly, though, the Queen's primary concern had been to stop her cousin marrying abroad and giving another foreign power a foothold on the British mainland—something she would have gone to almost any lengths to prevent. She probably realised quite early on that Mary would never accept Robert Dudley without the sort of collateral she was neither willing nor able to provide, but that would not have inhibited her from prolonging the negotiations with every appearance of serious intent, buying valuable time and keeping the Scots guessing. Elizabeth had no equal when it came to playing this sort of diplomatic grandmother's footsteps and was quite capable of keeping it up long after everyone else was exhausted.

In February 1565 the plan was still, officially, very much alive. Early in the month Thomas Randolph sought out the Queen of Scots to deliver a 'very loving' letter from Elizabeth and found her at St Andrew's, picnicking in a merchant's house with only a handful of attendants and thoroughly enjoying the novel experience of 'living like a bourgeois wife'. She was reluctant to interrupt her holiday by any discussion of 'great and grave matters' but, after three days 'passed wholly in mirth', Randolph finally managed to corner her for a serious talk. Much of it was taken up with Mary's reiterated desire for good relations with Elizabeth. 'How much better were it', she said yet again, 'that we two being Queens so near of kin, neighbours and living in one isle, should be friends and live together like sisters, than by strange means divide ourselves to the hurt of us both!' The English reputed the Scots poor, she went on, 'but yet you have found us cumbersome enough! We have had loss, ye have taken hurt! Why may it not be between my sister and me, that we living in peace and assured friendship may give our minds that some as notable things may be wrought by us women, as by our predecessors have been before?'

When Randolph turned the conversation to the Earl of Leicester, Mary said: 'My mind towards him is such as it ought to be of a very noble man, as I hear say by very many; and such one as the Queen your mistress, my good sister, doth so well like to be her husband if he were not her subject, ought not to mislike me to be mine. Marry! what I shall do, it lieth in your mistress's will, who shall wholly guide and rule me.'

Mary had still made no firm commitment. Until Elizabeth proceeded farther she must continue to rely on the advice of those that 'seem to tender most my profit . . . and wish me most good' and, reported Randolph, neither Maitland nor her brother Moray were willing to press her 'without that principal point whereon your Majesty stays.' All the same, he now felt there were real grounds for optimism and his annoyance and bewilderment were understandably acute when, barely a week later, the news reached him that Lord Darnley had been given licence to travel to Scotland.

Just why Elizabeth chose this particular moment to allow Darnley to go north remains a mystery—unless, as seems most likely, she was deliberately throwing him across Mary's path. It is virtually impossible now to unravel the dense cocoon of intrigue and counter-intrigue enveloping the whole affair, but there is no doubt that the Earl of Leicester played a prominent part in urging the Queen to abandon her negative policy. He may well have pointed out that she could not hope to postpone Mary's marriage indefinitely, that she might at any time decide to take matters into her own hands (the

Cardinal of Lorraine was currently promoting a match with the new Duke of Guise) and, in any case, sooner or later one of the 'two Queens in one isle' would have to marry and provide an heir. Darnley might be a negligible youth, but he had both English and Scots royal blood in his veins and should surely be capable of fathering a son. Why not at least let the Queen of Scots take a look at him and see what happened?

Elizabeth who, the previous September, had confessed to being in a labyrinth over Scottish affairs, may simply have yielded to her favourite's persuasions against her better judgement, and no doubt Leicester's influence carried a good deal of weight. The balance of the evidence, though, suggests that she had reluctantly come to the conclusion that Darnley, as the best available candidate, must now at last be brought into the game. Born in Yorkshire, where his parents owned large estates, he was technically an English subject and his mother would remain in London as a hostage for his good behaviour. He was very far from being an ideal choice, but he would certainly be infinitely preferable to another foreign connection.

Mary had not so far shown any public signs of interest in the Lennox cousin, three years her junior, who, apart from his breeding and girlish good looks, was of no particular account. But her initial reaction, when they met at Wemyss Castle on 17 February, was favourable. He was the 'properest and best proportioned long man' she had seen and made a welcome addition to her court. Darnley's arrival had naturally aroused great curiosity among the Scots. 'A great number wish him well', wrote Randolph, but others doubted whether this 'fair jolly young man' was fit for any high position.

A week later the jolly young man dutifully sat through one of Mr Knox's sermons and after supper danced a galliard with the Queen at the Earl of Moray's house. He was still making an excellent impression. 'His behaviour is very well liked, and hitherto so governs himself that there is very great praise of him.' He and Mary were now constant companions, but Thomas Randolph believed 'her grace's good usage and often talk with him' proceeded rather 'of her own courteous nature' than from anything more serious. Perhaps the wish was father to the thought, but so far the cousins seemed no more than just good friends.

Then, in the middle of March, Randolph received instructions from London to offer Mary 'gentleness etc.' but to tell her that Elizabeth had decided not to make any formal move to recognise her title 'until she be married herself or be determined not to marry.' Despite the ambassador's efforts to soften the blow, Mary took it badly, complaining that she had been deliberately deceived and fed with vain hopes in matters that were never intended. She did not blame Elizabeth for being reluctant to concede 'that which perchance any would be loath to do', but she did resent having been kept so long in suspense and finally answered with nothing. She would try not to fail in 'any good offices' towards the Queen of England, but would find it very difficult ever to trust her again. Moray and Maitland made no attempt to conceal their feelings, and the unfortunate Randolph, who was having to bear the full brunt of their angry chagrin, asked to be recalled.

Elizabeth's démarche, of course, marked the definitive end of the Leicester marriage negotiations and Darnley now had the field to himself. At the beginning of April he was lucky enough to fall ill with an attack of measles, with the Queen in anxious attendance at his bedside. In the intimacy of the sickroom romance flourished, and by the time the invalid was on his feet again Mary was in love. On the fifteenth Randolph reported gloomily from Berwick that she seemed about to forsake all other offers and 'content herself with her own choice', despite the 'inconveniences and dangers like to ensue.' Already, he wrote, people were saying openly that Elizabeth had sent Darnley to Scotland on purpose to match the Queen 'meanly and poorly'—a slander he was loyally doing his best to refute, although he obviously more than half believed it himself. Certainly if Elizabeth's purpose had been to use Darnley as bait to trap Mary into a misalliance likely to bring her nothing but unhappiness, she had succeeded brilliantly. The Queen of Scots at twenty-one was a warm-blooded young woman, impatient for a husband in her bed as well as the added status and protection that marriage and children would give her. Darnley had been brought to her notice at a time of mounting frustration and disappointment, and in the circumstances it is not in the least surprising that she should have seen him as an answer to prayer. She did not guess that beneath the surface of this tall handsome princeling, with his pretty manners and courtly accomplishments, lay a spoilt, loutish, unstable youth with all the makings of a vindictive bully.

From now on events moved with startling speed, and the ink had scarcely dried on Randolph's latest despatch before Maitland of Lethington was riding into London to ask for Queen Elizabeth's

consent to the marriage. It was not forthcoming. Elizabeth was, or
professed to be, greatly surprised and offended at such an unsuitable
suggestion, but the Spanish ambassador heard there was a suspicion
that the match had been arranged 'with the concurrence of some of
the great people here'—the Countess of Lennox, in particular, was
publicly boasting that it was already a settled thing. The Queen,
unamused, put her under house arrest and announced that she was
sending Sir Nicholas Throckmorton to Scotland to put a stop to this
nonsense at once. However, Guzman de Silva remarked, 'day after
day goes by and he does not depart.'

Throckmorton eventually departed on 5 May and saw Mary ten
days later, when he painstakingly set forth his sovereign's 'misliking
and misallowance of her hasty proceeding with the Lord Darnley, as
well for the matter as for the manner, wherein she erred by
unadvisedness and rashness: and the said Lord Darnley and his
parents had failed of their duties by their arrogant and presumptuous
attempts to enterprise such matter . . . without making your majesty
privy thereunto, being your subjects.' Mary retorted that she *had*
informed Elizabeth, 'as soon as she was resolved of the man and the
matter.' She was astonished at the Queen's disapproval, having
always understood that she was free to choose any nobleman in
England or Scotland, and thought no one would be more generally
acceptable than Darnley, 'he being your majesty's kinsman and hers
and participating of the English and Scottish blood.'

Although handicapped by his private knowledge that her choice
was not, in fact, quite so 'evil taken' in England as his instructions
indicated, Nicholas Throckmorton did what he could to persuade
the Queen of Scots that she had misinterpreted Elizabeth's 'liberal
permission', that Darnley would not do at all, 'for many just causes',
and that the marriage would seriously endanger Anglo-Scottish
friendship. They argued for some time, but Throckmorton could see
that Mary was determined to go ahead whatever happened, 'albeit the
matter is not yet consummated, neither shall be (as she hath willed
me to ascertain your majesty) these three months, in which time she
will use all means to procure your acceptance. . . . Yet I find her so
captivated either by love or cunning (or rather to say truly, by
boasting or folly) that she is not able to keep promise with herself,
and therefore not most able to keep promise with your majesty in
these matters.'

It certainly looked as though Mary was allowing her infatuation to blind her to all considerations of statecraft, of caution, or even basic commonsense. Thomas Randolph, back in Edinburgh with Throckmorton, was profoundly shocked by the change he saw in her. 'I know not how to utter what I conceive of the pitiful and lamentable estate of this poor Queen, whom ever before I esteemed so worthy, so wise, so honourable in all her doings: and at this present do find so altered with affection to the Lord Darnley, that she hath brought her honour in question, her estate in hazard, her country to be torn in pieces! . . . This Queen in her love is so transported, and he grown so proud that to all honest men he is intolerable, and almost forgetful of his duty to her already, that has adventured so much for his sake. What shall become of her, or what life with him she shall lead . . . I leave it to others to think!'

In London, Queen Elizabeth's advisers were thinking more of the political than the all too likely personal consequences of the Queen of Scotland's headlong romance, and William Cecil, who regarded the approaching union of these two grandchildren of Margaret Tudor with undisguised misgiving, wrote a detailed aide memoire on the subject, headed 'The Perils and troubles that may presently ensue . . . to the Queen's Majesty and safety of this realm upon the marriage of the Queen of Scots to the Lord Darnley.' Two perils in particular were discussed at a Council meeting on 4 June—'a plain intention to further the pretenced title of the Queen of Scots, not only to succeed the Queen's majesty . . . but to occupy the Queen's estate' and the inevitable encouragement of the Romish religion on which that pretenced title was founded. Darnley, as some of those present pointed out, might be even more of a menace than a foreign prince, for he and his mother were already known and popular figures among the English papists, 'and a small portion of adversaries at home in our own bowels is always seen more dangerous than treble the like abroad.'

A list of desirable precautionary measures—including a new drive against Catholicism, a show of force along the Border and some relaxation of the Queen's displeasure towards Mary's principal rival, Lady Katherine Grey, still languishing in disgrace and detention— was drawn up for royal consideration. But Elizabeth remained curiously lukewarm. She sent the Earl of Bedford back to his post as Governor of Berwick. She ordered Darnley and his father to come home—a command which was unsurprisingly ignored. She sent Lady Lennox to the Tower and gave another Scottish envoy, John Hay of

Balmerino, a hostile reception. Otherwise, despite the obvious risk involved in allowing two strong contenders for her throne to consolidate their respective claims, as Guzman de Silva put it, she did nothing to hinder the progress of events.

Mary had now obtained the blessing of her French relations and of the King of Spain, who instructed his ambassador in London to inform Lady Margaret Lennox that not only would he be glad for her son to be king of Scotland, 'but also to be king of England if this marriage is carried through.' Thus encouraged, the Queen of Scots was pressing on with her wedding preparations, regardless of the Queen of England's disapproval and regardless of the storm signals flying nearer home, where the fact that Darnley was reputed to be a Catholic had less importance than the fact that he was a Lennox Stewart and, on his mother's side, a Douglas.

The Queen had already quarrelled violently with the Earl of Moray, whose support had done so much to ensure the success of her first four years in Scotland. The row had ostensibly been about religion, but James Stewart was known to oppose his sister's marriage, no doubt foreseeing the inevitable diminution of his wealth and influence, while Mary, according to the ubiquitous Thomas Randolph, had gone so far as to accuse him of wanting to set the crown on his own head. Moray had left the court in a considerable huff and was now making rebellious noises off-stage. The Hamiltons, too, foresaw their ruin and the loss of their jealously-guarded position as the 'next heirs', which the Lennoxes had always disputed with them, and there were other Scottish noble families with plenty of old Scottish reasons for disliking the Lennox Stewarts. 'The rumours here are wonderful', wrote Randolph; 'men's talk very strange; the hatred towards Darnley and his house marvellously great.'

In spite of this, and in spite of the fact that Darnley's obnoxious behaviour was rapidly alienating even those that were 'his chief friends', Mary was still besotted, bewitched so Randolph had come to believe. 'Her councillors now are those she liked worst: the nearest of her kin the farther from her heart.' Even Maitland had fallen out of favour and the Queen was relying more and more on her secretary for French affairs, the Italian musician David Riccio, who was thick as thieves with Darnley. The wedding date was set for 29 July and on the twenty-eighth the Queen issued a proclamation declaring that she intended to 'compleit the band of matrimony in face of halikirk' and that her bridegroom was to be 'namit and stylit King of this our kingdome.' At six o'clock on the following morning Mary became 'a married wife' for the second time in the Chapel Royal at Holyrood Palace according to the Catholic rite, but the new King, it was noticed, left before the nuptial mass.

Queen Elizabeth did not send congratulations. Instead she despatched John Tamworth, a gentleman of her privy chamber, to convey once again her deepest disapproval of the whole proceeding and her annoyance over the underhand dealing and 'craft' of the Lennox family. Tamworth was also instructed to urge Mary to make up her quarrel with Moray and to warn her not to try and introduce any religious changes in her realm or to listen to any 'intelligences and advices' hostile to England.

Tamworth got short shrift from the Queen of Scots and 'some sharp words that biteth to the quick.' The greatest princes in Christendom had consented to her marriage and she knew of no good reason why Elizabeth should dislike it. As for Moray, she would thank the Queen of England not to meddle in her affairs. She and her husband were ready to continue to live in friendship with their southern neighbour, on condition that Elizabeth agreed to settle her succession on the Scottish line, and what about releasing the Countess of Lennox from captivity?

Mary, it seemed, was now very much in command—Tamworth described her as being 'marvellous stout'—and it looked as if the old days of gentle deference to her 'good sister's' judgement were gone for good.

VI

The Killing at Kirk o'Field

The Queen of Scotland had no leisure to enjoy her honeymoon, for within a fortnight of her marriage the Earl of Moray and the old Duke of Châtelherault, with Campbell of Argyll, Lord Rothes and Kirkcaldy of Grange were up in open revolt. The mortal hatred now flaring between Mary and her half-brother was commented on both by John Tamworth and Thomas Randolph, who hinted that Moray knew some disgraceful secret about the Queen's relationship with David Riccio, while Moray publicly justified his rebellion on the grounds that Mary was planning to overthrow the Protestant religion.

A more likely explanation lies in Moray's furious resentment at the elevation of the Lennoxes, especially the oafish Darnley. He must have known very well that Mary was in no position as yet to tamper with the established religion and was, in fact, going out of her way to conciliate the kirk. No doubt James Stewart had often reflected bitterly on the consequences of his father's unfortunate omission of the formality of marrying his mother, but had hitherto seemed content with exercising power from behind the throne. Now, it would appear, he saw a chance to make a bid for power on his own account, but he miscalculated his moment badly. As always in a crisis which called for bold, decisive action Mary showed to her best advantage, riding out of Edinburgh at the head of her troops in high spirits, with a pistol at her saddle bow and swearing revenge on her enemies. Moray failed to rally any worthwhile support and the Chaseabout Raid, as the brief campaign was dubbed, ended in his discomfiture.

To what extent the rebel lords had been encouraged by promises of assistance from England is difficult to assess with accuracy. Certainly there had been some promises and some financial aid, and Moray himself later protested that he would never had taken the field 'but being moved thereto' by Elizabeth and her Council. There's no question, either, that a situation in which Moray and Maitland were confirmed in their ascendancy over a sovereign who had lost much of her credibility and was, moreover, now trapped in an unpopular and unequal marriage would have suited the Queen of England very nicely. Quite possibly this was what she had envisaged when she despatched Darnley to Scotland. If so, Elizabeth was also guilty of miscalculation, seriously underestimating Mary's fearlessness, her determination and the speed of her reactions.

To the English agents on the spot it had been plain from the start that the rebels would be 'clean overthrown' without the Queen's majesty's assistance, but covert encouragement and a little money was one thing, open intervention in an insurrection which clearly did not command any widespread local support quite another. Elizabeth was not going to risk becoming involved in failure, although she offered the lords asylum in England if they felt their lives were in danger.

Early in October Moray and Châtelherault crossed the Border at Carlisle and Moray presently set out for London. He had a long private interview with the Queen and Secretary Cecil on the evening of the twenty-second and the following day, in a scene specially staged for the benefit of the French ambassador, Elizabeth received him in formal audience and solemnly rebuked him for the sin of rebellion against his sovereign lady. Moray, probably not too cast down, then retired to Newcastle to await developments. There had been talk at Whitehall of sending some suitable personage to Scotland to discuss the various points at issue between the two countries and try to settle the rebels' grievances 'in accordance with reason and justice.' There was also talk of sending an embassy to demand once again that the Queen of Scots should ratify the Treaty of Edinburgh on the understanding that her title to the English succession would not be prejudiced. But in the end nothing was done. The Queen of England, too, was content to wait on events.

Mary, meanwhile, had pardoned the Earl of Huntly's son, sworn enemy of the Earl of Moray, and had recalled from exile James Hepburn, 4th Earl of Bothwell. In December 1561, Bothwell (whose father had stood proxy for James IV at that long ago betrothal ceremony at Richmond Palace) had caused considerable scandal by provoking an armed affray with the Hamiltons in the streets of Edinburgh over a local prostitute, and was subsequently accused by an hysterical Earl of Arran of plotting to kidnap the Queen. He had been confined in Edinburgh Castle on Moray's orders but escaped without undue difficulty and, after a picturesque series of adventures, took service at the French court with the Scottish Archers of the Guard. His homeward journey in the autumn of 1565 was equally fraught with incident when he narrowly evaded capture by English pirates off the Northumbrian coast.

Bothwell was an ugly customer, arrogant, foul-mouthed and violent, but he was also a useful man to have on one's side in a fight. He had old scores to settle with Moray and the Hamiltons, and the reputation of being a hardline Anglophobe. Mary welcomed him kindly, forgave his past misdemeanours—even his reported comment that she and Elizabeth did not make one honest woman between them—and gave him the key military post of Lieutenant of the Borders where the Hepburn family power was concentrated.

Having thrown off the tutelage of Moray and Maitland and to all intents and purposes broken with the Queen of England, the Queen of Scots was now seeking to strengthen her ties with the Catholic powers, previously somewhat neglected. In September she wrote to the Pope and to the King of Spain, commending herself to their protection and asking for money. Before the end of the year she was dropping hints to her friends in France that if all went well she might soon be in a position to do 'some good anent the old religion.'

If Mary was really hoping to restore the old religion, or, rather more plausibly, to break the stranglehold of her overbearing nobility and their paymistress in London, she would certainly need all the outside help she could get. One of the principal grievances of the rebel lords had been that their Queen had turned away from her natural councillors and was giving her confidence to 'crafty and wily strangers'; men such as David Riccio, 'commonly called among us Seigneur Davy', another Italian, Francisco Busso, an Englishman called Fowler and the lawyer James Balfour. Not only were these 'unworthy persons' usurping the places of their betters, but they were enriching themselves in the process, than which nothing could have been more calculated to raise the hackles of the noble mafiosi and alienate even those members of it who had sided with the Queen against Moray.

Riccio in particular was singled out for attack. Seigneur Davy had first come to Scotland in 1561 in the train of the Savoyard ambassador. He was an ugly little man, but 'a merry fellow and a good musician' with a fine bass voice, and Mary took him into her household to complete her quartet of singers. Soon he was helping out with her personal papers and towards the end of 1564 had been promoted to become her private secretary with charge of that growing section of her correspondence which she preferred to keep secret.

To a ruler in Mary's position—isolated as she was by religion, background and outlook, and now trying to strike out on a line of her own—a man like Riccio, possessing some natural ability, wholly dependent on her protection and thus wholly devoted to her interests, represented an invaluable tool. But the Queen of Scotland was playing a terribly dangerous game. James Melville warned her bluntly of the risks she was courting and Thomas Randolph, still uncomfortably hanging on at his post in Edinburgh, kept up a steady flow of doomful despatches. Riccio, a stranger and a varlet, had the whole guiding of Queen and country. Mary and all about her were 'so ill spoken of that worse cannot be thought than is common in men's mouths', while she herself was so changed as to be hardly recognisable by one who had known her in those happy days when she listened to worthy counsel and 'her praise ran through all nations.' Now, Randolph reported, 'I may well say that a more wilful woman, and one more wedded unto her own opinion, without order, reason or discretion, I never did know or hear of.'

As for the King, he was turning out much as expected, spending his days hunting and hawking, his evenings getting drunk. At the end of October Randolph heard the first rumours of the Queen's pregnancy, but already there were signs that her marriage was going badly. By the New Year it appeared to be heading rapidly for the rocks. Where, only a few months before, the talk had been all of the King and Queen, of his Majesty and hers, now 'the Queen's husband' was the most common word, and coins minted with Henricus placed before Maria were withdrawn from circulation.

The King's objectionable social behaviour, too, was beginning to cause embarrassment. There had been a nasty scene at a public entertainment in Edinburgh which ended with the Queen leaving in tears after trying unsuccessfully to restrain her husband from drinking too much, and hints were being dropped of worse habits than drunkenness.

The domestic friction at Holyrood had attracted immediate attention in London and Newcastle as well as Edinburgh from all those with an interest in putting a stop to any unseemly flirtations with papistry and seeing a properly constituted, pro-English regime re-established in Scotland. The exiled lords, chafing just across the Border, had no time to lose, since the Queen remained inflexible in her determination to confiscate their property when Parliament assembled in March, but her marital difficulties had supplied them with just the weapon they needed. The King was known to be already much aggrieved by his wife's refusal to grant him the crown matrimonial and it proved a simple matter to work on his thwarted ambition, his vanity and his jealousy—to suggest to him that 'that villain Davy' had done him 'the most dishonour that can be to any man.'

In fact, despite the scurrilous rumours going about that he was the real father of her child, there is no more reason to suppose that David Riccio was ever Mary Stewart's lover than there is to suppose that Robert Dudley was ever Elizabeth Tudor's, but her undisguised preference for his cheerful, uncritical society, though understandable, was in the circumstances, extremely foolish. Six years earlier Caspar von Breuner had wondered aloud why no Englishman could be found to stab milord Robert with a poniard. In Scotland, as its Queen should surely have realised, men suffered from fewer inhibitions when it came to the liquidation of an unpopular public figure.

By early February the opposition's plans were well advanced. Maitland of Lethington, writing to William Cecil on the ninth, regretted the recent interruption of amity between the two Queens and their realms, but praised God that 'nothing is on either part so far passed but all may be reduced to the former estate, if the right way be taken.' The right way, of course, meant chopping at the very root—'you know where it lieth.' A few days later, Thomas Randolph informed the Earl of Leicester that he now knew for certain that the Queen of Scots bitterly repented her marriage and hated her husband and all his kin, who had 'practices in hand . . . to come by the crown against her will. I know that if that take effect which is intended', he went on, 'David, with the consent of the King, shall have his throat cut within these ten days. Many things, more grievous and worse than these are brought to my ears; yea, of things intended against her own person.'

The main outline of the plot—of which the removal of Riccio was merely a necessary and pleasurable preliminary—involved conferring the crown matrimonial on 'King' Darnley, together with a promise to uphold his right to succeed his wife (if they had no children) against the Hamilton claim. In return Darnley undertook to secure the free pardon and return of the exiles, to prevent the forfeiture of their estates, to support them in the exercise of the reformed religion and generally maintain them 'as a good master should.' The fact that Darnley's preferment had been the original cause of the revolt was no longer of importance now that Moray and Maitland had found a use for him as the figurehead of their new government. As for the Queen, she would, at best, be relegated to a purely ceremonial role and given no further opportunity to meddle in affairs of state.

All this was known in London, but Queen Elizabeth saw no reason to warn her 'good sister'. Edinburgh seethed with spies and double agents and it would be odd indeed if Elizabeth did not have some inkling of the nature of Mary's correspondence with her friends abroad over the past few months—especially of the letter which her messenger Francis Yaxley had carried to the King of Spain, assuring him of the Queen of Scots' earnest desire to restore the Catholic religion in both the island kingdoms, and asking for Spanish help in the matter of the English succession. The Queen of England, therefore, was not about to put any obstacle in the way of those who sought to clip her busy cousin's wings.

The Scottish Parliament met on Thursday, 7 March and Mary personally attended the opening session to demand a bill of attainder against her rebel lords. The Duke of Châtelherault had been forgiven, on condition that he remained abroad for five years, but the Earls of Moray, Argyll, Glencairn and Rothes, the Lords Ochiltree and Boyd, Kirkaldy of Grange and the rest, were summoned to stand trial by parliament on the following Tuesday.

The sequel was bloody and immediate. On the evening of Saturday, 9 March as the Queen, now six months pregnant, was entertaining a few close friends—including, naturally, Seigneur Davy—in her 'cabinet' at Holyrood, a gang of thugs, escorted by the King and led by the sinister figure of Patrick Lord Ruthven, a steel cap on his head, his armour showing beneath his gown, burst into the tiny supper room by way of the privy staircase. In the brutal scene which followed the wretched Riccio was dragged out screaming into the adjoining room, through the presence chamber beyond, where the Earl of Morton and Lord Lindsay were waiting, and savagely stabbed to death within earshot of the Queen who, so she always insisted, was being threatened with a loaded pistol aimed at her belly.

Mary herself believed, and it seems a reasonable assumption, that the murder had been deliberately staged to produce the maximum amount of shock and horror in the hope that she would miscarry and die. But even in this nightmarish moment, betrayed by her husband and held prisoner by men who snarled that they would cut her in collops if she attempted to appeal to the townspeople gathering outside, the Queen of Scotland was to display formidable qualities of courage, resolution and self-control. On hearing that Riccio was beyond help, she is said to have dried her eyes, declaring 'no more tears—I will think upon revenge', and she certainly thought to some purpose during that long, fear-filled night.

The King was obviously the weak link and throughout the following day Mary worked steadily to undermine his confidence, 'certifying him how miserably he would be handled if he permitted the lords to prevail.' The lords, it seemed, were planning to hold her prisoner at Stirling Castle until her child was born and, after that, as the mother-to-be no doubt pointed out, neither of its parents' lives would be worth a day's purchase to the party in power. These 'persuasions' had their desired effect on the chicken-hearted Darnley, and Mary was further encouraged by the news that her friends Bothwell and Huntly had escaped from the palace during the uproar of the previous evening—making a hasty and unconventional exit through a window overlooking the lion-pit.

The Queen had done well to seize her opportunity, for by the Sunday evening the Earl of Moray was back in town. His sister greeted him with apparent relief. According to James Melville, she embraced him, exclaiming that 'if he had been at home he would not have suffered her to be so uncourteously handled', and exonerated him from complicity in the murder. Next day Moray, Morton and Ruthven visited her again, exhorting her humbly 'to cast off her care, to study for that which might be her safety, weal and honour, promising for their parts obedience and service as became true and faithful subjects.' Mary played her part in this grim little charade by promising to forgive them and to 'put all things in oblivion as if they had never been.' Parliament had already been dissolved by a proclamation issued in the King's name, and now the Queen told the lords kneeling before her 'to make their own security in that sort they pleased best and she should subscribe the same.' She even, it is said, drank to them to seal the bargain. Then, turning her charm on Maitland of Lethington, she begged him to have the guard on her removed, seeing she had granted all their requests.

Some of the conspirators were inclined to be suspicious of this unexpected capitulation, but it was urged that the Queen's signature on any 'pacification' would be valueless if she were still a prisoner. Moray and Maitland, too, appear to have been rather disconcerted by their henchmen's violence—worried perhaps over the effect it might have on Queen Elizabeth. At any rate, they agreed to call off the Douglas cut-throats who had occupied the palace precincts during the weekend and went off to have dinner at the Earl of Morton's house, unwisely leaving Darnley behind.

Mary stayed in her rooms, feigning illness, until the coast was clear. At about eight o'clock she sent for John Stewart of Traquair, captain of the royal guard, Arthur Erskine, her master of the horse, and her page Anthony Standen and asked them to help her to escape. A few minutes after midnight she and Darnley made their way unobtrusively down the privy stairs and out through the kitchen quarters. Erskine and Traquair had horses waiting and after five hours' hard riding the fugitives were over twenty miles away at Dunbar Castle on the Lothian coast.

The King's defection and the Queen's escape brought the attempted *coup* to an abrupt end, and a week later Mary was back in Edinburgh at the head of a businesslike little army commanded by the Earl of Bothwell. By any standards it had been a remarkable exploit, but especially so for a young woman of twenty-three in an advanced stage of her first pregnancy.

Mary had also been able to drive a wedge between the conspirators by formally pardoning the Earl of Moray and the rest of the Chaseabout exiles. Her displeasure was now reserved—and nobody could quarrel with that—for those who had broken into her house, slain her 'most special servant' in her own presence, treasonably held her captive and put her in fear of her life. Morton, Ruthven, Lindsay and their followers were thus compelled to flee in their turn, making for Newcastle where, in James Melville's felicitous phrase, they found 'the other lords' nests yet warm.' William Maitland had not been a member of the murder party at Holyrood, but his had undoubtedly been the organising brain behind the Edinburgh end of the plot and he therefore felt it prudent to remove himself temporarily from the Queen's vicinity. Even John Knox, who had of course led the kirk's outcry against Davy and had publicly approved the deed, left town in a hurry. No steps were taken against the King—indeed his 'innocence' was publicly proclaimed—but he cut an ignominious figure, cold-shouldered by his wife and universally despised. Mary now reconciled Moray, Glencairn and Argyll with Bothwell, Huntly and Atholl and these six formed the nucleus of a newly constituted Privy Council. Thomas Randolph, who had been declared *persona non grata* in February, reported from Berwick that he heard the Queen was seeking by all means to quiet her country, and on the surface at least it seemed that her bold, prompt action had once again won her a famous victory.

Mary lost no time in publishing her version of her recent gruesome experience to the world and had dictated an impassioned letter to the Queen of England from Dunbar. The news was received in London with proper disapproval. When the Spanish ambassador saw Elizabeth early in April she was wearing a miniature of the Queen of Scots hanging from a gold chain at her waist and told him fiercely that if she had been in Mary's place, she would have seized her treacherous husband's dagger and stabbed him with it.

Now that the Earl of Moray was restored to favour, Anglo-Scottish relations improved and Mary wrote to Elizabeth asking her to be godmother to her child. But the reports which William Cecil was receiving from his agents in Edinburgh were doing nothing to soften his mistrust of Mary, and Elizabeth strongly suspected her cousin of trying to stir up trouble in Ireland—never a very difficult feat.

The Queen of Scots' baby was born in Edinburgh Castle on 19 June 1566. It was a boy, apparently strong and healthy. Five days later the new English ambassador, Henry Killigrew, was brought to the Queen's bedside to offer his sovereign's congratulations which were graciously received, although Mary was still too weak to say more than a few words, spoken faintly 'with a hollow cough'. Killigrew was then introduced to the infant, whom he found 'sucking of his nurse', and afterwards saw him 'as good as naked, I mean his head, feet and hands, all to my judgement well proportioned and like to prove a goodly prince.'

The announcement of the birth was brought south by Sir James Melville, whose Memoirs are the only authority for the famous story of Elizabeth's bitter and uncharacteristic outburst that 'the Queen of Scots was lighter of a fair son, while she was but a barren stock.' It may be true, but Melville was writing many years after the event and may equally have been doing a little embroidery. When they met again the following day, he recalled, the Queen of England welcomed him with 'a merry countenance', saying that the joyful news of the Queen her sister's safe delivery had 'recovered her out of a heavy sickness which had holden her for fifteen days.' She would be glad to accept the invitation to stand gossip, or godmother, but when Melville slyly remarked that this would give her Majesty 'a fair occasion to see the queen, which she had so oft desired', Elizabeth only smiled and said she wished her estate and affairs might permit it. However, she promised to send 'both honourable lords and ladies to supply her room.'

One result of the birth of her son was a definite strengthening of Mary's position *vis-à-vis* the English succession among a section of the English establishment. Melville recorded that the Earl of Leicester was now her 'avowed friend' and had been doing his best to persuade the Queen of England to declare the Queen of Scots 'second person'. Also, according to Melville, the Duke of Norfolk, the Earl of Pembroke and several others 'showed themselves more openly her friends after they understood the birth of the prince.'

Sir James was therefore advised to approach Elizabeth again, saying he was assured that she had only been waiting until Mary became a mother before taking 'the same fair opportunity of satisfying the minds of many, as well in England as in Scotland, who desired to see that matter out of doubt.' He had, after all, he reminded her wistfully, brought good news from his Queen, and would be happy to carry home the equally good tidings of 'that so long delayed declaration.' If he had been hoping to catch Elizabeth in sentimental mood, he was to be disappointed. She replied only that the birth of the prince would certainly be a spur to the lawyers investigating the legal aspects of the case. As always, she sincerely hoped it could be decided in Mary's favour and would send news of any developments by the lords going north for the christening. But Melville could see she was still at her old game of 'driving time.'

The baby prince was already being hailed in some quarters as the future King of England, and Elizabeth herself may well have seen in Mary Stewart's son—doubly descended from the main Tudor stem—a possible long-term solution to the nagging problem of the succession, that 'good provision' by Almighty God which she had hopefully relied on for so long. In the meantime, however, the problem was refusing to lie down, and in the autumn of 1566 another confrontation with Parliament could no longer be postponed.

Motherhood might have strengthened the Scottish Queen's title in the eyes of one political faction, but it had done her no good with the House of Commons and there were ominous signs that the increasingly militant Protestant left-wing was planning to mount an organised campaign of agitation to have the whole question of the succession thrashed out in public and settled without more ado. The Queen of Scots could hardly stand aside from such a debate, and in her turn demanded the right to send commissioners to Westminster to represent her if the matter should be raised in Parliament, where, as the Spanish ambassador reported, the heretics were furiously in favour of Katherine Grey or, alternatively, the Earl of Huntingdon. Add to this the Queen of England's well known determination not to allow the matter to be discussed at all, and every ingredient of a first-class row seemed to be simmering nicely.

The Queen's advisers were relucant to turn up the heat but, finally, at a Council meeting on 12 October, the Duke of Norfolk ventured to remind her Majesty of the petitions presented by the Lords and Commons in 1563 which still awaited her final answer. Would she now permit both Houses to debate the twin issues of her marriage and the succession? Her Majesty most emphatically would not. The succession was her business and she wanted no advice from anyone on how to handle it. She had no intention of being 'buried alive' like her sister, and had not forgotten how people had flocked to her at Hatfield in the summer of 1558. She meant to have no such journeyings during her lifetime. As for her marriage, everyone knew that that was not far off. Parliament should do its duty, which did not include meddling in her private affairs.

It was perfectly true that talks had been going on about a possible marriage with Archduke Charles of Austria for the past three years, and for a time William Cecil had allowed himself to become quite optimistic, but in 1566 there seemed very little, if any, prospect of a royal wedding taking place in London in the foreseeable future. The Archduke's Catholicism, the Queen's stubborn refusal to commit herself to an engagement to any man she had not seen, and the House of Habsburg's equally stubborn refusal to send one of its sons 'on approval' were, as always, proving insurmountable obstacles to progress. Although Elizabeth, again as always, was wringing the last drop of diplomatic advantage out of her current courtship, Guzman de Silva—by far the most perceptive of King Philip's ambassadors to the court of St James—saw no reason to alter his opinion that while the Queen thoroughly enjoyed the business of being courted and having all the world running after her, she would end up by marrying Robert Dudley or no one.

Elizabeth had been driven to summon Parliament by acute financial necessity and when the subsidy bill came up for its first reading, the House of Commons—or at any rate a vocal and recalcitrant pressure group within the House of Commons—was quick to seize its opportunity, making it plain that there would be no supplies until the succession and the Queen's marriage had been fully discussed. Government efforts to cool the situation met with no success and the reply to one councillor who urged a little more patience was uncompromising: 'We have express charge to grant nothing before the Queen gives a firm answer to our demands. Go to the Queen and let her know our intention, which we have in command from all the towns and people of this Kingdom, whose deputies we are.'

Elizabeth told Guzman de Silva that the Commons had offered to vote her £250,000 if she would allow the nominating of Katherine Grey as her successor to be debated, but she had refused. Apart from the fact that she had no intention of letting Parliament interfere in the matter at all, she was not going to make bargains. The money she was asking for was for the common good and should be given freely and graciously. De Silva sympathised with her predicament, but pointed out that if she married the Archduke all this trouble would automatically come to an end. She was aware of that, replied the Queen, and meant to go ahead without further delay. De Silva's information was that negotiations with Vienna had come to a standstill, but he kept his scepticism to himself.

The House of Lords was as concerned as the Commons, but hesitated to precipitate a head-on collision with their sovereign lady. On 22 October, therefore, an imposing deputation, headed by the aged Lord Treasurer, waited on the Queen in her Privy Chamber. One by one the peers reminded her yet again of the need to provide for the future in good time, and one by one they begged her to declare her will in the matter of the succession. Elizabeth's answer gave no hint of surrender. The Commons, she exclaimed, were no better than rebels and would never have dared to treat her father in such a way. As for the Lords, they could do as they pleased and so would she.

Three days later the Lords agreed to combine with the Commons to exert joint pressure on the Queen. Elizabeth felt herself cornered and reacted accordingly. De Silva heard that she had called the Duke of Norfolk a traitor, or something very like it. The Earl of Pembroke and the Marquis of Northampton also felt the rough edge of her tongue and not even the Earl of Leicester was immune. Elizabeth said she thought that if all the world abandoned her, he would not, and when Robert hastily protested his willingness to die at her feet, she retorted crossly that that had nothing to do with the matter. Then, having ordered them all to get out of her sight and stay out of it, she flounced off to pour her grievances into the receptive ear of the Spanish ambassador who, in her present state of isolation, seemed the only friend she had.

Meanwhile, the Commons were staging what amounted to a sit-down strike— after nearly a month virtually no government business had been transacted—and tension was mounting. Early in November, just as the Lords and Commons were about to return to the attack, the Queen took the initiative herself, ordering a delegation of thirty members from each House to appear before her. She had already said that she would marry, she told them, and would never break the word of a prince for her honour's sake. She could only say again that she would marry as soon as she conveniently could, adding 'and I hope to have children, otherwise I would never marry.'

Turning to the succession, she made another of her infrequent references to her own experience as 'a second person', when she had 'tasted of the practices against her sister' and stood in danger of her life as a result. She had then had 'great occasions' to listen to the siren voices of men now sitting in the Commons, whom she could have named if she chose, and knew only too well how vulnerable—and how dangerous—the heir presumptive could become in the hands of an ambitious or dissatisfied faction. It was, therefore, not convenient to settle the succession, she informed her audience, 'nor never shall be without some peril unto you and certain danger unto me.' If she ever did see a suitable opportunity to name an heir, then she would 'deal therein for your safety, and offer it unto you as your Prince and head, without request; for it is monstrous that the feet should direct the head.'

One thing Elizabeth made abundantly clear. 'Though I be a woman, yet I have as good a courage, answerable to my place, as ever my father had. I am your anointed Queen. I will never be by violence constrained to do anything.'

This was one of those occasions when Elizabeth left no doubt in anyone's mind 'whose daughter she was', and it is therefore indicative of the strength of feeling roused by the subject that the House of Commons was still defiantly prepared to proceed with its controversial suit for the limitation of the succession. The Queen retaliated by forbidding any further discussion of the subject, ordering the members to 'satisfy themselves with her Highness's promise of marriage.' This led to another revolt—Paul Wentworth, a leader of the militants, going so far as to question whether the Crown had authority to prevent the Commons from debating a matter of urgent public concern.

By the middle of November the main issue at stake was no longer the succession or the Queen's marriage, but royal violation of Parliamentary privilege, and it was beginning to look as if a serious constitutional crisis might be impending. De Silva heard that 'the insolence of these heretics and their hankering after liberty in everything' was infuriating the Queen, but Elizabeth, now faced with a choice between dissolving Parliament, going without her much needed supplies and admitting a damaging defeat at the hands of the radical Protestants or giving way, wisely gave way. On the twenty-fifth she lifted her embargo, an action 'most joyfully taken of all the House', and it seems that an arrangement was reached in some behind-the-scenes negotiations whereby the Commons agreed to drop the succession debate in return for recognition of their right to freedom of speech. Thus Elizabeth got her way in the end. The succession remained a contest open to all-comers and her marriage plans remained as indeterminate as ever. But the episode had provided a salutory reminder of the continuing, implacable hostility towards the Queen of Scots among an influential and articulate section of the community. Nor had agitation been confined to Westminster. Broadsheets and handbills had been widely circulated through the city—some even appearing mysteriously in the Queen's own apartments—and the law students at Lincoln's Inn had held a disputation which found that 'by all the laws and customs of England' Mary Queen of Scots, as a foreigner born outside the realm, could not succeed to the crown 'even if she were the nearest in birth and the ablest.'

At one point in the argument it had looked as if the problem might be about to solve itself, for towards the end of October Mary was taken violently ill at Jedburgh, where she had gone to hold a justice eyre, and for a while her life was despaired of. However, her remarkable constitution and the devotion of her physician triumphed over prolonged attacks of vomiting, fainting fits and convulsions, and after about ten days, though still far from well, she was able to resume her tour of the Borders.

Maitland of Lethington, recently restored to royal favour, told James Beaton, Archbishop of Glasgow, resident in France, that the Queen's sickness, so far as he could understand, had been caused by 'thought and displeasure' and that the root of it was the King. 'For she has done him so great honour . . . contrary to the advice of her subjects, and he, on the other part, has recompensed her with such ingratitude, and misuses himself so far towards her, that it is heart-breaking to her to think that he should be her husband, and how to be free of him she sees no outgait.'

M du Croc, the French ambassador, also writing confidentially to Archbishop Beaton, agreed with Maitland that Mary's recent collapse had been brought on by 'deep grief and sorrow' over the breakdown of her marriage. Nor did he see any prospect of a reconciliation between husband and wife. Darnley had shown no sign of mending his ways since the Riccio murder, and 'the Queen cannot perceive him speaking with any nobleman but presently she suspects some plot among them.'

In view of her past experience, these suspicions were understandable and back in June Henry Killigrew had remarked on the factions visible on the Scottish Council—'an uncertain and disquiet sort of men.' Certainly deep divisions existed only just beneath the fragile calm of the surface. In July the Earl of Bedford reported that Bothwell now carried all credit with the Queen and was, in consequence, becoming 'the most hated man among the noblemen in Scotland.' At the same time, Bothwell and Huntly were nervously jealous of the favour being shown to the Earl of Moray, 'for they were upon contrary courses.' However, in the late autumn of 1566 all were temporarily united in the determination to get rid of the King.

At the end of November Mary arrived at Craigmillar Castle, some two miles south of Edinburgh, and there she took the opportunity to have a full and frank discussion of her marital problems with her principal advisers—Moray, Maitland, Bothwell, Huntly and Argyll. Not surprisingly no independent record of these very private talks exists, but it seems clear that a bargain was struck whereby the lords undertook to find a way of getting the Queen her freedom, while in return she agreed to pardon the Earl of Morton and the rest of the surviving Riccio murderers still in exile. It is also reasonably certain that a 'bond' to this effect was drawn up and signed by a majority of the lords.

On 12 December the court went into residence at Stirling for the baptism of Prince Charles James, which took place on the seventeenth according to the Catholic rite and with as much splendour as his mother could contrive. The Earl of Bedford had come north for the occasion, bringing with him a magnificent gold font as a gift from Queen Elizabeth and a message to say that if the baby had already outgrown it, then Mary must keep it for her next child. Needless to say, Bedford brought no news about the succession, but he was instructed to urge the Queen of Scots to agree to 'a mutual confirmation of a treaty of perpetual amity'—the Treaty of Edinburgh again—and to repeat Elizabeth's assurances that this would in no way prejudice her title 'to be next heir after us and our children.'

The Countess of Argyll stood proxy for the Queen of England at the papistical christening ceremony, but Bedford himself, a man of strict Protestant convictions, did not enter the chapel and neither did the Earl of Bothwell, although he was in charge of the arrangements and did not suffer from religious convictions of any shade. Another notable absentee, both from the service and the festivities which followed, was the baby's father. The King remained skulking in his apartments and du Croc, who repeatedly refused an invitation to visit him, told Archbishop Beaton that his 'bad deportment' was incurable, and no improvement could be expected for reasons which the ambassador preferred not to commit to paper. 'I cannot pretend to tell how it may all turn out', wrote du Croc on 23 December, 'but I will say that matters cannot subsist long as they are without being accompanied by many bad results.'

On Christmas Eve, yielding to the persuasions of Moray, Bothwell and the others, Mary finally signed the Earl of Morton's pardon and the King, faced with the prospect of the imminent return to Scotland of a bad-tempered, unforgiving body of men whom he had so flagrantly betrayed the previous spring, retreated precipitately to the Lennox family stronghold at Glasgow. There he became ill with either smallpox or syphilis—most probably the latter, especially in view of his well-known sexual proclivities.

During the first weeks of the New Year the air was thick with rumours of plots and counter-plots. While she was still at Stirling the Queen had been warned that her husband was planning to have the prince crowned and seize control of the government in his son's name, but when she attempted to investigate further, the story was denied and 'a bruit of how the King should be put in ward' substituted. Certainly this seemed more likely. Morton and his followers had wasted no time in re-crossing the Border and Bothwell and Maitland met him for a quiet talk at Whittinghame in East Lothian on or about 18 January, after which it was noticed that he and Bothwell had 'packed up' a friendship—an alliance which boded no good for the King. As James Melville put it, 'the days were evil and it was a busy time.'

Rumours of something unpleasant brewing for the hapless King of Scotland were already current in London and on 18 January Guzman de Silva reported that 'the displeasure of the Queen of Scotland with her husband is carried so far, that she was approached by some who wanted to induce her to allow a plot to be formed against him, which she refused, but she nevertheless shows him no affection.'

Writing to Archbishop Beaton on 20 January, Mary herself made no secret of her feelings. 'As for the King our husband, God knows always our part towards him; and his behaviour and thankfulness towards us is semblably well known to God and the world.' The Queen had no illusions about the malice of her husband, his father and all their folks, 'if their power were equivalent to their minds. But', she went on, 'God moderates their forces well enough, and takes the means of execution of their pretences from them: for, as we believe, they shall find none, or very few approve of their counsels and devices imagined to our displeasure or misliking.'

Although she said nothing about it to Beaton, an old friend and loyal supporter, on the very day this letter was written Mary left Holyrood for Glasgow to visit her estranged husband. Exactly why she chose to make such a journey in the dead of winter to see a man she so openly despised and distrusted is still a matter for conjecture. It has been suggested that the Queen's normally kind heart had been touched by the King's illness and that she genuinely wanted to make a fresh start. More credibly, it is said that she wanted to have him where she could keep an eye on him, in view of the persistent rumours that he was plotting against her. Another hypothesis, which takes the existence of an illicit relationship with Bothwell for granted, is that the Queen was afraid she was pregnant and everyone would know the child could not be her husband's unless marital relations were resumed in a hurry.

There remains an even simpler explanation. If Darnley were to be disposed of—and it was common knowledge that the Douglases at least were after his blood—then he would first have to be dislodged from Glasgow, where he was surrounded by Lennoxes and comparatively safe. His wife, with her royal authority and famous charm, was the only person likely to be able to persuade the victim to leave his refuge without a fuss and this is just what she proceeded to do—apparently promising that the past should be forgotten, that in future they would be at bed and board together and that 'she would love him and use him as her husband.'

The newly reconciled couple left for Edinburgh round about 27 January 1567, the King travelling in a litter with his disfigured features concealed by a taffeta mask. It seems that they were originally bound for Craigmillar, the Queen having stipulated that before they could come together the invalid must be 'purged and cleansed of his sickness', and at Craigmillar she could be with him and not far from the little prince, who had recently been transferred from Stirling to Edinburgh for greater security.

Darnley, however, possibly remembering some sinister stories he had heard about the conference there the previous autumn, objected to Craigmillar and in the end it was agreed that he should complete his convalescence at the old provost's lodging at Kirk o'Field. This was a modest house in the quadrangle attached to the former collegiate church of St Mary-in-the-Field, lying just within the Edinburgh town wall, south of the Cowgate and roughly halfway between Holyrood Palace and the Castle—a site occupied today by the buildings of Edinburgh University.

The King and his servants were established at Kirk o'Field, a pleasant enough spot on rising ground and surrounded by gardens, by Saturday 1 February. The provost's lodging, which now belonged to the Balfours, had been standing empty, but a selection of tapestries and furniture, including a bed hung with violet velvet, was hastily brought out of store to make the two main rooms habitable, while a second bedroom was prepared for the Queen on the floor below.

Whatever her motives in persuading her husband to return to the capital, Mary showed every sign of fulfilling her promise to put the past behind her. During that week she visited Kirk o'Field every day, sleeping in the room beneath her husband's on the Wednesday and Friday nights, and Darnley who had left Glasgow with considerable misgiving, is said to have written to his father on the Friday reporting an improvement in his health which he attributed to the 'good treatment of such as hath this good while concealed their good will; I mean of my love the Queen, which I assure you hath all this while, and yet doth, use herself like a natural and loving wife. I hope yet', he went on, 'that God will lighten our hearts with joy that hath so long been afflicted with trouble.' Few people shared the King of Scots' simple optimism. James Melville was to remember that it was widely suspected that his days were numbered, but no one cared to warn him because of his well-known inability to keep anything to himself.

On Sunday, 9 February it was announced that the King would be returning to Holyrood on the following day. That Sunday, the last before Lent and by tradition a day of carnival, was a busy one for the Queen, crammed with social engagements. In the morning one of her favourite servants, Bastien Pages, married Christiana Hogg, another member of the royal household, and Mary attended their wedding breakfast. At four o'clock in the afternoon she was present at a dinner given for Robertino di Moretta, the departing Savoyard ambassador, at a house in the Canongate and afterwards went on to Kirk o'Field 'accompanied with the most part of the lords that are in this town.'

Those lords *not* present included Maitland of Lethington, the Earl of Morton and the Earl of Moray, who had gone to St Andrews to visit his sick wife. But there was still a large enough party at the old provost's lodging to fill the King's rooms and make them a scene of cheerful conviviality. Argyll was there and Gilbert Kennedy, Earl of Cassilis. So was the Earl of Huntly and the dark, saturnine figure of Bothwell, splendidly turned out in black and silver, moved about among the company. The nobles played at dice and the Queen sat chatting cosily by her husband's bed until about eleven o'clock, when she suddenly remembered that she had promised to look in on Bastien's wedding masque and got up to go. Darnley protested—he had apparently been expecting her to sleep downstairs again that night—but she reminded him that tomorrow they would be together again permanently and anyway she was riding to Seton early next morning. According to one account, she kissed him and, pulling off one of her rings, gave it to him as a pledge of her good faith. Then she was gone. The torches of the royal cavalcade bobbed away down the slope to the Cowgate and darkness settled over Kirk o'Field.

Back at the Palace, Mary put in a brief appearance at the wedding party before retiring to her private apartments where she held a conference with Bothwell and John Stewart of Traquair, the same who had helped her to escape from Holyrood eleven months before. After Traquair left, Mary and Bothwell had a brief conversation à deux. The Queen was now ready to go to bed, but Bothwell went off to his own quarters, changed his clothes and went out again. Quite a number of people had business abroad that night.

Soon after two o'clock in the morning of Monday, 10 February, the citizens of Edinburgh were startled awake by the rumble of a mighty explosion which seemed to come from the direction of Kirk o'Field. Many 'rose from their beds at the noise' and residents of the nearby Blackfriars Wynd came rushing out of their houses in alarm. Three-quarters of a mile away at Holyrood, the sentries patrolling the grounds asked one another 'what crack was that?' and Queen Mary, roused by the sound 'as of a volley of twenty-five or thirty cannon', sent to know whence it came. By the time the messengers came panting back about an hour later with the horrifying news that the house at Kirk o'Field had been destroyed 'by the force of powder' so completely that hardly one stone was left standing, and that the dead body of the King had been found lying in the garden some sixty paces away, the whole palace was astir.

Lord Bothwell, who had been virtuously in his bed, got up and went to the Queen and so did Secretary Maitland, the Earls of Argyll, Huntly and Atholl. Everyone seemed stunned while this 'monstrous chance was in telling', but while one account says that Mary showed heroical presence of mind, sending 'the most part of them that were then about her to inquire out the manner of the doing' and ordering the soldiers of the royal guard to follow, another describes her as collapsing in tears of grief.

Two things only emerged with any clarity from the general 'amazedness' of that night: the Queen had been widowed in circumstances of appalling violence, and Scotland was about to be plunged into a major political scandal.

VII

She Is Not Worthy To Live!

The first news of the outrage at Kirk o'Field was passed to London by William Drury, commanding at Berwick, and reached London on 14 February. 'The case is a strange one', commented Guzman de Silva cautiously, 'and has greatly grieved the Catholics.' On the nineteenth Robert Melville, brother of James, arrived with the official version of the tragedy, which was that the assassins had intended to blow up both the King and Queen of Scotland and it was only by a fortunate chance that the Queen had escaped.

Mary herself, writing to Archbishop Beaton, declared her firm belief that it was not chance but God himself who had preserved her, and expressed her intention of taking rigorous vengeance. The Scottish Council in a letter to the Queen Mother of France followed an identical line. 'The authors of this crime very nearly destroyed the Queen in the same way, with most of the lords at present in her suite, who had been with the King in his chamber until nearly midnight. Her Majesty might easily have remained there all night, but God has been so gracious to us that these assassins have been despoiled of a part of their prey, and has reserved her Majesty to take the vengeance which such a barbarous and inhuman act deserves. We are making enquiries, and have no doubt that in a short time we shall succeed in discovering those who have perpetrated this deed.'

This sounded plausible enough, yet within a matter of days it was being whispered in London and Paris that Mary and her friends already knew the identity of the criminals and were unlikely to take any very rigorous vengeance on themselves. Guzman de Silva cross-examined Robert Melville in an attempt to 'get at the bottom of the suspicions as to who had been the author of the crime', but Melville either could not or would not tell him anything definite. The ambassador found it hard to credit that so virtuous and pious a lady as the Queen of Scotland could have been a party to her husband's murder; all the same, it is clear that a seed of doubt had been planted and when Moretta, 'the Duke of Savoy's man', reached London on his way home from Scotland on 24 February, he brought little reassurance. 'His account of the matter is almost the same as that published', reported de Silva, '. . . although he makes certain additions, which point to suspicion that the Queen knew of, or consented to the plot. When I asked him what he thought, or had been able to gather as to the Queen's share in it, he did not condemn her in words, but did not exonerate her at all. He thinks, however, that all will soon be known, and even gives signs that he knows more than he likes to say.'

Not everyone was being so discreet. Well before the end of February placards had begun to appear on the streets of Edinburgh accusing the Earl of Bothwell and even the Queen herself of murdering the King. In England, the 'heretics' were publishing her complicity as a fact and the Lennox family were in no doubt either where to lay the blame. Queen Elizabeth had sent two senior ladies, William Cecil's wife Mildred and Lady William Howard, to break the news to the dead man's mother and de Silva heard that in the first agony of her grief Margaret Lennox had cried out bitterly against her daughter-in-law. This, he felt, was understandable in the circumstances, but it was Elizabeth's attitude which was obviously going to be crucial and the Spaniard took the first available opportunity to sound her on the subject.

She spoke of the tragedy with much apparent sorrow, he reported, and said she thought it very extraordinary, but could not bring herself to believe that the Queen of Scotland could be guilty of so dreadful a crime, 'notwithstanding the murmurs of the people.' De Silva offered an opinion that the rumours were being deliberately spread by those who were out to injure Mary's reputation 'and make her odious in this country with respect to the succession.' He advised Elizabeth to be on the alert to prevent undue elation among the opposite party 'who were strong and might cause trouble'—meaning, of course, the supporters of Katherine Grey, though he was careful not to mention any names. Elizabeth replied that she had already taken precautions against this and de Silva added a few words of wisdom about the need for solidarity among princes to frustrate the evil designs of 'bad subjects and rebels'. He also improved the occasion by pointing out the 'inconveniences' which might result if Mary were now to be driven by desperation back into the arms of France.

Although the news of Darnley's death had probably not come as any great shock of surprise, the Queen of England was bound to take a very serious view of the case. Whatever his faults, the unfortunate 'long lad' had been her subject and closely related to her, and on 24 February, two days after her conversation with de Silva, she sent Henry Killigrew back to Scotland with a letter to Mary which sounded an almost brutally blunt note of warning. 'My ears have been so astounded and my heart so frightened to hear of the horrible and abominable murder of your husband and my cousin', it ran, 'that I have scarcely spirit to write; yet I cannot conceal that I grieve more for you than him. I should not do the office of a faithful cousin and friend, if I did not urge you to preserve your honour, rather than look through your fingers at revenge on those who have done you "tel plaisir" as most people say. I counsel you so to take this matter to heart, that you may show the world what a noble princess and loyal woman you are. I write thus vehemently not that I doubt, but for affection.'

On 1 March Guzman de Silva told the King of Spain that 'every day it becomes clearer that the Queen of Scotland must take steps to prove that she had no hand in the death of her husband, if she is to prosper in her claims to the succession here.' But every day it was also becoming clearer that the Queen of Scotland's well-known resilience of spirit in times of crisis had failed her on this occasion. In spite of the vehemently expressed advice of the Queen of England, the shocked reactions of her friends abroad and the anguished appeals for justice from her dead husband's family, in spite of the openly hostile posters being nailed to the door of the Tolbooth, on the Market Cross and other equally prominent sites, in spite of the anonymous voices heard crying in the night for vengeance and the preachers thundering daily from the pulpits, during those crucial weeks when her whole future hung in the balance, when, if ever, it was vital to move quickly and resolutely, not merely to establish her own innocence but to call some person or persons to account for the killing at Kirk o'Field, Mary did nothing. Worse than that, she was continuing to bestow smiles, confidence and other, more tangible, tokens of her regard on the man whom public opinion, rightly or wrongly, had unanimously and unhesitatingly cast in the role of first murderer. The Earl of Bothwell was to be seen swaggering through the streets of the capital, his dagger ostentatiously loose in its sheath and fifty armed Hepburns trotting at his heels, briskly offering to

wash his hands in the blood of his accusers, while the Queen stood by
with apparent complaisance or rode out on excursions to her
favourite resort at Seton to recreate herself with some gentle games of
golf.

All the reports reaching London during March from the professional
Scotland-watchers stationed at Berwick reinforced the general
conviction that Bothwell had murdered Darnley with the connivance
of the Queen, and before the end of the month Sir William Drury was
reporting 'the judgement of the people is that the Queen will marry
Bothwell.' There was certainly no doubt that, for the time being at
least, Bothwell was riding high.

Few murders have been more exhaustively discussed and dissected
by succeeding generations than that of Henry Stewart Lord Darnley,
but undisputed facts concerning it can still be written on the back of a
postcard. One of those facts, however, must be that, like the murder
of David Riccio, it was a corporate act, approved in advance by every
member of the inner coterie of power in Scotland. Whether that
coterie included the Queen remains a matter of heated controversy,
although circumstantial evidence that it did is very strong. Mary, at
twenty-four, had proved herself to be an astute, daring and forceful
young woman. Despite her sheltered childhood, she had grown up in
a world where intrigue and violence were commonplace, and since her
return to Scotland she had had plenty of first-hand experience of
both. That she knew, or wanted to know, the details of the murder
plan is unlikely; that she knew a murder was intended seems an
inescapable conclusion. It is stretching credulity beyond reasonable
limits to believe that she did not realise, when she signed the pardon
for Riccio's murderers, that she was also signing her husband's death
warrant. By the same token, it is somehow very difficult to accept
that she did not know, or at least guess, when she deliberately
brought Darnley back to Edinburgh a month later, that she was
bringing him to his death.

As for the events at Kirk o'Field on the night of 9/10 February
1567, these are so blurred by the fog of accusation and counter-
accusation, recrimination and exculpation, partisanship and prejudice,
by the suppression, misrepresentation and garbling of testimony,
that we are never likely now to penetrate to the truth. That Bothwell
was among the executants is not disputed. He and about half-a-
dozen of his henchmen were certainly responsible for setting off that
famous explosion—the chief purpose of which seems to have been to

confuse the issue by focussing attention on the deed rather than the doers, and lend credence to the official story that the Queen and her attendant lords had been among the intended victims.

16th century gunpowder was a lethal enough weapon (Bothwell appears to have narrowly escaped being blown up himself), but it was also an unpredictable one. It is therefore in the highest degree improbable that any practised assassin—and there were some very practised assassins at large in Edinburgh that night—would have trusted to gunpowder alone. Indeed, as far as it is possible to be certain, Darnley did not die in the explosion. The evidence, such as it is, leads to the presumption that, alarmed by suspicious noises off (it was an old northern custom to burn one's enemy's house over his head), Darnley and his valet had managed to get out through a first floor window, only to walk straight into the hands of the waiting Douglases, who despatched them with a minimum of noise and fuss amid the falling debris of the old provost's lodging.

But, apart from the perennial fascination of any murder mystery, the details of the case are not really important. It had been an open secret for nearly a year that Darnley was a marked man and no one would have been disposed to blame the Queen unduly for conniving at this drastic solution to her marital problems, if only she had played out the game according to the rules. Even in 16th century Scotland it was necessary to keep up appearances, and a suitable scapegoat had to be produced for the satisfaction of the world.

Here the evidence points logically enough to the presumptive existence of a plot within a plot, known to no more than a chosen few, which had pre-selected Bothwell as the sacrifice. Bothwell, always something of a loner and suspected of having 'a mark of his own that he shot at'—namely marriage with the Queen—was already unpopular among his peers. He had been manoeuvred into undertaking the most spectacular role at Kirk o'Field, and almost within hours of the crime a well-orchestrated and deadly propaganda campaign was being directed against him. No one, for obvious reasons, wanted too thorough an investigation, but if things had gone according to plan there can be little doubt that there would have been a hurried 'show' trial, as hurriedly followed by the execution of Lord Bothwell and his principal cronies, after which life would have returned to normal with everyone—especially the Earls of Moray and Morton and William Maitland of Lethington—quietly pleased over a useful piece of tidying up.

As it was, the Queen had had to complicate a perfectly straight-forward affair by falling in love with Lord Bothwell, and when he did actually stand trial on 12 April it was to clear his name—and clear his way to Mary's bed and throne—rather than the reverse. The trial itself—a private prosecution brought by the Earl of Lennox, who was understandably reluctant to show his face in a town seething with Bothwell's Borderers—was plainly intended to be a cover up of the most cynical kind, and Lennox in desperation appealed to the Queen of England to secure a postponement.

There had been hardly any communication between the two Queens in the weeks since the murder but now Elizabeth, with memories of the Amy Robsart scandal still fresh in her mind, wrote urgently to Mary. 'For the love of God, Madame, use such sincerity and prudence in this matter, which touches you so nearly, that all the world may feel justified in believing you innocent of so enormous a crime.'

This letter, carried post haste from Berwick by the hands of the Provost Marshal, reached Edinburgh at sx o'clock on the morning of 12 April, but the Provost, shouldered rudely aside and refused access to the Queen, was left with plenty of leisure to stand in the crowd and watch as the Earl of Bothwell proceeded 'with a merry and lusty cheer' to the Tolbooth. There, while two hundred of his men kept the door, he was solemnly 'made clean of the said slaughter' in the absence of Lennox, the plaintiff or 'pursuer'.

The imminent prospect of Bothwell's acquittal had been the signal for a thoroughly irritated Earl of Moray to leave Scotland again. He reached London, en route for the Continent, on 16 April and had a long private conversation with Elizabeth next day. On the nineteenth he paid a courtesy visit to the Spanish ambassador and confirmed the rumours that Bothwell's wife was about to divorce him. He also said he had heard 'that the divorce would be effected in order that the Queen might marry Bothwell, but did not believe it, considering the Queen's position and her great virtue, as well as the events which have take place.'

Other people were less sanguine. The French ambassador in London was certain the marriage would take place, and now came a letter from Kirkcaldy of Grange with the ominous information that Bothwell had held a supper party for 'most of the noblemen' to demand their consent in writing to the Queen's marriage 'which he will obtain—for she has said she cares not to lose France, England and her own country for him, and shall go with him to the world's end in a white petticoat ere she leave him.'

The rise to power of this ruthless strong man clearly threatened the whole fabric of the Anglo-Scottish alliance. Kirkcaldy, a sturdy Protestant and Anglophile, urged Elizabeth to revenge the murder of Darnley and thus 'win the hearts of all honest Scotsmen', but, wrote William Cecil gloomily on 23 April: 'Scotland is a quagmire. Nobody seems to stand still, the most honest desire to go away, the worst tremble with the shaking of their conscience.' Two days later the Privy Council met to discuss the situation, but before anything could be done to try and halt the calamitous trend of events north of the Border, those events took another lurch for the worse.

On Monday, 21 April Mary had gone to Stirling to see her son, now restored to his nursery there under the guardianship of the Earl of Mar, and as she rode back to Edinburgh on the following Thursday she was waylaid by Bothwell with a party of 400 horsemen and 'carried off' to Dunbar Castle. 'Judge ye if it be with her will or no!' wrote Kirkcaldy of Grange sardonically. Certainly everyone at the time was convinced that the abduction and the 'rape' which is said to have taken place at Dunbar had been a put-up job arranged 'so that if anything comes of the marriage, the Queen may make out that she was forced into it.'

When news of this latest outrage reached London, Queen Elizabeth, greatly scandalised, told Guzman de Silva about it herself and he also heard the story from the messenger 'who is a good Catholic and an intimate acquaintance.' There were worried faces at Whitehall and a good deal of talk about having the ten-month-old Prince James brought to England to be cared for by his Lennox grandmother, but otherwise the Queen of England seemed content to pursue a policy of wait and see. As it turned out, she hadn't long to wait for further developments. On 15 May the Queen of Scots married the Earl of Bothwell, a divorced man, according to the rites of the Protestant church and Catholic Europe openly despaired of her.

Giovanni Correr, Venetian ambassador in Paris, was of the opinion that Catholicism in Scotland had been 'deprived of all hope of ever again raising its head', and Mary's attempts to present her third marriage as a matter of political necessity were received with cold disbelief in the courts of Europe. The young King of France and his mother told Archbishop Beaton that the Queen of Scotland 'had behaved so ill and made herself so hateful to her subjects' that they

felt unable to give her either help or advice, and the Pope let it be
known that he would have nothing more to do with her 'unless by
and by he shall discover in her some sign of improvement in life and
religion.' Nor was opinion in Protestant England any more
favourable. Guzman de Silva reported that the Bothwell marriage
'seems to have scandalised people here very much, and has caused
sorrow to many who see the evils it will bring in its train.' Elizabeth,
he wrote on 7 June, 'expresses great surprise at events in Scotland,
and deplores them very much as touching the honour of that Queen.'

Even the most uncritical admirers of the Queen of Scots have been
hard put to it to condone her marriage to Bothwell, who had been
created Duke of Orkney by his bride a few days before the wedding.
But with the benefit of hindsight, it is possible to see that hole-and-
corner ceremony at Holyrood, marked by none of the pleasure and
pastime 'wont to be used when princes were married', as a logical
culmination of the train of events set in motion by Mary's disastrous
quarrel with the Earl of Moray in the spring of 1565, when she had
unleashed forces which, for all her personal courage and resource, she
could not hope to control, and which, for all her quick wits and native
intelligence, she only dimly comprehended.

Surrounded as she now was by an impenetrable morass of
treachery, feuding and faction, it is perfectly understandable that she
should have turned, with the optimism of desperation, to the one
man who had shown himself consistently loyal to her interests, who
alone seemed to possess the power and the will to support her and
who, like so many of his type, had an undoubted fascination for
women. It was understandable, but it was also suicidal.

A variety of hypotheses have been put forward to account for
Mary's apparently total suspension of judgement in the period
following Darnley's death, ranging from witchcraft to epilepsy, from
guilty conscience to nervous breakdown, or—most recently—that
she may have been subject to attacks of porphyria, which is now
believed to have caused the intermittent madness of her remote
descendant George III. The great majority of her contemporaries,
however, could only assume that the Queen of Scots had yielded to
'spite and appetite' and allowed her illicit passion for Bothwell to run
away with her. In any case, her fellow sovereigns and the hard-headed
professional men who managed their affairs were less interested in her
motivation than in the likely political consequences of her bizarre
rampage of self-destruction.

These consequences were already being foreshadowed in the reports of William Drury and Kirkcaldy of Grange. It was not, of course, to be supposed that the Scottish nobility would permit Bothwell to enjoy his ill-gotten gains for a moment longer than they could help, and as early as 1 May an active group of dissidents, including the Earls of Morton, Argyll, Atholl and Mar, had assembled at Stirling to discuss plans publicly announced as being to pursue the King's murderers, to set the Queen at liberty—or, rather more accurately, to separate her, by force if necessary, from Bothwell—and to ensure the safety of the Prince. A written agreement, or Band, always a favourite instrument of conspiring Scottish lords, was drawn up to this effect and Guzman de Silva also heard that 'the said lords had considered the raising of the child to the throne . . . the government being carried on by them in his name.'

Although they put up a brave front, the isolation of Mary and Bothwell was becoming increasingly obvious. 'The company at Court increases not of one nobleman more than were at the marriage', wrote Drury on 25 May. Maitland of Lethington stayed until 6 June, when he slipped away to join the Confederate Lords without observing the formality of taking leave, and on the following day the Queen and her husband also left Edinburgh for Borthwick Castle on the edge of Bothwell's Border country, where they hoped to gather their forces—Mary had already been obliged to melt down Elizabeth's gold font for money to pay the troops. On 11 June, after returning from a disappointing recruiting campaign, Bothwell ran into an advance party of confederates laying siege to the Castle. He got away by the skin of his teeth, leaving Mary to conduct a spirited exchange of insults with the enemy who, baulked of their prey, presently retired towards Edinburgh. The Queen, 'dressed in men's clothes, booted and spurred', then rode through the night to join her husband and together they reached the coastal fortress of Dunbar.

The final confrontation came early in the morning of Sunday, 15 June about eight miles east of the capital on rising ground overlooking the Esk river, the rebel army flaunting a banner showing the near naked body of Darnley lying under a tree with the infant Prince James kneeling beside it, holding up a scroll which enclosed the words: 'Judge and avenge my cause, O Lord.' The Confederate Lords might be very much more interested in destroying Bothwell than in avenging the cause of his alleged victim, but the forlorn ghost of the late and generally unlamented King had provided them with a propaganda weapon of the most potent kind.

There was no battle at Carberry Hill. As the day wore away in parleys and delays the royal troops, despite the Queen's 'great persuasions and encouragements', showed a disheartening tendency to melt into the background or suggest that terms had better be made. In the end, at about eight o'clock in the evening, Mary agreed to surrender to the lords apparently believing that she would be respectfully treated, and on condition that her husband would be allowed to leave the field unmolested. The couple embraced for the last time; Bothwell, with about thirty companions, took the eastward road; and Mary, still wearing the short red petticoat, velvet hat and scarf she had had to borrow at Dunbar, was escorted back to Edinburgh through the summer dusk, the banner of the dead man and the kneeling child going before her.

The story of that dreadful night, with the mob yelling 'Burn the whore! Kill her! Drown her! She is not worthy to live!' under the windows of the Provost's house by the Market Cross, is sufficiently well known. The following day the Queen was hurried away under close guard to her first prison at Lochleven and the reign of Mary Stewart was over.

Elizabeth's initial reaction to the news from Scotland was cautious and on 23 June she wrote to her cousin, still in reproachful vein, but 'for your comfort in such your present adversity, as we hear you are in, we are determined . . . to send with all speed one of our trusty servants not only to understand your state, but thereon so to deal with your nobility and people, as they shall find you not to lack our friendship and power.'

The trusty servant selected for this unenviable task was Sir Nicholas Throckmorton, and he received his instructions on 30 June. These made it clear that Elizabeth did not condone Mary's past behaviour, which 'almost made her Majesty think to deal no more with her by way of advice, but look on her as a person desperate to recover her honour, as other princes her friends and near kinsfolk also judge.' Carberry Hill had, however, altered the situation and the Queen of England summarised her objectives for Throckmorton under three heads: 1) to restore Mary's personal liberty, it being against God's (and Elizabeth Tudor's) ordinance for a prince and sovereign to be forcibly restrained by subjects; 2) to secure the punishment of Darnley's murderers—i.e. Bothwell; and 3) 'to preserve the young prince from all danger.' Elizabeth showed particular concern about her godson's future—the fear that he might be spirited off to France as once his mother had been was clearly haunting her—and Throckmorton was to do his utmost to get the child safely to England, where 'he might be placed in custody of his grandmother, with all security of hostages etc. that can be devised.'

Sir Nicholas also carried a list of matters to be imparted to the Scottish lords which included a strong protest at their action in offering such violence to their sovereign 'as to commit her to any manner of prison', and a warning against the dangers of accepting aid from France. Elizabeth would herself further any of their reasonable demands, but her Majesty 'found it strange, that till they met their sovereign in the field, she had never heard from them in any credible sort, nor indeed hitherto by any authorised person.'

Throckmorton set out for Scotland on 1 July in no very optimistic frame of mind. 'I am sorry to see the Queen's majesty's disposition alters not towards the lords', he wrote to Cecil from Berwick, 'for when all is done, it is they which must stand her in more stead than the Queen her cousin which is void of good fame.' His preliminary interview with Maitland of Lethington confirmed his forebodings. The lords' distrust of Elizabeth's intentions was unconcealed. They had not forgotten her treatment of Moray after the Chaseabout fiasco and did not mean to risk being left 'in the briars' a second time. 'It were better for us you would let us alone', said Maitland frankly, 'than neither do us nor yourselves good, as I fear in the end it will prove.' As for releasing the Queen, which Elizabeth had made a pre-condition of English support, that was out of the question in present circumstances.

By 14 July Throckmorton had reached Edinburgh and was able to send a fuller report. The Queen was 'in good health' at Lochleven and waited on by about a dozen ladies and gentlewomen and two 'chamberers', one a Frenchwoman. According to his information, the principal reason for her detention was her defiant refusal to abandon Bothwell, who was still at large somewhere in the north. On the contrary, the ambassador was told, she 'avoweth constantly that she will live and die with him; and sayeth if it were put to her choice to relinquish her crown and kingdom, or the Lord Bothwell, she would leave her kingdom and dignity to live as a simple damsel with him.'

Throckmorton had not been allowed to see Mary, but it did not take him long to find a way of getting a message to her, and on the eighteenth he informed Elizabeth she had sent him word that 'taking herself to be seven weeks gone with child', she would rather die than agree to renounce Bothwell and thus acknowledge herself to be with child of a bastard. Mary's pregnancy, if genuine, seemed likely to make the situation still more explosive and Throckmorton believed her now to be 'in great peril of her life.'

A General Assembly of the Church was about to convene at Edinburgh and the preachers, led by the prestigious figure of John Knox, were keeping public indignation at seething point. Some of Bothwell's underlings had by this time been rounded up, but it was being openly said that the Queen had 'no more liberty to commit murder or adultery than any other private person', and Knox confidently predicted a great plague from God on the whole nation if she were allowed to escape her just deserts. As for the lords, they were in an edgy mood, at once nervous and belligerent, which did not bode well for the prisoner in Lochleven Castle.

Nicholas Throckmorton was continuing, very much against his better judgement, to press for Mary's release, but at a late night conference on 20 July—a day appointed for 'continual preaching and common prayer'—he was warned off by Lethington in the plainest possible terms. 'To my great grief I speak it', said the Scottish Secretary, 'the Queen my mistress may not be abidden amongst us, and this is not the time to do her good, if she be ordained to have any.' Throckmorton had reliable information that the lords intended to press ahead with the coronation of young James, with the Queen's consent if they could get it. 'Otherwise they are determined to proceed against her publicly by such evidence as they can charge her with.' 'It is to be feared', added Throckmorton grimly, 'when they have gone so far, these lords will think themselves unsafe while she lives, and take her life.'

By the same post, Queen Elizabeth's envoy told William Cecil that he could see very little point in his staying in Edinburgh, unless her Majesty was prepared to change her tune and agree to negotiate with the *de facto* government to have their prince—or, indeed, their king 'if their designs take place'—brought to England on such conditions as they would accept for 'such a jewel'. As these conditions included official recognition of young James as his godmother's heir presumptive, Throckmorton was not hopeful of a successful outcome. In this he was quite right. Elizabeth had no intention of entering into any negotiations with the Scottish lords while their Queen remained in captivity, and she made this crystal clear in a letter dated 27 July.

'Our pleasure is', she wrote, 'you shall continue prosecution of your first charge to procure the Queen's liberty, and licence to speak with her that she may understand how much we mislike her doings, and induce her to accord to that most for her honour and the safety of her realm: for (as you know) we have ever desired to proceed evenly betwixt her and her people.' Elizabeth was not impressed by the lords' 'colourable defences' of their doings and Throckmorton was to 'require them to be better advised how they proceed further: and plainly denounce to them that if they determine the deprivation of the Queen their sovereign lady of her royal estate, we are determined . . . that we will take plain part against them, to revenge their sovereign for example to all posterity.' 'What warrant have they in Scripture, as subjects, to depose their prince?' demanded the Queen of England furiously. None. The contrary, in fact, and Throckmorton was to quote them the 'express words' of St Paul to the Romans. 'What law find they written in any Christian monarchy, that subjects may arrest the person of their princes, detain them captive and proceed to judge them? None such we are assured is in the whole Civil Law.'

Elizabeth detested the murder of Darnley and Mary's marriage to Bothwell as much as any of the Scottish lords, but that was no excuse for them, 'being by God's ordinance subjects, to call her, who also by God's ordinance is their superior and prince, to answer to their accusations by way of force, for we do not think it consonant in nature, that the head should be subject to the foot.' The Queen of England was well aware that she might be acting against her own interests by the stand she was taking, that she might well be putting the whole precious, painfully acquired Scottish alliance at risk: 'But we shall not consent for private profit, to what our conscience will not allow, but trust as hitherto in the good will and favour of Almighty God, at whose hands we have found no lack.'

Events in Scotland were now moving faster than the royal couriers and by the time this particular thunderbolt arrived from London Mary had miscarried of twins, according to her own account dictated in later years to her secretary Claude Nau (Throckmorton heard she had had 'two fits of an ague' and was keeping to her bed); she had been forced to sign an instrument of abdication; little James had been crowned king at Stirling and Nicholas Throckmorton was pressing urgently for his recall. 'For as the case stands with this miserable Queen', he told William Cecil, 'it shall be to little purpose for me to have access unto her, and I see no likelihood to win anything at these men's hands.' He told both Cecil and the Earl of Leicester that he feared the tragedy in Scotland would end violently in the Queen's person, as it had begun in the persons of 'David the Italian' and her husband. The conditions of her imprisonment were now stricter than ever and although he had so far managed to preserve her life—'to what continuance I am uncertain'—Throckmorton was convinced that nothing would so surely hasten her death as 'the doubt that these men may conceive of her redemption to liberty and authority by the Queen's majesty's aid.' To Elizabeth he wrote that it was no longer practicable to attempt to follow her original instructions and he was having as much as he could do to save Mary's life. Even the Hamiltons, who had previously appeared to be willing to support her, were now ready to agree to her death and Throckmorton, experienced as he was in the ways of the political world, was finding it difficult to credit that noblemen 'could have such double faces and such traitorous minds'.

Elizabeth's first reaction to the news of the abdication was to recall her ambassador. Four days later, after a talk with Guzman de Silva, she changed her mind and dictated another furious letter ordering Sir Nicholas to stay at his post and threaten the Scots with every kind of vengeance if they so much as touched a hair of Mary's head—a message he was to declare 'as roundly and sharply as he can, for sure she is he cannot express it with more vehemency than she means and intends.'

This unwelcome communication, dated 11 August, was enclosed with a covering letter from William Cecil telling Throckmorton that the Queen had sent for him hastily at five o'clock that afternoon and had 'entered into a great offensive speech that nothing was thought of for her to do to revenge the Queen of Scots' imprisonment and deliver her.' Cecil, who was as worried as Throckmorton about the possible consequences on the Scottish alliance, had done what he could to pacify her, but 'she increased so in anger against these lords that in good earnest she began to devise revenge by war.' Cecil tried to point out that this might do no more than drive the lords to desperation, 'and if the worst happened to the Queen (of Scots), her Majesty would be very sorry, yet malice would say she did it to urge

them to rid away the Queen.' Just then, most opportunely thought
Cecil, Throckmorton's latest batch of letters was delivered, and
seeing her Secretary's arguments backed up by the man on the spot,
Elizabeth 'began to pause'.

The Queen of England was in a very awkward position. It is
clear enough that she felt no personal sympathy for Mary's
predicament—more the exasperated contempt of a thorough-going
professional, with experience of the personal sacrifices often required
of reigning monarchs, for the gifted but irresponsible amateur whose
conduct had not only created a serious international crisis but
threatened to bring the institution of monarchy, and especially of
queenship, into disrepute. There's no doubt that Elizabeth's
problems would have been considerably reduced if her cousin had
been 'rid away', as Cecil put it, in the summer of 1567, but whatever
her shortcomings Mary was still an anointed and a sovereign prince
and as such, in Elizabeth's book, that meant she must be supported at
whatever inconvenience.

Cecil believed his mistress was moved by two 'special causes'—
one, that she should not appear partial against the Queen of Scots,
and two, 'that by this example none of her own be encouraged.' The
second was pretty certainly the more compelling reason. Elizabeth
Tudor, always a supreme realist, never made the mistake of taking
her special relationship with her own subjects for granted, and if
other subjects so close to home were allowed to get away with laying
violent hands on their queen, it might give some people some very
undesirable ideas.

But despite the uncompromising attitude adopted by the Queen of
England, the situation in Scotland continued to look extremely
black—the one gleam of light on the horizon being the fact that the
Earl of Moray was now on his way home. He had passed through
London at the end of July and spent several days in private talks with
the English government. He also saw the Spanish ambassador and
told de Silva that he would try to find some formula by which Mary
could eventually be restored to a conditional state of liberty. There
would, however, be many difficulties in the way, not the least of them
being the existence of documentary evidence—a letter written in her
own hand on three sheets of paper—which proved beyond doubt that
she had been 'cognisant of the murder of her husband.' Moray was
deeply grieved, he said, for the honour of his father's house and could
not tell how the matter would end. 'From all of which', wrote de

Silva on 2 August, 'I gather that the lords can depend upon him better than his sister can, although he says he will do his best for her.'

Ten days later Moray arrived in Edinburgh to a rapturous welcome and Nicholas Throckmorton, who had just succeeded in wringing a promise out of Maitland that 'this woeful Queen shall not die any violent death unless some new accident chance', wasted no time in urging him to go to Lochleven 'to comfort his sister after her long and grievous affliction; and to be favourable to her.' But the reunion between brother and sister, which took place on 15 August, can have brought little comfort to Mary Stewart. In a long, emotional interview which spread itself over two days she had to listen to some very plain speaking on the subject of her 'unadvisedness and misgovernment'. Moray did promise that, while there could be no question of setting her free for some time to come, he would use his influence to preserve her life and honour, but added a strong warning that her future would depend very largely on her own good behaviour and especially on an 'evident demonstration' that she minded no revenge against the Confederate Lords.

The Queen, Moray told Throckmorton, was in excellent health and had sent a message thanking Queen Elizabeth for her kind offices. 'And as she was beholding to your Majesty for this your favour employed for her relief already, so she desired your Majesty would be pleased, and to procure that she may live with you in England in what sort and manner it should please your Majesty to appoint; for truly she had no desire to live in her own country, nor any other but there in your realm.'

Moray returned to Edinburgh on 19 August and on the twenty-second was proclaimed Regent to rule in the name of King James VI. There was now very little left for Nicholas Throckmorton to do. He had dutifully 'declared' the message contained in Elizabeth's last letter to Moray and Maitland but found them unmoved by threats. They meant no harm to their Queen, said Maitland blandly, none in the world, and as soon as they saw some 'moderation' of her present passion she would have nothing but good at their hands. In the meantime, they had no intention of risking their lives, estates and reputations by letting her loose. If the Queen of England insisted on going to war against them, they would be sorry but would not change their minds. 'You must think, my Lord Ambassador', remarked the Lord of Lethington, 'your wars are not unknown to us; you will burn our Borders, and we will do the like to yours; and whensoever you invade us, we are sure France will aid us, for their league standeth fast, and they are bound . . . to defend us.' As for any English attempts to suborn rival factions such as the Hamiltons, Maitland could safely predict how those would end—'they will take your silver, and laugh you scorn when you have done, and agree with us.' Moray, when appealed to, fully associated himself with Maitland and the others, pointing out that if Elizabeth would only look around her 'she will find more profit for her and her realm to fortify and assist us, than to be against us.'

Throckmorton was considerably hampered by the fact that in his heart he agreed with every word uttered by his two antagonists (he had practically run out of adjectives to describe the general horribleness of the Hamiltons) and knew that they knew it, while everyone seemed to know that his mistress had no real intention of going to war on her cousin's behalf. The Scottish lords, with a good deal of valuable assistance from their Queen, had succeeded in their objective of establishing another royal minority, a situation which had always suited them very well in the past, and nothing was going to make them back down now.

The whole of Throckmorton's mission had been something of a charade, played out for the benefit of world opinion, but it had achieved something. Mary had been spared the indignity of trial by a 'people's court', and she was still alive. She might yet recover some limited freedom of action, which most people felt was as much as she deserved. To what extent she owed her life to Elizabeth's and Throckmorton's exertions is, like so much to do with her, still debated in certain quarters, but the fact remains that the Confederate Lords would have had nothing much to lose and a great deal to gain by killing her after Carberry Hill, had they not, for all their brave words, been a little afraid of the Queen of England and reluctant to push her too far. It is also a matter of record that, of all the European heads of state, the Queen of England alone made any effort to help the Queen of Scots. The Vatican had publicly abandoned her to her fate. The King of Spain, who had more important things on his mind that summer, did nothing at all, while as for the French—Throckmorton reported on 13 August that M de Lignerolles, the new envoy who travelled over with Moray, had come with decidedly conciliatory instructions and was using himself very mildly 'all to the contentation of these men.' The French, he told Cecil after a conversation with de Lignerolles, 'do not take greatly to heart how this Queen speeds, whether she lives or dies. The mark they shoot at is to renew their old league.' It seemed, though, that there was no immediate danger of the events of 1548 repeating themselves. The new Regent was luckily far too scrupulous a Protestant to risk his nephew's moral welfare in papist France.

Nicholas Throckmorton departed thankfully for home on 30 August. He had spent an uncomfortable, frustrating and at times, so he believed, actively dangerous two months in Scotland, and his mission had ostensibly been a failure. Nevertheless, it is likely that neither he nor Elizabeth, and certainly not William Cecil, were too dissatisfied. Elizabeth was employing her abundant histrionic talent in keeping up a quite convincing display of 'offence' over Moray's proceedings. She sent a small sum of money to the Hamiltons (with precisely the result foretold by Maitland) and made an approach, through her ambassador in Paris, to the French government suggesting a joint policy of trade sanctions against rebel Scotland. All this, though, was little more than a public relations exercise. Once it became clear that France, now embroiled in another religious civil war, had neither the inclination nor the resources for meddling in Scottish affairs, and that Mary was no longer in any imminent peril, Elizabeth relaxed and, to all intents and purposes, accepted the *status quo* in Scotland. She stuck to her refusal to recognise the Earl of Moray's regime and, after Throckmorton's recall, official diplomatic contact between the two countries came to an end, but the Scottish Regent and the English Secretary of State continued to correspond privately and Moray was not too despondent about the situation. 'Although the Queen's Majesty your mistress outwardly seem not altogether to allow the present state here', he remarked in one of his letters to Cecil, 'yet doubt I not but her Highness in heart likes it well enough.'

He was probably quite right. With her deeply felt conservative and legitimist prejudices, Elizabeth would have much preferred to see Mary restored to her throne on a nominal basis at least, but at the same time she cannot, 'in heart', have been too sorry to see her volatile cousin placed under restraint. Her Secretary of State was not sorry at all. William Cecil had always had a high opinion of the Earl of Moray—indeed he had once gone on record as describing him as 'not unlike, either in person or qualities, to be a king'—and was frankly relieved, after all the feminine crotchets of the past few years, to have a sober, rational and godly man with whom it would be possible to do business back at the head of affairs in Scotland.

Certainly, a welcome improvement in the state of Scottish affairs was soon apparent. The Earl of Bedford wrote from Berwick in September that he found the Regent 'most willing to continue the peace and quietness of the Borders', and a month later the Regent himself was able to tell his friend Cecil that 'the realm draws to a great quietness, and no appearance of any stir unless the same be practised by foreign enemies.'

The crisis in Scotland had, of course, been considerably eased by the elimination of the Earl of Bothwell who, after a brief career as a pirate off the Orkneys, had been chased as far as Scandinavia by Kirkcaldy of Grange. There he was unlucky enough to fall in with the kinsfolk of his discarded mistress, Anna Throndsen and was destined to spend the rest of his life in a variety of Danish prisons. At a Parliament held in Edinburgh in December (when, for the first time, it was publicly announced that the Queen was 'retained' for being of counsel with those who murdered her husband), the Earls of Huntly and Argyll went over to Moray and he seemed to be consolidating his position very satisfactorily. In January 1568, William Drury could announce gleefully that the Border country had not been 'in quieter or surer state' for the past forty years.

The occasional reports percolating out of the island fortress of Lochleven were not quite so reassuring. Mary, it appeared, was rapidly recovering her nerve and her self-confidence. 'She waxes fat, and instead of choler makes show of mirth', Drury had written as early as the end of September, and a month later, from the Earl of Bedford, 'the Queen . . . is merry and wanton as at any time since she was detained.' More ominously, she had already 'drawn divers to pity her, who before envied at her and would her evil.' The old magic was at work again, and during the autumn suspicions arose concerning 'the over great familiarity' between the prisoner and the dashing young George Douglas, brother of Sir William, the Lord of Lochleven. By the spring of 1568 rumours were circulating that 'the Queen's liberty, by favour, force, or stealth, is shortly looked for' and in April Guzman de Silva passed on news of an abortive escape attempt to the King of Spain.

It was not surprising—Queen Elizabeth had warned the Confederates all along that they were foolish to expect to be able to keep a young woman of Mary's calibre in detention for the rest of her life—and on Sunday, 2 May the inevitable happened. With the eager assistance of George Douglas, who was, of course, 'in a fantasy of love with her', and another, junior member of the clan, the Queen of Scots escaped from Lochleven while her gaolers were at supper.

Riding west with a small party of loyal adherents she made for Hamilton Castle, where the Hamilton family, increasingly irked by Moray's assumption of a power which they regarded as rightfully theirs, seized both the Queen and the opportunity she had given them to dislodge the usurper and re-establish their position next door to the throne. Weather-cocks like Huntly and Argyll joined them and a gratifying amount of support flowed in from the still predominantly Catholic south-west in response to appeals for help issued in the name of the 'undoubted and righteous Queen' of the realm of Scotland. The Regent, who happened to be conveniently close at hand in Glasgow, issued his own proclamation, calling on the lieges to rally to his side 'for the preservation of the King's person and authority', and the matter was somewhat precipitately decided at the village of Langside on 13 May.

The Queen's forces outnumbered the Regent's, but their hearts were not really in the fight—or at least their leaders' were not—and Moray's men had the advantage of the generalship of Kirkcaldy of Grange. Mary did not stay to see the end. In panic fear she fled south, guided by John Maxwell, Lord Herries, scarcely stopping for food or sleep until she had reached Dundrennan, about seventy miles away on the Kirkcudbrightshire coast. Here she wrote to her cousin Elizabeth hastily outlining her most recent misfortunes. 'I am now forced out of my kingdom', she went on, 'and driven to such straits that, next to God, I have no hope but in your goodness. I beseech you, therefore, my dearest sister, that I may be conducted to your presence, that I may acquaint you with all my affairs.'

The reasoning which lay behind the Queen of Scots' determination to seek asylum in England (if, indeed, reason was involved) remains obscure, not the least mysterious aspect being the fact that there was really no need for such a desperate measure. Langside had been a serious defeat but it had not been a rout and need not have been the end of the campaign. The Queen was in no immediate danger of re-capture. Lord Herries, as head of the important Maxwell family whose own loyalty was beyond question, had personally guaranteed her safety in his territory for the next forty days, and she could perfectly well have waited long enough to take stock of her position and see how the rest of the country reacted, especially now that the shadow of Bothwell had been lifted. She could at least have waited to see how Elizabeth reacted. If all else failed, she would still have had time to find a ship in one of the western ports and sail for France by the same route she had taken as a child.

France would certainly seem to have been the obvious refuge for Mary Stewart. Despite its generally lukewarm attitude towards her in recent months, the French government would have found it hard not to receive her kindly and to support her cause. On a more practical level, she was still a queen dowager with inalienable rights and a comfortable income from her French estates. She also had the vital links of language and religion and influential friends and relations. The Guises were still a power in the land. The Cardinal of Lorraine was active in the Court, and young Duke Henry showed every sign of developing into as prominent and resplendent a figure as his father had been. Yet Mary rejected this obvious solution to her problems.

Was it an instinctive revolt against the prospect of returning to the scene of her youthful triumphs as an anxious fugitive and supplicant, or an instinctive recoil from the patient malevolence of 'the Italian woman', her former mother-in-law? Was she drawn inexorably onwards by that elusive chimera, the English succession? Or was she temporarily beyond thought, in the grip of one of those reckless, irrational destructive impulses which had already twice brought her to the edge of disaster?

We are never likely to know. All we do know is that Mary Queen of Scots, acting, as she later admitted, against the advice of her best friends, chose deliberately and unnecessarily to throw herself on the mercy of strangers who had no particular reason to love her. On the afternoon of Sunday, 16 May, exactly a fortnight after her escape from Lochleven, she went down to the shore escorted by Lord Herries, Lord Fleming, Lord Claud Hamilton and a tiny handful of devoted attendants and embarked in one of the rough little craft normally used for inshore fishing or carrying coals and lime across the Solway Firth. This undistinguished conveyance entered the harbour at Workington, a small fishing port near the mouth of the River Derwent, at about seven o'clock that evening and the travellers sought shelter for the night at Workington Hall, Lord Herries, as their spokesman, announcing that he had carried off an heiress whom he was hoping to bestow on the son of his old friend Sir Henry Curwen. Henry Curwen was away from home, but one of his servants, a Frenchman, recognised the Queen, muffled in a borrowed cloak and hood, the moment she crossed the threshold and told a member of her entourage that he had formerly seen Her Majesty in better plight than now.

VIII

A Small Gilt Coffer

Mary's first act on the morning after her arrival in England was to write again urgently to Elizabeth, once more recapitulating all her woes from the date of the Riccio murder and graphically describing her present predicament—pitiable enough for an ordinary gentlewoman, let alone a queen. She had been obliged to flee for her life with nothing in the world but the clothes she stood up in, and begged her cousin to send for her as soon as possible.

By a curious irony, on that same day, Monday, 17 May Elizabeth was writing from Greenwich to congratulate Mary on her escape from Lochleven, but still regretting that her infatuation for 'ung malheureuse meschant' (i.e. Bothwell) should have made her so careless of her estate and honour and lost her so many friends. Elizabeth offered to help the Queen of Scots to recover her throne, provided she made no attempt to bring in aid from France, which the Queen of England must regard as an unfriendly act, and added a warning that 'those who have two strings to their bow may shoot stronger, but they rarely shoot straight.'

Mary, meanwhile, had no sooner despatched her letter by the hand of Lord Herries than she was ceremoniously waited on by a deputation of local gentry who proceeded to escort her a few miles inland to the town of Cockermouth. There Sir Richard Lowther, deputy governor of Carlisle, 'made his attendance on her' in the absence of the governor, Lord Scrope, and it was agreed that she should spend that night in the house of a well-to-do merchant, Master Henry Fletcher. The Queen used this brief respite to do something about her most pressing problem, clothes. Henry Fletcher is said to have presented his guest with thirteen ells of crimson velvet and a black cloth gown was hastily made up for her on credit. Anxious not to be outdone in matters of hospitality Richard Lowther 'ordered her charges at Cockermouth to be defrayed' and himself provided horses to carry the Queen and her train to Carlisle.

Lowther, not at all certain about the protocol governing the reception of refugee queens and much harassed by the sudden awesome responsibility which had descended on his shoulders, felt the only safe course was to detain the exotic visitor at Carlisle Castle pending further instructions. His couriers must have ridden fast, for news of Mary's presence in their midst had reached Queen Elizabeth and her Council by 20 May. Although it cannot have been entirely unexpected, it still caused a considerable stir and the Privy Council met in emergency session to discuss the situation. According to both the French and Spanish ambassadors, Elizabeth's first impulse had been to take Mary's part and receive her at Court, but this instinctive desire to show solidarity with the afflicted Queen of Scotland had been hurriedly over-ruled by a majority of councillors 'who leant to the side of the Regent and his government.'

'I think they must be somewhat embarrassed', wrote Guzman de Silva. '. . . If this Queen has her way now, they will be obliged to treat the Queen of Scots as a sovereign, which will offend those who forced her to abdicate, so that, although these people are glad enough to have her in their hands, they have many things to consider. If they keep her as if in prison it will probably scandalise all neighbouring princes, and if she remain free and able to communicate with her friends great suspicions will be aroused. In any case', he added with studied understatement, 'it is certain two women will not agree very long.'

The Privy Council was only too conscious of the many things they had to consider, but some action had to be taken quickly to relieve Sir Richard Lowther, who was already having to fend off the bullying attempts of the Earl of Northumberland, well known for his papistical tendencies, to remove Mary from his custody. Elizabeth therefore sent Lord Scrope and Sir Francis Knollys, her Vice-Chamberlain and an old and trusted friend, to take charge at Carlisle and explain as tactfully as possible that the Queen of England could not admit her 'dearest sister' to her presence 'by reason of this great slander of murder, whereof she was not yet purged.' If, however, she would put her future into Elizabeth's hands and undertake not to bring a foreign army into Scotland, then the Queen would be happy to do everything she could for her relief and comfort.

Mary made no attempt to conceal her disappointment when this message was conveyed to her on the evening of 28 May. In the twelve days which had passed since her arrival, frightened and exhausted, on the English coast, her naturally buoyant spirits had bubbled up again and she had aready written to the Earl of Cassilis telling him that she expected to be back in Scotland at the head of an army, French if not English, before the end of the summer. It never seems to have occurred to her that the Queen of England might refuse to see her, and she shed tears of angry frustration over Knollys and Scrope before hurrying away to write again to Elizabeth. She had evidently not made it clear that her principal reason for coming to England had been her urgent desire to lay all her grievances before her cousin in person, to complain of the unjust treatment she had received and to clear herself of those wicked calumnies being spread against her by her ungrateful subjects—subjects whom she had previously pardoned at Elizabeth's own request.

Mary now proposed to send the faithful Lord Herries to London with a request that Elizabeth should 'believe him as myself, and forthwith to let me have your answer in writing, whether it would be agreeable to you if I were to come without delay and without ceremony to you, and tell you more particularly the truth about all that has happened to me, in contradiction to their lies.' This, she indicated, should be more than enough to convince any right-minded person of her innocence of any crime and of the absolute justice of her cause.

If, for any reason, Elizabeth was unable or unwilling to help, then Mary felt sure her cousin would not refuse to let her go and seek assistance from her friends abroad, of which, she thanked God, she was not destitute. She thought it harsh and strange, after all she had suffered, that she should now be detained 'in manner a prisoner' and ended by begging Elizabeth for some sign of natural affection 'for your good sister, cousin and firm friend.'

If the Queen of Scots was dissatisfied by her present situation, so too was Francis Knollys. He had, in his often quoted estimation, found Mary to have 'an eloquent tongue and a discreet head', with 'stout courage and liberal heart adjoined thereunto.' She was already beginning to turn the heads of the susceptible gentlemen around Carlisle who had come flocking to pay their respects and listen sympathetically to the impassioned recital of her wrongs with which she favoured all her visitors—a fact that caused Knollys, himself a hard-line Protestant, to worry about the seditious rumours which might be spread if once the impression gained ground, in a district notoriously given to 'papistry', that this charming and unfortunate lady was being unfairly treated by the Queen.

Knollys was also seriously worried about the risk of another escape. He did not for a moment doubt the Queen of Scots' courage to make the attempt, or her ability to climb out of her bedroom window if need be. The devoted George Douglas was actually living in the Castle, while a growing number of her friends and their hangers-on were gathered in the town, and no restrictions had yet been placed on letters and visits.

As the days passed and it became more and more difficult to keep up the polite fiction of her 'guest' status, Sir Francis' anxiety and embarrassment increased, as did his impatience for some 'resolute order and direct way with this Queen.' He and Scrope were really in an impossible position. They had been instructed not to let their charge escape, but had been given no authority to control her activities or to detain her against her will.

Knollys was convinced that Mary meant nothing but trouble and after an uneasy fortnight in her company saw no reason to change his opinion. 'This lady and princess is a notable woman', he wrote on 11 June. 'She seemeth to regard no ceremonious honour beside the acknowledgement of her estate regal. She showeth a disposition to speak much, to be bold, to be pleasant, and to be very familiar. She showeth a great desire to be avenged of her enemies. She showeth a readiness to expose herself to all perils in hope of victory.' In fact, it seemed 'the thing that most she thirsteth after is victory' and she was not at all particular about the means used to achieve it. 'Now what is to be done with such a lady and princess?' enquired Francis Knollys of his friend William Cecil.

Despite all the anxious discussion going on round the council table and the memoranda flowing from William Cecil's busy pen, the answer to that question was never really in doubt. Although Queen Elizabeth was naturally more concerned than some of her advisers with saving her cousin's face, she was in broad agreement with them on the fundamental issue that Mary Stewart must never again be allowed to enjoy unrestricted possession of the Scottish throne. Nor did she quarrel with Cecil's conclusion that she would be obliged to 'intermeddle', if for no other reason than that 'the Queen of Scots has heretofore openly challenged the crown of England, not as a second person after the Queen's majesty, but afore her.' In practical terms this meant accepting responsibility for Mary's safe-keeping, at least for the time being. It was obviously out of the question either to hand her back to Moray and the lords or to let her go to France, where her Guise kinsfolk would inevitably stir up a hornets' nest of faction on her behalf.

No one in government circles viewed the prospect of, as Francis Knollys put it, nourishing the exiled queen in their bosoms with any relish. On the contrary, wrote the historian William Camden, 'they reasoned lest she (who was as it were the very pith and marrow of sweet eloquence) might draw many daily to her part which favoured her title to the crown of England, would kindle the coals of her ambition, and leave nothing unassayed whereby they might set the crown upon her head.'

The reports coming in both from Carlisle and Berwick, where William Drury 'marvelled to hear how divers are gladded with the Queen of Scots' escape' and warned that she had many well-wishers northwards, served to reinforce Cecil's gloomy conviction that Mary would 'practise with her friends for this crown', embolden all evil subjects and become even more of a menace in England than she had been in Scotland. Elizabeth, too, was worried about the situation. 'As well she may be', reported Guzman de Silva, 'for the Queen of Scots has certainly many friends, and they will increase in number hourly, as the accusations of complicity in the murder of her husband are being forgotten, and her marriage with Bothwell is now being attributed to compulsion and fear.' Friends, he added sagely, 'easily persuade themselves of the truth of what they wish to believe.'

It was plainly essential from Elizabeth's point of view that Mary's murky past should not be forgotten, for it offered the only half-way legal excuse for holding her in England and the Queen had to be able to justify herself to her fellow sovereigns—especially the King of France, who was hurriedly informed that her Majesty meant to take her cousin's causes into her protection and would proceed to consider how best to 'reduce her honourably in concord with her subjects.' As a first step towards this laudable goal, Elizabeth announced her intention of setting up a court of enquiry to hear both sides of the Scottish dispute and herself act as an impartial arbitrator between them. To emphasise her neutral stance, a letter was despatched to Moray requiring him to suspend hostilities against Mary's party in Scotland, though it seems that another message containing a warning to get on with his mopping-up operations as quickly as possible went by more private channels.

On 12 June Henry Middlemore, Nicholas Throckmorton's cousin and one of the most promising of the younger civil servants, arrived at Carlisle to see the Queen of Scots and outline the English government's plans for her immediate future. He also brought a letter from Elizabeth in which the Queen of England promised to be so careful of Mary's life and honour that no parent could have them more at heart, but again refused to receive her until she had been 'honourably acquitted' of the crimes charged against her. 'Whatever my regard for you, I can never be careless of my own reputation.'

Middlemore delivered this discouraging communication at the beginning of a long, stormy and unproductive interview. He repeated Elizabeth's assurances of friendship and protection and tried to point out that if she were to receive and entertain the Queen of Scotland before her 'justification' it would look as if 'her Majesty would rather wink at her grace's faults, than have the truth known or justice done.' It would not help Mary's cause to destroy Elizabeth's credit as an impartial judge and give the world an excuse for saying that she 'little regarded the murder of her near kinsman' or the infamy her cousin had incurred by marrying the principal murderer.

Mary was not impressed. As Knollys had predicted, this cool approach to the situation did nothing to satisfy her fiery stomach, or her 'bloody appetite to shed the blood of her enemies.' She complained passionately about deliberately created delays and reiterated her demands to be allowed to go and seek help elsewhere—from the Grand Turk if necessary. As for the suggestion that a trial should be made of her 'innocency', the Queen of Scots 'had no other judge but God, neither none could take upon them to judge of her: she knew her degree of estate well enough.' It was true she had previously offered to submit to the Queen of England's judgement but, reported Henry Middlemore, '"how" sayeth she, "can that be, when the Queen my sister will not suffer me to come at her?"'

To Mary Stewart it was as simple as that. If she could only 'come at' her cousin and tell her side of the story as one queen to another, any unworthy suspicions Elizabeth might be harbouring would be dispelled without further ado. As it was, her enemies on the English Council were being given a free hand to conspire against her with her own rebellious subjects and Queen Elizabeth was apparently quite willing to receive *them*. Mary wept and raged at the unfairness of it all, impervious to Middlemore's reasoned arguments, his promises and pleas for patience, and when he told her, hoping 'to make a pleasant parting', that she was soon to be transferred from Carlisle to some other place where she might enjoy more pleasure and liberty she at once asked if she was to go as a prisoner.

Middlemore was due to go on to Scotland to confer with the Earl of Moray and thankfully left Francis Knollys to cope with the task of moving his charge to the greater security of Bolton Castle, an isolated stronghold on the Yorkshire moors, without resort to actual coercion. Mary, understandably reluctant to leave her vantage point on the Border, insisted that she would not stir unless taken by force and was also still flatly refusing to discuss her affairs with anyone but the Queen of England in person.

The Queen of England thought her cousin's obstructive attitude 'very strange.' 'Your innocence being such as I hope, you need not refuse answer to any noble personage I shall send', she wrote on 30 June. While as for the difficulties Mary was making about the simple matter of changing her residence—'pray do not give me occasion to think that your promises are but wind.' 'Good sister, be of another mind', pleaded Mary. 'Win the heart, and all shall be yours and at your commandment. I thought to satisfy you wholly, if I might have seen you. Alas! do not as the serpent that stoppeth his hearing, for I am no enchanter, but your sister and natural cousin.' But the serpent in London remained obstinately deaf. Whatever impression to the contrary she may have contrived to make on the Spanish ambassador, it seems highly unlikely that Elizabeth had, even for a moment, ever seriously intended to give the Scottish enchantress an opportunity to outshine her at her own court.

The Queen of Scots hung on at Carlisle until mid-July, banging her head against the stone wall of her gaolers' stolidly courteous but implacable determination to remove her. 'Surely', reported the much-tried Knollys, 'if I should declare the difficulties that we have passed, before we could get her to remove, instead of a letter I should write a story and that somewhat tragical!' However, being a fairminded man, he added that once she realised tears and tantrums were having no effect, Mary had given in gracefully and shown herself 'very quiet, tractable and void of displeasant countenance' on the journey to Bolton.

Before the end of the month she had given way on another, more crucial issue, agreeing to commit her cause to be heard by Elizabeth, not as a judge—nothing like that—but as 'her dear cousin and friend.'

The Queen of England intended to summon the noblemen of Scotland to give an account of themselves before a panel of commissioners. If they failed to justify their actions to her satisfaction (and she told Lord Herries that she expected them to fail), then she would restore the Queen of Scots to her former state, by force of arms if necessary. It was not quite so clear what she meant to do if the lords did succeed in making out a case for having deposed their sovereign, but she assured Herries that whatever happened she would continue to look after Mary's interests, and make every effort to arrange an honourable reconciliation between the Scottish queen and her subjects. In return for these good offices, Mary was required formally to renounce all claim and title to the English throne during Elizabeth's lifetime (or that of her increasingly doubtful offspring), to ratify the Treaty of Edinburgh, abandon her French alliance in favour of a 'straight league' with England, abolish the mass altogether in Scotland and instead 'receive the common prayer after the form of England.'

This was not what Mary had wanted. But after nearly two and a half months' unsuccessful agitation and with little or no encouragement forthcoming from abroad—the French ambassador told her frankly that he thought she was better off where she was—she seems to have reached the conclusion that she had better settle for what she could get; especially since Elizabeth's message as delivered by Lord Herries appeared to contain a promise that she would be conditionally restored whatever the outcome of the enquiry.

Moray also accepted the Queen of England's terms, though he was not entirely happy about them either. He resented being cast in the role of defendant and was distinctly nervous that Elizabeth did indeed intend somehow to restore his sister whatever happened, in spite of certain private assurances to the contrary. The English Council shared his unease, and had already expressed its collective misgivings over the prospect of Mary's restoration, even in name only, 'considering the comforts and aids from her kindred, and also from Rome, whereby she may vanquish all both here and in Scotland.' For once she was back on her throne, what possible oaths and promises could be imagined to withstand her appetite for the English crown?

William Cecil was equally sceptical. 'The Queen's Majesty', he wrote to Henry Norris in France early in August '. . . meaneth to have the matter between the Queen of Scots and her subjects heard in this realm and compounded, as I think, with a certain manner of restitution of the Queen and that limited with certain conditions; which how they shall be afterwards performed, wise men may doubt.'

Wise men continued to doubt, but it seems the Queen of England continued to hope that it might yet be possible to strike a bargain with the Scots by which Mary could be returned home in some purely nominal capacity, while the Earl of Moray remained in effective control as Regent. Elizabeth was no doubt aware that, given the deep-rooted passions of vengeful hatred, fear and distrust on both sides, the chances of reaching such a compromise were remote and it is hard to say whether she ever rated them very seriously—the Spanish ambassador believed that the English had always intended to sell the Queen of Scots down the river and keep her in 'an honourable prison.' Nevertheless, any settlement which would preserve the decencies and secure the Anglo-Scottish alliance without forcing Elizabeth to take on the expense, responsibility and social embarrassment of holding her cousin and sister queen in detention possessed obvious appeal and was at least worth trying for.

Mary, too, was doing her best to keep her options open. She edified the godly Francis Knollys by listening to Protestant sermons up at Bolton and seeming outwardly 'not only to favour the form, but also the chief articles, of the religion of the gospel.' When some of her orthodox friends took alarm, she made a public reaffirmation of her devotion to Rome, saying coolly to Knollys in private that she could not be expected to risk losing France and Spain and her friends in other places by appearing to change her religion, at least until she was assured that Queen Elizabeth meant to keep faith with her. She was now bringing all her charm to bear on Knollys. 'She hath of late not only used me very courteously', he reported at the end of August, 'but also pressed me marvellously, as though she conceived I could persuade her highness to show her great favour, and grant access to her presence.'

Mary had by no means given up hope of getting access to Elizabeth, but she wrote submissively on 5 September that since she perceived how disagreeable her coming would be, she would abandon the idea for the present. 'I will cease to admonish you about any thing; do as you think best, seeing the confidence I have in you. . . . Whenever you think there is any thing wherein I can serve you, I shall be ready to do so, either after your disputes [the enquiry] are begun, or after you have, according to your promise, reinstated me in my authority. Meanwhile, I will have patience, contenting myself with offering, in every thing that is in my power, to devote myself entirely to you without exception.'

Another letter, written some three weeks later to her childhood friend Elisabeth of Valois, now married to the King of Spain, told a rather different story. Mary complained about the Queen of England's bossy determination to direct her affairs regardless of her own wishes, and went on to remark wistfully that if only she could count on a little outside help, she felt sure she 'could easily teach this queen what it is to intermeddle and assist subjects against princes.' The whole of the north of England was devoted to the Catholic faith and since her arrival Mary had gained the hearts of many good people, 'so that they are ready to hazard all they possess for me and my cause.' She had been offered many inducements to change her religion but, whatever might be said to the contrary, she had no intention of doing so and meant to die in the Roman Catholic faith. If the Kings of France and Spain would now acknowledge her as their sister and ally and take her under their protection, the Queen of England would not dare refuse to restore her and help her punish her rebels. Mary would then be able to ensure that her son was raised as a good Catholic. Indeed, if she had her choice, James would be sent to be brought up in Spain and married to one of King Philip's daughters, while for her part she would be prepared to 'risk every danger to re-establish the ancient and good faith throughout this whole island.'

After some three months' intensive behind-the-scenes activity by all the interested parties, the court of enquiry which was to settle the Queen of Scots' future finally opened at York on 4 October. Of the three principals, only Moray was present in person, accompanied, among others, by his second-in-command the Earl of Morton, Lord Lindsay and Maitland of Lethington. Mary's team was headed by Lord Herries and John Lesley, Bishop of Ross, and the English adjudicators were the Duke of Norfolk, the Earl of Sussex and that reliable old warhorse Sir Ralph Sadler.

The proceedings opened with a statement of Mary's complaints against her rebellious subjects presented by Lord Herries. The other side countered with a recital of the Queen's misbehaviour following the Darnley murder, ending in her 'voluntary' abdication. Mary's commissioners retorted by pointing out that her marriage to Bothwell had not taken place until after his 'acquittal' and that it had been recommended by a significant body of opinion among the nobility. As for her abdication, far from being voluntary, it had been extorted from her under threats of extreme violence.

All this, though, was mere finessing while Moray waited an opportunity to play his ace. On 10 October three members of the Scottish delegation came, quite off the record they insisted, to show their English opposite numbers 'such matter as they have to condemn the Queen of Scots of the murder of her husband.' This 'matter' consisted of a series of letters apparently written by Mary to Bothwell between January and April 1567 and which had, according to the official Scots account, been discovered in a silver casket taken from one of Bothwell's confidential servants in June of that year. If accepted as genuine, they would provide damning evidence of the Queen's moral turpitude and of her guilt as an accessory before the fact of Darnley's murder.

Controversy over the Casket Letters—were they Mary's unaided work, were they forgeries pure and simple, or an ingenious amalgam of the Queen's own letters and love letters written to Bothwell by another woman—is still very much alive, but as the original documents, with one possible exception, vanished during the fifteen-eighties, the question is never likely to be resolved now. What mattered at the time was not so much their authenticity—though no one who actually saw them seems to have doubted them—but the use which might be made of them.

In October 1568 the existence and substance of the Casket Letters had been known to a select few in the world of high politics for more than a year, but they had remained strictly classified. Even now Moray was not prepared to produce the originals, still less put them in evidence before the court of enquiry, until he had been given a cast-iron guarantee that, if he were to take the irrevocable step of charging his sister with murder, the Queen of England would 'sustain' him, recognise his regime and either hand Mary over to him or, preferably, undertake to keep her safely under lock and key in England. Failing this, all the indications were that he would make every effort to conclude a separate peace with the Marian faction, leaving Elizabeth out of the reckoning. The assembly at York was, in fact, rapidly dissolving into a sticky morass of intrigue. 'This cause is the doubtfullest and dangerest that ever I dealt in . . .', wrote the Duke of Norfolk to William Cecil. 'You shall find in the end as there be some few in this company that mean plainly and truly, so there be others that seek wholly to serve their own private turns.'

The Duke did not add that he, too, was not without his private interests in the outcome of this doubtful cause, for it was during the York conference that he was first propositioned by Maitland of Lethington, who suggested that he might care to consider becoming Mary Stewart's fourth husband.

It was hardly surprising that the old idea of solving the problem of the Queen of Scots by means of an English marriage should now have recurred both to men like Maitland with compelling personal reasons for not wanting to see old scandals raked up, and to others who honestly believed that some form of reconciliation would be a more seemly, as well as a more equitable method of settling the whole unsavoury business. Apart from these considerations, Mary, adulteress and murderess or not, was still a first-rate matrimonial prize, for the trifling matter of her marriage to Bothwell could easily be set aside. Even the high-minded Francis Knollys had been moved to reflect on the political and religious advantages of marrying her to an Englishman of suitable rank (his favoured candidate was George Carey, who happened to be his wife's nephew as well as Queen Elizabeth's cousin), while Norfolk, a widower in his early thirties, was irresistibly attracted by the prospect opened up by Maitland.

When rumours of these matchmaking activities filtered through to London, and they filtered with remarkable speed and accuracy, an immediate change was noticed in Elizabeth's attitude. 'The Queen's Majesty', wrote Cecil, 'is now at the pinch so careful for her own surety and state as I perceive the Queen of Scots shall not be advanced to greater credit than her cause will serve. And I think that is rather to put her back than to further her.' Cecil was immensely relieved and so was the Earl of Sussex. 'God hold the Queen's majesty in the mind . . . she is in, and put in her councillors' hearts to advise her thereto.'

God evidently listened to this appeal. At a Council meeting on 30 October it was agreed that Moray should be given the assurances he wanted and urged to press the murder charge against Mary. Four days later Elizabeth announced that the enquiry was to be transferred from York to Westminster and summoned all the principal councillors and peers to attend.

It was a fateful decision and unquestionably had a lot to do with the doubts being cast on Norfolk's good faith, for Thomas Howard occupied a unique position in the English hierarchy. As the country's leading aristocrat, with the blood of the old royal house in his veins and closely related to the Queen through her mother, he commanded enormous personal influence and respect. As a great territorial magnate he commanded personal power on an almost mediaeval scale. He was also a popular figure, generally regarded as standing aloof from the sordid scramble of career politics. But now it appeared that even Norfolk had his price, and the first hint that that price was Mary Queen of Scots did more to harden Elizabeth's view of Mary's future than all William Cecil's well-argued memoranda.

The adjourned enquiry re-opened in London at the end of November and on Friday the twenty-sixth Moray produced his so-called Eik, or addition, a document formally accusing Mary of complicity in the murder of Darnley. The proceedings now began to take on an increasingly Kafkaesque quality. Mary's commissioners protested that they were not authorised to answer to anything other than those matters already raised at York and demanded an audience with Elizabeth to require, on their sovereign's behalf, 'that for answer of these infamous calumniations, the said Queen might come in proper person to the presence of her Majesty, and there before her council and nobility, and such ambassadors as were here in this realm for any foreign princes, to answer for herself for defence of her innocency.' This was expectable. Rather less expectably, they told Leicester and Cecil in private conversation that they were prepared, on their own authority, to agree to some compromise or 'appointment' between Mary and her subjects 'for her honour and the weal of her country, with surety to Moray and his party.'

But Elizabeth would not agree to a compromise which might leave a permanent stain on Mary's reputation. She could not forget her office as a friend and sister, she said and thought it better to have Moray's allegations examined and seen to be unfounded, and he and his accomplices duly punished for 'so audaciously defaming' their sovereign. Nor did she think it suitable that Mary, being a Queen, should be forced to come and answer for herself. When Herries and Ross persisted, she would only repeat that she thought it better for their Queen's honour to have her cleared, 'as she trusted she should be', and her accusers reproved without any need either for her to answer in person, or to have the matter 'wrapped up by any appointment.'

On Monday, 6 December Mary's commissioners registered a final protest against any further hearings unless she was allowed to appear in person before Queen Elizabeth, and then formally withdrew from the proceedings. As soon as they had gone, the Lord Keeper Nicholas Bacon, as spokesman for the now much enlarged English commission, solemnly informed the Earl of Moray and his party that her highness thought it very strange that they, 'being native subjects of the Queen of Scots, should accuse her of so horrible a crime, odible both to God and man' and invited them to prove their case.

The rest of that week was taken up with an examination of the documentary evidence against Mary. The notorious Casket—'a small gilt coffer not fully a foot long'—made its first public appearance. Depositions by some of Bothwell's servants (now all rather conveniently dead and unavailable for interrogation) were produced, together with a mass of other documentation—Acts of Parliament, Acts of Attainder, marriage contracts and acts of divorce.

The enquiry moved to its climax on Tuesday of the following week in a carefully stage-managed public relations exercise at Hampton Court Palace. Elizabeth had summoned all the lords of her Privy Council, plus six other earls 'as the principal persons of her nobility', and after being sworn to secrecy this august assembly was given a full account of 'the state of the cause of the Queen of Scots, now at some stay as her commissioners have refused further conference.' The record of the proceedings, both at York and Westminster, was read aloud to them and all the documents made available for their inspection, after which they were told they knew as much about the affair as the Queen and her Council.

As for the Queen of Scots' request to come and vindicate herself in person, Elizabeth was only too anxious that 'some good answer may be made by the said Queen', but unless and until that answer was made and Mary 'some wise purged', she meant to stick to her resolve not to risk the contamination of direct contact with an accused murderess—especially now that the case against her looked so black. Properly impressed, the six earls—they were Northumberland, Shrewsbury, Huntingdon, Westmorland, Worcester and Warwick —thanked the Queen for her openness in showing them the state of this great cause so plainly, 'wherein they had seen such foul matters as they thought truly in their conscience that her Majesty's position was justified.'

Having gained this valuable propaganda point, the English government was ready for the next step—to be seen to be making every effort to induce the Queen of Scots to offer a reasoned defence.

On 16 December Elizabeth informed Mary's commissioners that she was willing to re-open the enquiry if their mistress would agree to answer the Earl of Moray's charges, either through her properly accredited representatives or, if she preferred, in her own person to a delegation of noblemen who would be sent to wait on her at Bolton. Herries and Ross were strongly advised to urge her not to suffer herself 'to be noted culpable of such horrible crimes only for lack of coming to her Majesty's presence', for there would be no surer way to procure her condemnation than for her to refuse to answer.

Elizabeth followed this up four days later with a letter to Mary. Her sorrow over her cousin's misfortunes had been doubled, she wrote, 'in beholding such things as are produced to prove yourself cause of all the same. . . . Nevertheless, both in friendship, nature and justice, we are moved to cover these matters, and stay our judgement, and not to gather any sense hereof to your prejudice before we may hear of your direct answer thereunto.' And she went on, 'we cannot but as one prince and near cousin regarding another, most earnestly as we may in terms of friendship, require and charge you not to forbear from answering; and for our part, as we are heartily sorry and dismayed to find such matters of your charge, so shall we be as heartily glad and well content to hear of sufficient matter for your discharge.'

Meanwhile, various plans for Mary's future were being discussed. There was no longer any question of restoring her to her throne under any conditions—not at any rate for the foreseeable future—or of allowing her to leave the country. But Elizabeth still wanted, if at all possible, to avoid the odium of being forced to hold her against her will. She was also manifestly determined to avoid being forced into publishing a guilty verdict. Quite apart from the international scandal and complications this was likely to cause, the Queen of England had not forgotten that the Queen of Scots, whatever horrible crimes she might have committed, was still *de facto* heir presumptive to the English throne (indeed, the recent death of Katherine Grey had left her with no serious competitor) and the domestic scandal and other complications which would inevitably follow her open condemnation were such as Elizabeth preferred not to contemplate.

By the time the proceedings at Westminster came to an end, it had been generally agreed to adopt William Cecil's suggestion that the Queen of Scots should remain deprived of her crown and Moray left to continue his regency undisturbed. Cecil considered this the best way for England, but not the easiest. There was just a chance, though, that Mary could still be persuaded to accept the situation gracefully, to resign voluntarily in favour of her son and consent to live in England for 'a convenient time', with the charges against her dropped and 'committed to oblivion.' It seemed worth a try and Francis Knollys was sent a list of points to be used as bargaining counters. These included the threat of having her guilt and infamy notified to the world, her own closer confinement, and the recognition by Elizabeth of Moray's regime. Knollys was also instructed to argue that if Mary did return to Scotland she would be bound to find herself dependent on the Hamiltons and their faction for support, in which case neither she nor her child could expect to have 'long continuance'. At least she would be safe where she was and if she would agree to have James educated in England, 'it may be beneficial to her supposed title to this crown.'

Probably to no one's great surprise, Mary flatly refused to consider any proposition which might be interpreted as an admission of guilt. She would rather die, she declared, than resign her crown, and the last word in her life would be that of a Queen of Scotland. Perhaps it was just as well. The Earl of Arundel put his finger on a not insignificant aspect of the 'Catch 22' predicament in which both queens were now trapped when he remarked in a letter to Elizabeth: 'One that has a crown can hardly persuade another to leave her crown because her subjects will not obey. It may be a new doctrine in Scotland, but is not good to be taught in England.' Mary continued vehemently to insist on her complete innocence and told Knollys that she could easily demolish her accusers' case, but had never meant to answer except in person before Elizabeth. 'For', she exclaimed, 'I am not an equal to my rebels, neither will I submit myself to be weighed in equal balance with them'— another argument which could hardly fail to appeal to Elizabeth Tudor.

On 26 December Francis Knollys reported that he did not believe the Queen of Scots would ever be brought to answer, other than by a blanket denial, 'without her assurance beforehand that howsoever the matter fall out, that yet the judgement shall fall on her side.' In short, she was demanding a not guilty verdict in advance, just as Moray had demanded a guilty one.

Mary had seen the original Eik, produced at Westminster in November, in which Moray and his accomplices had, among other things, 'falsely, traitorously and mischeantly lied, imputing to us the crime whereof they themselves are authors, inventors, doers and some of them proper executors', but now she was demanding an opportunity to examine the other 'alleged principal writings'—those infamous forgeries purporting to be her privy letters. On 13 January 1569 she was informed that Elizabeth did not mean to deny her 'the sight of the true copies of the said writings', but wanted her to realise that once they had been delivered, 'of necessity she must make answer, without any cavillation for lack of her admittance to the presence of her Majesty or such like.' The Queen of Scots was also solemnly adjured to remember that once her answer was made and the matter thus put 'upon direct trial', she would have to be judged 'either innocent or culpable of the horrible crimes, whereof she is as yet but accused, and not convinced; and if she should not by her answer prove herself innocent, then of necessity the Queen's majesty can never with her honour show her any favour.' The Queen's majesty, therefore, wanted Mary to think very carefully about the possible consequences of a guilty verdict, and wanted her assurance in her own handwriting that she understood them and would be prepared to abide by them. The warning was too obvious to miss and Mary did not miss it, but it naturally did not make her like her cousin any better.

In fact, by now the decision, such as it was, had already been taken. Moray was agitating to be allowed to return to Scotland and the affair which had been occupying everyone's attention for so long had to be brought to some sort of conclusion. Elizabeth would not pronounce a final judgement until she had heard the Queen of Scotland's answers to the charges brought against her, but on 10 January, using Cecil as her mouthpiece, she let it be known that whereas nothing had yet been deduced against the Earl of Moray and his adherents 'that may impair their honour or allegiance', equally 'there had nothing been sufficiently produced nor shown by them against the Queen their sovereign whereby the Queen of England should conceive or take any evil opinion against the Queen her good sister.' In the circumstances, the Queen of England did not feel justified in detaining Moray and his friends any longer, and would suffer them to depart 'in the same estate in the which they were of before their coming within this realm.' Mary, though, must stay where she was. Elizabeth had undertaken 'the order and redress of her causes' and as this had not yet been satisfactorily accomplished (due, it was to be inferred, to Mary's general lack of co-operation) she could not let her cousin go.

The great enquiry was thus reduced to a non-event, its outcome one which the Bishop of Ross had predicted with remarkable accuracy the previous October, when he told Mary that Elizabeth's 'determined purpose' would be to hold matters in suspense, while at the same time making the enemy 'utter all they could to your dishonour, to the effect to cause you to come in disdain with the whole subjects of this realm, that ye may be the more unable to attempt anything to her disadvantage.' When they had done their worst, he went on, the Queen of England would not come to any immediate decision, 'but transport you up in the country, and retain you there, till she think time to show you favour, which is not likely to be hastily, because of your uncles in France and the fear she has herself of your being her unfriend.'

In all her dealings with the Scots, Elizabeth, as was perfectly right and proper, had put her country's interests first and had come best out of the settlement she imposed in January 1569. Her rival's wings were clipped and a friendly regime remained in power in Scotland while, in typically Elizabethan fashion, no doors had been finally closed. True, the Queen of England was left to entertain an unwilling, unwanted and potentially dangerous guest, but one could not have everything. In any case, Mary might yet have her uses as a pawn in the diplomatic chessgame and by keeping control of her person, Elizabeth could be reasonably assured of keeping a controlling influence over Scottish affairs.

Moray had no reason to complain, either. He was no worse off than he had been before—actually he was a good deal better off, having got rid of his sister, and when he left London on or about 19 January he took with him a loan of £5,000 from the English exchequer. Even Mary was in no worse plight than she had been before her dramatic exit from Lochleven, and even she could count a few blessings. Her life was more secure now than at any time since Carberry Hill. She had made no concessions. Her reputation was still, officially, intact and she had not been left without a gleam of hope for the future. She, naturally, did not see it that way, but in the context of the harsh world of 16th century *realpolitik* her present position was as good if not a little better, than she could realistically have expected.

Arrangements for her accommodation now had to be put on a more permanent footing and another custodian appointed. Francis

Knollys had been pleading to be relieved since the summer and Elizabeth's choice of replacement had fallen on George Talbot, sixth Earl of Shrewsbury, a nobleman of the first rank and an extremely wealthy one—a necessary qualification this, since the honour of playing host to a captive queen was likely to prove an expensive business. Another qualification was the fact that the Earl's estates extended widely across the north Midlands, well away from London and the coast as also from the sensitive Border region. In all he owned seven sizeable houses and his wife, a rich woman in her own right, possessed two more. Between them, therefore, they would be able to provide an ample choice of residence for their charge and in mid-January Knollys and Lord Scrope received instructions to escort the Queen of Scots to Tutbury Castle in Staffordshire and hand her over into Shrewsbury's keeping.

Mary's last weeks at Bolton were miserable for all concerned. In her bitter chagrin at the outcome of the Westminster conference, the Queen of Scots had written to Lord John Hamilton and the others still holding out at the fortress of Dumbarton that Elizabeth had betrayed her, that her son was to be handed over to the English, that Moray would be assured of the Scottish succession if James died without heirs and would hold Scotland 'in manner of fee of the Queen of England', that English garrisons were to be established at Edinburgh and Stirling Castles, and Dumbarton besieged and taken for the English. Elizabeth was obliged to issue a public denial of these damaging reports, which did nothing to improve her temper and caused additional unpleasantness between the cousins. Mary was also making trouble over the move from Bolton, threatening to refuse to go 'without violence' and Francis Knollys, distracted with worry over the terminal illness of his wife, was reaching the end of his endurance.

The party finally set forward on 26 January, Mary 'with an evil will and much ado', on a journey which turned into a nightmare of bad weather, bad roads, illness and misunderstandings. Lady Livingstone, one of the Queen's favourite attendants, fell sick at Rotherham and had to be left behind. Then Mary herself collapsed with the familiar 'pain in her side', resulting in a further delay at the house of a Mr Fulgeham near Chesterfield while she recovered. The Earl of Shrewsbury had asked that she should be taken temporarily to his house at Sheffield, as Tutbury was not yet ready for her, but at the last moment another message arrived to say that Lady Shrewsbury had sent all the hangings from Sheffield to Tutbury and had furnished it as well as she could with her own stuff, so it was Tutbury after all—a large, dilapidated medieval castle, exposed to every wind that blew and used nowadays only as an occasional hunting lodge. It was a place which Mary always hated, but her first meeting with Shrewsbury passed 'without sign of offence.' Knollys had been braced for a scene over the order that her retinue was to be reduced from sixty to thirty persons, 'besides her women and grooms of the stables', by the removal of such superfluous Scots and Frenchmen 'as do no other service but practise unmete things', but to his surprise she accepted it with apparent docility. Mary evidently wished to make a good impression on Shrewsbury and on 16 February his lordship was able to report that 'this Queen continues very quiet in outward behaviour, and talks only of indifferent matters, with mild and seemly words when the Queen's majesty is mentioned.'

The Earl had been instructed to treat his involuntary house guest with all the respect due to her rank and nearness in blood to Elizabeth, and while Mary was certainly a prisoner in the sense that she could not choose where she lived, that her visitors were carefully screened and her correspondence censored—in theory, at least—her material circumstances were hardly those of an ordinary prisoner. She might complain vigorously about the draughts and discomforts of Tutbury, but she was never at Tutbury for long and although the discomforts of country house living were admittedly notorious, they were the same for everyone. The Queen of Scots' meals were served on silver plate, she sat on a royal dais beneath a cloth of estate and her rooms were furnished with Turkey carpets and tapestries, with chairs upholstered in crimson cloth of gold and stools embroidered with gold on crimson satin. Her suite may have been reduced but it was still considerable—forty-two persons are listed on a check-roll dated October 1569—and included such old friends as Mary Seton, one of the famous Maries who had gone with her to France all those years ago, Bastien Pages and Christiana Hogg, whose wedding the Queen had attended on that momentous Sunday in February 1567, and young Willy Douglas who had rowed her ashore from Lochleven Castle and now served her as a valet de chambre or gentleman usher. She had a physician, a secretary and also now a priest, though an English visitor who saw her shortly after her arrival at Tutbury, reported that she heard the English service 'with a book of the psalms in English in her hand'.

She was able to ride and enjoy the pleasures of the chase, as she had at Bolton, and soon struck up a friendship with Shrewsbury's formidable countess, Elizabeth, better known as Bess of Hardwick, with whom she shared an interest and skill in the fine needlework over which so many ladies spent so many hours. The Earl worried that his prisoner's 'daily resort' to his wife's chamber might be taken amiss by the authorities, but assured Cecil that their talk was altogether of 'trifling matters'.

To the outward eye Mary was accepting her lot with as much resignation as could be expected. In her letters to Elizabeth she continued to harp on the theme of the poor, forsaken stranger princess who had fled so trustingly for succour to her nearest kinswoman. But now, she wrote, a few days before leaving Bolton, 'I cannot but deplore my evil fortune, seeing you have been pleased not only to refuse me your presence, causing me to be declared unworthy of it by your nobles; but also suffered me to be torn in pieces by my rebels . . . not allowing me to have copies of their false accusations, or affording me any liberty to accuse them.' Nevertheless, despite the fact that the Queen of England apparently preferred to believe the word of traitors and rebels before that of her cousin and sister queen, Mary still sought her aid alone and yearned only for her friendship and favour. She knew she was in Elizabeth's power and could do nothing but appeal to God and to her, 'for other support I have none.'

Elizabeth was not unduly impressed by this affecting picture of the poor, helpless prisoner. She was still annoyed by Mary's efforts to stir up trouble in Scotland and told her rather curtly to quiet herself, according to 'the princely good heart' that God had given her, and be assured, 'if no impediments are ministered to us by yourself . . . we will take care of your causes as in honour we shall always answer to your trust reposed in us.'

As it happened, Queen Elizabeth was wise to be sceptical about the sincerity of Mary's 'trust', for the Queen of Scots had already embarked on her long and ultimately disastrous career of intrigue and had succeeded in opening a channel of communication with Guerau de Spes, the new Spanish ambassador in London, who informed King Philip that 'she certainly seems a lady of great spirit and gains so many friends where she is, that with little help she would be able to get this kingdom into her hands.' De Spes had contrived to send a reliable messenger to Bolton and on 8 January reported triumphantly: 'The

Queen of Scotland told my servant to convey to me the following words: "Tell the ambassador that, if his master will help me, I shall be Queen of England in three months, and mass shall be said all over the country."'

IX

A Determination with the Queen of Scots

Throughout the whole period of her captivity the Queen of Scots was ready at all times to open her heart to everyone, English or Scots, French, Italian or Spaniard, who showed the slightest sign of being willing or able to help her, and had warned Francis Knollys frankly enough the previous October that if she continued to be held 'perforce', he might be sure 'that then being as a desperate person' she would use any attempts which would serve her purpose, either by her friends or by herself. But in 1569 her most realistic hopes of freedom still lay with the Queen of England, who would have been happy enough to be rid of her if only a really fail-safe formula for her restoration could be found.

In April the defection of some of the leaders of her party in Scotland, although it caused Mary to sit weeping inconsolably all through supper one evening, seemed to Elizabeth to offer an opportunity of re-opening talks about a possible reconciliation with the Regent and early in May the Bishop of Ross, who had now become Mary's principal spokesman and 'ambassador' in England, was able to inform his mistress that he had had a long conversation with the Queen in the garden at Westminster and had found her highness apparently sincerely concerned for her welfare.

The old request to allow Mary to go back to France was evidently raised again, for the Bishop reported that 'the Queen finds it not good you go to France for divers inconveniences: one that sometime ye acclaimed her crown and doubts not but the Cardinal (of Lorraine) and your friends will make you do the same yet.' John Leslie retorted by saying that if Elizabeth feared for her surety from Mary's friends in France, the remedy was in her own hands—she had only to help her cousin herself and then the Queen of Scots would have no need to turn to strangers. Elizabeth promised an answer 'by advice of her council', but would first have to be satisfied on several matters—

especially 'the matter of the title'. The point had been made repeatedly over the past year that the Queen of England could never forget that the Queen of Scotland had once challenged her lawful title to her crown and could not let her go until proper reparation had been made for this 'great offence'—in other words, of course, until Mary had formally and publicly retracted any such challenge. Nevertheless, Ross felt definitely optimistic. 'I see her Majesty here and her nobility seem more careful of your honour and weal than ever I saw them before', he wrote on 2 May, 'which puts me in good hope of speedy resolution.'

Few matters of Elizabethan diplomacy were ever speedily resolved, but on this occasion the Queen wasted no time in despatching a discussion document setting out possible ways and means by which Mary might be returned to Scotland without prejudice to Moray's regime for consideration by the Regent and his party. The delay came from Moray, who viewed the prospect of his sister's return under any conditions with undisguised revulsion, and his reply, making it clear that he would negotiate only on the basis of a confirmation of Mary's abdication, did not arrive until early August. Elizabeth, although she can scarcely have been surprised, was irritated by this display of intransigence and threatened 'to proceed of ourselves to such a determination with the Queen of Scots as we shall find honourable and meet' without further reference to the Regent who, she evidently considered, was getting above himself.

But while she had no hesitation in reminding the Earl of Moray of his inferior status, the Queen of England could not afford to risk disturbing the precarious equilibrium in Scotland at a time when the political outlook, both at home and abroad, was becoming increasingly unsettled. In France, where religious civil war still raged intermittently, the government of Charles IX and Catherine de Medici was not exactly looking for trouble, but in the general turmoil there was always a danger that the ultra-Catholic Guise faction might get the upper hand at any time. The Guises, who remained dedicated to the extermination of heresy in general and the promotion of the Queen of Scots' cause in particular, were openly hostile towards Elizabeth and her ambassador in Paris was constantly coming across vague but disquieting rumours of Guisard plots.

Trouble of a more immediate nature was brewing across the North Sea where the Netherlands, England's traditional allies and trading partners, were in open revolt against their Spanish overlords. Philip had never taken much interest in his Dutch and Flemish territories, regarding them chiefly as a useful source of revenue, but the spread of a radical form of Protestantism—especially in the north and east and the great commercial centre of Antwerp—had prompted him to turn an unforgiving eye on their affairs. The King of Spain might be obliged to tolerate the heresy of other nations for reasons of political expediency; in no circumstances would he tolerate it within his own dominions and in 1567 he had sent the notorious Duke of Alva from Italy with an army of ten thousand 'blackbeards' to carry out a policy of blood and iron in the disaffected provinces.

The thought of this kind of force within a day's sail of their south-eastern coastline was not a comforting one for the English, particularly in view of the fact that Anglo-Spanish relations began to deteriorate rapidly at the end of the sixties. There had been a series of unfortunate incidents, culminating in the English seizure of a quantity of bullion on its way up the Channel to pay Alva's troops in the Netherlands—an outrage which caused the fire-eating Guerau de Spes to dance up and down with fury and goaded the Duke of Alva into slapping an embargo on English trade. Although, technically speaking, the money in question was still the property of the Genoese bankers who were lending it to Philip and had no objection to transferring their business to another client, the seizure could hardly be described as a friendly act, and in February 1569 the King of Spain was sufficiently irritated to agree with his ambassador in London about the general desirability of deposing the Queen of England and giving her crown to the Queen of Scots.

As it happened, not only Philip had been ruffled by the incident of the Spanish pay-ships. An influential group of right-wing English councillors, nominally led by the Duke of Norfolk, regarded it as a dangerous and unnecessary piece of provocation and a disagreeable instance of the growing effrontery of William Cecil. These individuals, who included the Earls of Arundel and Pembroke, the Marquis of Northampton and possibly the old Marquis of Winchester, favoured a policy of appeasement towards the great European powers, in view of England's apparent vulnerability to attack. They favoured the release of Mary Stewart, her recognition as heir presumptive and her marriage to the Duke of Norfolk. They also wanted to get rid of the upstart Secretary Cecil, in which they could count on the support of the Earl of Leicester, and the year had begun with a conspiracy to bring Cecil down in the good old-fashioned way. It was the kind of scheme which had succeeded more than once in Henry VIII's day, but times had changed, as Elizabeth made very clear by direct intervention on her faithful Secretary's behalf, and the conspirators were forced to retreat in disarray. Their unofficial plans for Mary's future, however, remained under active consideration.

The idea of solving the problem of the Queen of Scots by means of an English marriage attracted support not only from disgruntled Catholic sympathisers and impoverished feudal magnates like the Earls of Northumberland and Westmorland, who saw Mary's release and rehabilitation as a stepping stone to their own aggrandisement, but also from those at the other end of the religious spectrum—from men like Nicholas Throckmorton and even the Earl of Moray—afraid that Elizabeth was bent on restoring Mary without adequate safeguards and who felt that 'by this marriage her highness and the realm might take commodity.'

The matter was discussed with the Bishop of Ross and through him with the Queen of Scots, who was naturally much encouraged by this evidence of interest and support from such important members of the English nobility as Arundel, Pembroke, Leicester and, of course Norfolk himself. In reply to an approach made early in June, she promised to put herself entirely at the Queen of England's disposal once she was restored to her throne and agreed to consider the Duke of Norfolk's suit, although she stipulated that Elizabeth's consent must first be obtained. In fact, she was eager for the match and had already begun to correspond affectionately with Norfolk. The unfortunate Bothwell, still languishing in his Danish prison, no longer entered into her calculations and towards the end of June the French ambassador reported that the affair seemed so far advanced that he thought it could not fail to proceed. 'The Queen of Scots', he went on, 'appears not only to consent but very strongly to desire it.' A month later Guerau de Spes believed it was all but settled, as a majority of the Council was now determined to have the Queen of Scots set at liberty 'on condition that she marries an Englishman', and he told Philip 'the Queen of Scotland says that, if she were at liberty . . . she would deliver herself and her son entirely into your Majesty's hands.'

There may have been nothing overtly treasonable in the Norfolk marriage scheme by itself, but it was noticeable that none of its promoters, least of all the bridegroom elect, could quite bring themselves to mention it to Queen Elizabeth. In the end it was the

Earl of Leicester, whose motives throughout remained somewhat obscure, who spilt the beans and the Queen then had it out with Norfolk, commanding him on his allegiance to deal no more in the Scottish matter. Elizabeth was under no illusions about the likely consequences of such an alliance, or who would be its dominant partner. When the French ambassador again raised the question of Mary's release early in September, she remarked sourly that the Queen of Scots did not appear to feel the want of her liberty very much, 'for she was able to find a husband even as it was.'

But if Mary was expecting some dramatic rescue attempt she was to be disappointed, for Thomas Howard Duke of Norfolk was no slayer of dragons. Thoroughly unnerved by his recent encounter with his sovereign lady, he bolted to the sanctuary of his East Anglian estates where, he was accustomed to boast, he thought himself as good a prince as any. The whole court, according to William Camden, 'hung in suspense and fear lest he should break forth into rebellion', but instead of taking the field Norfolk took unheroically to his bed with an ague. The Queen ordered him back to London, ague or no, and by the second week of October he had surrendered tamely to her officers and was in the Tower in preventive detention, William Cecil having advised his mistress that, after studying the words of the statute, he could not see how the Duke's actions were 'within the compass of treason.'

As for Mary, she had been hurriedly taken back to the hated Tutbury where she remained under strict guard, protesting volubly, the problem of her future looking as insoluble as ever. 'The Queen of Scots', wrote Cecil, summarising the situation for Elizabeth, 'is and shall always be a dangerous person to your estate. Yet there are degrees of danger. If you would marry, it should be less; whilst you do not, it will increase. If her person be restrained, here or in Scotland, it will be less, if at liberty greater. If by law she cannot marry while Bothwell lives, the peril is less, if free to marry, the greater. If found guilty of the murder of her husband, she shall be less a person perilous, if passed over in silence, the scar of the murder will wear out and the danger greater.'

A week or so later Cecil was still musing on the question of the disposal of the Queen of Scots who, by 'her great wit and sugared eloquence', seemed able to disarm 'even such as before they shall come to her company shall have a great misliking.' The Queen of England might keep her a perpetual prisoner, 'being her capital

enemy in claiming her throne' or—and here an unmistakable note of
wistfulness creeps in—she might follow the precedents to be found in
many histories of kings and princes in other times, 'that is by justice
to take her life from her.' More realistically, however, he concluded
that 'the Queen's majesty has most reason to send her to Scotland,
where her majesty is to provide that she may live the natural course of
her life in surety, and to that end is to have a sufficient number of
hostages.'

Before any further progress could be made in this direction,
ominous rumblings became audible from north of the Trent and in
November these erupted into the first and, as it turned out, the only
serious civil disturbance of the reign. The underlying causes of the
Rising in the North were as much social and economic as religious
and political while its leaders, the reactionary Earls of Northumberland
and Westmorland, were principally motivated by personal and
financial grievances against the central government. None of these
grievances, of course, were directly connected with Mary Stewart,
but in a part of the country where the old religion was still a powerful
force, the mere presence of the Catholic heiress provided a rallying
point and a figure-head. 'All the north is ready and only awaits the
release of the Queen of Scotland', wrote Guerau de Spes.

The release of the Queen of Scotland was obviously an essential
pre-condition for success. Had they achieved it, the rebel earls might
well have found themselves in a position to dictate terms to London.
They might even have received the foreign aid they had been angling
for all summer. But they never got closer than fifty miles from
Tutbury and, in any case, Mary had once more been hurried away,
this time to Coventry where she had to be temporarily lodged at an
inn—most unsuitable, as everyone agreed. Without her, the Rising,
badly timed, inadequately prepared and irresolutely led, was doomed
to end in smoke, just as that uncompromising realist the Duke of
Alva had predicted it would, and Northumberland and Westmorland
were forced to seek refuge over the Border in the bandit country of
Liddesdale.

From Queen Elizabeth's point of view, probably the most
significant and heartening feature of the whole miserable affair was
the fact that it had failed to attract any widespread popular support.
Although the Earl of Sussex, commanding in York, had not dared to
rely on the loyalty of his local levies and had lived through some
anxious days while waiting for reinforcements to reach him from the

south; although the northern earls had publicly proclaimed their intention of restoring 'the true and Catholic religion' and Sir Ralph Sadler reported gloomily that the gentry of the region were all Catholic in sympathy and the common people 'ignorant, full of superstition and altogether blinded with the old popish doctrine', still they had not responded in any meaningful numbers either to the call of the old faith or to the siren song of the Queen of Scots, despite her much vaunted allure. To the Queen of England it was a satisfying vindication of her intuitive certitude that her Catholic subjects—even those of the 'inly-working north'—would, when it came to the crunch, always put allegiance to the Crown before allegiance to the Bishop of Rome.

Nevertheless, the crisis was not yet over. The Borders were in a turmoil and in mid-January 1570 the assassination of the Earl of Moray by Hamilton of Bothwellhaugh removed a valuable ally, gave new impetus to Mary's party and threatened to plunge Scotland into civil war. Elizabeth's first reaction was to reassure the leaders of James's party. She sent Thomas Randolph to urge the Earls of Morton and Mar to stand fast and united, 'to preserve the state of religion from any alteration, and the Prince from all danger', to maintain the peace between the two realms and take steps to apprehend the English rebels still at large in their territory. In April, the Earl of Sussex was authorised to cross the Border and carry out a punitive raid against 'all such as helped the Queen's rebels' and a few weeks later Sir William Drury took an English force to Edinburgh to strengthen Morton's hand.

If William Cecil, his brother-in-law Nicholas Bacon and the Earl of Sussex had had their way, this policy would have been pursued to its logical conclusion, young James officially recognised as King, his professedly pro-English adherents given English troops and English gold to enable them to destroy his mother's party, and all Scotland—perhaps—brought firmly under English domination. But Elizabeth, well-versed in the untrustworthy ways of professedly pro-English Scots and their habit of taking English gold and using it for their own purposes, was reluctant to venture any further into the Scottish quagmire than was necessary to pursue her rebels and avenge the latest crop of Border outrages. Nor, in view of the current international situation, did she want to offer any unnecessary provocation to the French, and took the attitude that nothing could be decided until the future of the Queen of Scots had been settled.

At the end of April she called a council meeting and laid the familiar problem before her advisers—should Mary be released 'upon such assurances as might be devised' and restored to her kingdom, or should she be left as she was. Elizabeth herself, she declared, was 'free from any determined resolution' and invited each of those present to speak his mind. Needless to say, no decision was reached but a week later the Privy Council had begun work on drafting the terms on which they were prepared to consider the restitution of the Scottish Queen. In essence these remained the same as before—Mary must ratify the clause of the Treaty of Edinburgh 'concerning her pretence to the title and arms of the Crown of England' and agree not to marry 'nor treat of marriage' with any person born out of Scotland without the prior consent of Queen Elizabeth. She must also agree to a perpetual peace with the Queen of England 'according to the straitest bond that ever has been betwixt England and Scotland', undertake to maintain the Protestant religion and allow the leaders of her son's party to continue in their various offices.

The difficulty, as always, was to devise safeguards stringent enough to ensure that these terms would be observed once Mary had regained her liberty, and Elizabeth was now insisting that Prince James should be sent to England for a period of seven years as a pledge for his mother's good behaviour, together with a number of other hostages including the Earl of Argyll and the Lords Herries and Fleming. The strategic fortresses of Hume and Dumbarton were to be surrendered to English garrisons and it was to be enacted by the Parliaments of both countries that if the Queen of Scots broke any of the articles of the proposed treaty, she should be made to give up her throne to her son and forfeit all her rights to the English succession.

Despite the deep misgivings of a number of influential Englishmen, negotiations with Mary along these lines had begun by the middle of May. 'She is very willing to have her Majesty's favour', wrote Shrewsbury to Cecil on the twenty-fourth, 'and harps upon one string still, that if she might come to her Majesty's presence she would utter such things to her, both for the weal of the realm and her own contentment, as she doubted not but such a knot of friendship would be tied thereby as should not be undone again, and she would do by her Majesty's advise and persuasion what she would not otherwise be brought unto. She thinks it a hard matter to yield her son in pledge, and her strongholds, and says that if the Queen has any doubt of her good meaning and plain dealing, she may be pledge herself till all things are performed.'

During this same month an event took place which was to have an incalculable effect on the future of the Queen of Scots. In the early hours of the fifteenth a Catholic gentleman living in Southwark nailed a smuggled copy of the papal bull *Regnans in Excelsis* to the door of the Bishop of London's palace in St Paul's Churchyard, thus informing his fellow citizens that the Pope had finally excommunicated Elizabeth, 'the Servant of Wickedness', deprived her of her pretended title to her throne and absolved her Catholic subjects from their duty of allegiance.

The papacy's impulsive and unheralded declaration of war after more than a decade of uneasy *detente* had apparently been prompted by inaccurate and out-of-date information about the success of the Northern Rising, and on reports that the English Catholics were eager to throw off the yoke of their heretical sovereign but hesitated to act, lest by taking the law into their own hands they might be endangering their immortal souls. Popular reaction in Protestant England was immediate and predictable. Indignantly patriotic ballads, broadsheets and pamphlets flooded the market. Protestant bishops hurried into print, denouncing Pius V as a 'wilful and unlearned friar' and his bull as bold, vain and impudent, 'full fraught with blasphemy and untruth', while clergymen up and down the country loyally thumped their pulpits in outspoken defiance of the papal challenge.

In government circles, where an air of studied indifference prevailed, *Regnans in Excelsis* was dismissed as 'a vain crack of words that made a noise only.' Its implications were, nevertheless, profoundly disturbing and served to heighten the perennial English Protestant dread of a league of hostile Catholic powers dedicated to the extirpation of the gospel, for the Queen and her advisers naturally found it hard to credit that the Vatican would have taken such a decisive step without the prior knowledge and approval of its allies. In fact, it appears that the other Catholic powers had not been consulted and were in consequence both irritated and offended.

The French ambassador, de la Mothe Fénélon, who had been exerting strong pressure on Elizabeth to withdraw her forces from Scotland and come to terms with Mary, feared that this untimely launching of papal thunderbolts might well abort the latest round of talks, but Elizabeth did not break off negotiations with her Catholic heiress. On the contrary, she was pressing ahead and showing every sign of serious intent. When Cecil and Nicholas Bacon ventured to remonstrate, she snapped their heads off, declaring that she wanted to settle the business and meet the French king's wishes.

It was a convincing performance and in the summer of 1570 came near to persuading Fénélon and the Bishop of Ross that she was in earnest. It did not, however, convince Maitland of Lethington, who was now directing the policy of Mary's party in Scotland. 'When the Queen of England gives you good words', he wrote to Ross on 15 August, 'you do well to make semblance to believe her, and to hope for goodness at her hands. But, on my peril, in your heart trust never a word she speaks, for you will find all plain craft without true dealing. . . . The Queen of Scotland is in the Queen of England's hands, and I think she intends never (with her goodwill) to part with her.'

Maitland felt sure that all this talk of a treaty was merely a ploy to hoodwink the French and prevent or delay the sending of promised French aid to the Marians still holding out at Dumbarton; that Elizabeth was deliberately proposing conditions so harsh that Mary would have no choice but to refuse them. But what really mattered was the Queen's release and, if necessary, she must agree to anything to obtain it, for once she was a free agent Maitland had no doubt that means could be found 'to make both England and Scotland loath to enterprise far against her . . . I speak all to this end', he went on, 'that her liberty be procured whatsoever the conditions be. Press it the best. If we fail we must accept the worst.'

The Laird of Lethington may well have been right to be suspicious of Elizabeth's good faith. She had recently engineered the appointment of the Earl of Lennox as regent in succession to Moray, and as King James's grandfather he was not likely to attempt to strike out on an independent line. She had also instructed her representatives in the north to assure the King's party that, whatever reports they might hear to the contrary, she did not mean to alter the state of the King or the government of Scotland.

If the Queen of England was playing a double game, so too was the Queen of Scots. Towards Elizabeth Mary was all sweet compliance, but she had taken the first opportunity to re-open her secret correspondence with the Duke of Norfolk asking for his advice on any enterprise she might attempt and signing herself 'your own, faithful to death.' Nor was the Duke's own conduct exactly above board. In June 1570 he had made a formal, and voluntary, submission to the Queen, binding himself on his allegiance to abandon all thought of a marriage with Mary and never again to deal 'in any other cause belonging to the Queen of Scots' but only as his sovereign should command him. This undertaking, as was presently to emerge, was worth no more than the paper it was written on, but it achieved its immediate objective and in August his grace was released from the Tower and permitted to take up residence in his London house, although still under a degree of supervision.

Elizabeth, meanwhile, continued to pursue her policy of reconciliation in Scotland. In September a six months' truce was arranged between the rival factions, both of whom were invited to send deputations to London to discuss a settlement of their differences, and the Queen announced her intention of sending William Cecil and Sir Walter Mildmay to confer with the Queen of Scots, who had now been moved to pleasanter quarters at Chatsworth. To Mary she wrote in reproachful terms, reminding her that she owed the preservation of her life, when 'in circumstances of the greatest danger', to her English cousin and had repaid the obligation by attempting to stir up treason among the servants of her benefactress. Elizabeth was, however, ready to blot out the past and send two faithful councillors to treat with her in the hope of coming to 'some terms of agreement.'

Neither of the two faithful councillors relished their task, Cecil in particular complaining mournfully that he was being thrown into a maze (or the lioness's den) and 'knew not how to walk from dangers.' He seems, though, to have survived his first encounter with the Queen of Scots without falling victim to her 'sugared entertainment'. Everyone was very polite and non-committal and, after some demur, Mary conceded virtually all Elizabeth's demands. She evidently felt with Maitland that it was worth accepting any conditions to regain her freedom of action. Cecil and Mildmay were safely back in London before the end of October, leaving Mary to await developments pending the arrival of the commissioners from Scotland.

Queen Elizabeth used the interval to make friendly overtures to France and set the first of her French courtships in motion. Not that the Virgin Queen was for one moment seriously contemplating matrimony with either of the King of France's younger brothers who, other considerations apart, were respectively eighteen and twenty years her junior, but in an age when it was taken for granted at all levels of society that 'the knot of blood and marriage was a stronger seal than that which was printed in wax' the fact that Elizabeth Tudor still remained 'the best match in her parish' gave her a priceless asset when it came to negotiating with foreign powers. Unlike the improvident Mary, it was an asset which Elizabeth had no intention of squandering and she was to exploit it to keep the French in play throughout the greater part of the fifteen-seventies, just as successfully as she had exploited it to confuse the Hapsburgs during the sixties.

The burgeoning Anglo-French rapprochement was bad news for the Queen of Scots and when, at last, her son's commissioners, headed by the Earl of Morton, came south in February 1571 they brought no comfort either. The lords of the King's party made it painfully clear that they were as firm as ever in their refusal to consider their former Queen's return, unless she was prepared to acknowledge her reduced status as Queen Mother. They had no authority, they said, to negotiate on any other basis and asked leave to return home for further consultations with the Scottish estates. Elizabeth let them go, on the understanding that they would obtain fresh powers enabling them 'to treat for a perfect agreement for the full restitution of her majesty', and come back to England within two months ready to proceed. No one, though, was deceived. Mary wrote despairingly to Elizabeth that unless the abdication, extorted from her by force at Lochleven, was declared null, 'in vain shall I make offer for my restitution' and the Bishop of Ross made a spirited protest against the admission of 'such frivolous allegations and excuses whereby a good and godly agreement intended should be frustrated and delayed', but la Mothe Fénélon reported that he believed all hope of a settlement was now at an end.

Although the uncompromising attitude of Morton and his colleagues provided an excellent excuse for further delay, the overwhelming likelihood is that Elizabeth had already come to the conclusion that she could not risk letting Mary loose. Enough intercepted correspondence had come into the English government's hands over the past two and a half years to give them every reason to distrust the Queen of Scots and her promises, but most probably it had been the Norfolk affair—the discovery that 'a marriage was practised underhand without her privity between Norfolk and the Scotch queen'—which had decided the English queen and put paid to Mary's chances of freedom. Nothing could have been more calculated to arouse Elizabeth's worst fears than the knowledge that her closest kinswoman and heiress and her most prestigious subject were 'practising' together.

So Mary stayed where she was, but her cousin would do no more than keep her under restraint. When Parliament, still seething with angry patriotism, met in April, the Queen frustrated an attempt to exclude from the succession any person who 'hath (made) or hereafter shall make claim to the crown of England during her Majesty's life, or shall say she hath not lawful right.' This proposed 'addition' to a new treasons act, prompted by the papal excommunication, was clearly aimed at the Queen of Scots and had a good deal of support in both Houses, but Elizabeth would have none of it. 'This being brought unto us', she told the assembled Lords and Commons at the end of the session, 'we misliked it very much; being not of the mind to offer extremity or injury to any person. . . . And therefore, reserving to every his right, we thought it not good to deal so hardly with anybody as by that bill was meant.' She got her way, but if the members had known what she and her Secretary of State already knew, or guessed, about the activities of a certain Roberto Ridolfi, the pressure would have been more difficult to withstand.

Although labyrinthine in its ramifications, the ultimate objectives of the so-called Ridolfi Plot were straightforward enough—to depose Elizabeth, release the Queen of Scots and set her on the English throne with the Duke of Norfolk as her consort and, of course, restore the Catholic religion. These interesting feats—at any rate according to a blueprint offered for the King of Spain's approval—were to be accomplished by the native Catholics led by Norfolk and assisted by an army of six thousand or, better, ten thousand soldiers provided by the Duke of Alva from the Netherlands.

Coming as it did so soon after the fiasco of the Northern Rising, and based as it was on such a total disregard of political and geographical realities, it is hardly surprising that the Ridolfi Plot should today be regarded with a certain amount of scepticism. Indeed, there is a school of thought which maintains it was all a trap, painstakingly devised by William Cecil to ensnare, discredit and finally destroy both the Queen of Scots and the Duke of Norfolk. But while the traditional story of a dastardly Catholic plot should perhaps no longer be swallowed whole, a scheme to secure foreign Catholic help for Mary's release and restitution did undoubtedly exist. Exactly when and to what extent it was penetrated by Cecil and his agents remains a matter of conjecture.

Roberto Ridolfi himself was a member of a well-known Florentine banking family with longstanding English connections, and had been living and working in London for the past ten years. Lately, though, he had begun to find plotting a more stimulating occupation than banking and had taken it upon himself to act as general contact-man between Mary and the Bishop of Ross, Norfolk and some other disaffected members of the aristocracy, and the Spanish ambassador. He may or may not have also been acting as an *agent provocateur*. Certainly it was not until after his departure for Brussels, Rome and Madrid, taking with him letters of credence and 'Instructions' from his clients, in March 1571, that details of the conspiracy which bears his name started to come to light.

By May the English government had evidence of ciphered correspondence between Ridolfi and Ross, and of two mysterious letters addressed to '30' and '40' who were believed to be English noblemen. But, according to Guerau de Spes, writing to King Philip in July, they could get no further than a general suspicion, 'which will put them on the alert for the future as to who communicates with the Queen of Scots.' Then, towards the end of August, the fortunate curiosity of a Welsh draper conveying a parcel to Shrewsbury provided the vital clue. The Duke of Norfolk had been caught in the act of sending money and messages to Mary's partisans in Scotland and Cecil—or Lord Burghley as he had now become—was able to move in for the kill.

The Duke was re-arrested on 7 September, his secretaries taken in for questioning and all the finagling and double-dealing surrounding the Queen of Scots dragged out into the open. A search of Howard House revealed letters hidden under mats and the 'alphabets' or keys of ciphers under the rooftiles. The council's investigators also heard about 'writings' smuggled in and out of the Tower in bottles with specially marked corks and of 'a little dark privy house' which was used as a letter box for similarly private correspondence. In the light of these new developments the Bishop of Ross was examined again and, after it had been forcibly pointed out to him that neither his cloth nor his quasi-diplomatic status would protect him in a crisis of this nature, his lordship in a cold sweat told all he knew. It turned out to be a good deal.

Norfolk had retained just enough sense not to sign letters for

Ridolfi, but there can be no reasonable doubt that he was implicated up to the neck in that devious individual's fantasies. There is no doubt whatever that, despite his solemn undertaking to Elizabeth, he had continued to write letters to Mary, to lend her money and to advise her not only about her escape plans but on her recent negotiations with the Queen. Behind the grand facade Thomas Howard had the soul of a small-time crook, weak, greedy and venal, and he was lucky to have lasted as long as he did. By the end of November the case against him was complete and on 16 January 1572 he was brought to trial before his peers, convicted of high treason and condemned to death.

Although the Queen of Scots' own ambassador had not hesitated to incriminate her—'Lord, what people these are! What a Queen! What an ambassador!' exclaimed one Englishman in pious horror—Mary flatly denied that she had ever gone about to stir up a rebellion in England or intended any harm to the Queen her good sister, despite the fact, as she said, that 'the Queen hath maintained my rebels against me, to the taking away of my crown from my head.' She had not had any dealings with Norfolk 'since the time of his restraint' and denied having any connection with Ridolfi—'she never saw him, nor had to do with him'—though she did later admit having given him a financial commission. And so, wrote Ralph Sadler, who was standing in for Shrewsbury during the latter's absence at the Norfolk trial, 'and so she flyeth from all things which may touch her, and will needs be innocent of all manner of practices tending . . . to the peril of the Queen's majesty, or any other disturbance of this State.'

Sadler did not believe her, and neither did anyone else who had seen the evidence in the case. Nor is there any reason why she should have been so innocent. Mary was a fighter, 'a free and sovereign princess' who considered herself to be unjustly imprisoned. As a Catholic she now had moral grounds for regarding Elizabeth as a usurper and Ridolfi's hare-brained schemes were, of course, exactly calculated to appeal to her optimistic gambler's instincts. 'Her letters and discourses . . . being in cypher, to the Duke of Norfolk are found' wrote Burghley to the Earl of Shrewsbury after his ferrets had been through Howard House, and documents captured at Dumbarton, when the castle was finally taken in April 1571, showed that she had also been corresponding with the Duke of Alva. 'Ah, the poor fool will never cease until she lose her head', remarked the King of France prophetically after reading the reports of his ambassador in London.

Nevertheless, in the winter of 1571-2 there seemed no immediate prospect of this happening. Elizabeth was angry. She abandoned her policy of negotiation with Mary and, more significantly, abandoned her policy of protecting her cousin's reputation, allowing George Buchanan's *Detectio*—a violently anti-Marian account of the Darnley murder—to be published in England for the first time, with the Casket Letters appended. Mary's household underwent one of its periodic purges and there was a general tightening up of security, causing Guerau de Spes to complain to King Philip about the difficulties the Queen of Scots was experiencing in communicating with her friends, but this, it seemed, was as far as the Queen of England intended to go. Even the Duke of Norfolk was still alive. Three times the warrant for his execution had been signed and three times Elizabeth had revoked it at the last moment. 'The Queen's majesty hath been always a merciful lady and by mercy she hath taken more harm than by justice' lamented Lord Burghley to his friend and protégé Francis Walsingham after the first of these changes of heart. 'God's will be fulfilled and aid her majesty to do herself good' he sighed after the second one.

Matters were still in this uncertain state in March 1572 when Elizabeth succumbed to an acute attack of gastroenteritis caused, so she said afterwards, by eating some bad fish. It was the kind of accident which could happen to anyone at any time—every Elizabethan had good reason to know that in the midst of life they were in death—but Thomas Smith undoubtedly put the general feeling into words when he wrote from the embassy at Paris of 'the disorder, the peril and danger which had been like to follow if at that time God had taken from us that stay of the commonwealth and hope of our repose, that lantern of our light next God.'

The stay of the commonwealth made her usual rapid recovery, but this latest scare stiffened the Council in its resolve to summon another Parliament without delay. Strong pressure must have been brought to bear on the Queen to get her to agree, for she must have known very well that Parliament would demand the Queen of Scots' and the Duke of Norfolk's heads on the same charger. And so indeed they did. A committee of both Houses was immediately appointed to discuss the 'great cause' of the Scottish queen's future and after hearing its preliminary report the Commons proceeded to make it crystal clear what they wanted done about Mary Stewart. In the words of Richard Gallys, member for New Windsor, they wanted to 'cut off her head and make no more ado about her.' With scarcely a dissenting voice the clamour grew for a final solution to the problem of that sower of sedition and disturber of the peace, that notorious whore, adulteress and murderess, that monstrous and huge dragon. 'A general impunity to commit treason was never permitted to any' declared the Londoner and literary man Thomas Norton. Another member could see no reason why the Queen of Scots should not be dealt with as she deserved. She had come into England not as an enemy, but worse, as a dissembling friend, and under the guise of friendship had sought the destruction of the Queen's majesty. 'Shall we say our law is not able to provide for this mischief? We might then say it hath defect in the highest degree.'

As the debate continued, member after member added his voice to the general outcry for an axe, not an act. It was no use threatening Mary or warning her. As long as she lived nothing would prevent her and her friends from seeking to subvert the Protestant state, and the axe must be the next warning. Let the Queen, while she had her enemy in her hands, execute her quickly, lest hereafter she should come to be executed herself. If Elizabeth would not take action for her own safety, then she should think of her subjects. 'I have heard she delighteth to be called our mother', cried Robert Newdigate, member for Buckingham. 'Let us desire her to be pitiful over us her children, who have not deserved death.'

The parliament of 1572 was not just baying for blood. The sober knights and burgesses gathered at Westminster that spring could see their whole way of life, their peace and prosperity, the future peace and prosperity of their children and grandchildren being put at risk for the sake of a scruple of royal conscience, and they were frankly afraid. They knew what was happening in the religious civil wars ravaging France and the Netherlands. Enough people living in the south and east of the country had heard enough first-hand atrocity stories from Dutch, Flemish and Huguenot refugees to give them cause to be afraid. The English dread of popish plots, of invading armies of anti-Christ breathing fire and slaughter, may have been exaggerated, but they were very understandable. Many of the speakers in the Commons debate had made the point that their lives, their lands and their goods would be forfeit if the Catholic Queen of Scots succeeded to the throne.

But Queen Elizabeth was unmoved by all the urgent and piteous pleas being addressed to her. She was deeply grateful for so much loyal concern for her safety, but she was unmoved. Nor was she impressed by the numerous precedents for the putting to death of wicked kings industriously culled by the bishops from the Old Testament. 'Partly for honour, partly for conscience, for causes to herself known' she would not consent to a Bill of Attainder against Mary. To the consternation and near despair of her faithful Lords and Commons, she would not even agree to a bill excluding Mary from the succession. Norfolk had to be sacrificed, Parliament would not be cheated entirely of its prey, but the Scottish Queen survived.

Thus, for the second time, Elizabeth, by her deliberate personal intervention, had saved the life of the woman she now knew beyond a shadow of doubt to be her mortal enemy. It was a decision taken in defiance of the will of the nation as expressed by its elected representatives; against the combined weight of the House of Lords, the Privy Council, the church and the legal profession; against every argument of expediency, prudence and plain common sense urging her to strike at her enemy now, while there was still time.

Although she suffered from a quite un-Tudorlike squeamishness when it came to killing her own kinsfolk (was it perhaps because she herself had once known the fear of the axe?), Elizabeth is not likely on this occasion to have been motivated by sentiment. That April her representatives had signed the draft protocol of the Treaty of Blois, giving her a defensive alliance with France by which both countries contracted to come to the aid of the other if either were attacked by a third party, even on religious grounds, and in which both agreed to work jointly for a pacification in Scotland. Most significantly it contained no mention of Mary Stewart and no provision for her welfare. The Treaty of Blois, in fact, marked the final abandonment of Mary's cause by the King of France and gave Elizabeth what amounted to a free hand in settling the Scottish problem. This was a solid diplomatic gain which the Queen of England had no intention of jeopardising by proceeding to extremities against her cousin, whatever the provocation.

As it happened, both the Anglo-French treaty and the Queen of Scots nearly came to an untimely end that same summer, when the violent forces of sectarian hatred simmering just below the surface of French society erupted in a particularly horrific manner. The spark which ignited the explosion of the Bartholomew's Day Massacre is generally held to have been Queen Catherine de Medici's jealousy of the veteran Huguenot leader Admiral Coligny and his growing influence over her impressionable son. But what began as an attempt to curb the undesirable ascendancy of the Huguenot party by murdering its leader, ended in one of history's best remembered bloodbaths. In Paris alone the Catholic mob is estimated to have slaughtered between three and four thousand Huguenots until the very gutters, according to some accounts, ran with blood. The killing quickly spread to the provinces, and altogether something like ten thousand men, women and children were butchered during the last week of August 1572.

Reaction from abroad varied. Te Deums were sung in Rome which was illuminated as for a great victory, and the King of Spain sent his personal congratulations to the King of France. The Dutch insurgent leader, William of Orange, on the other hand, declared that Charles would never be able to cleanse himself of the bloody deed and even Ivan the Terrible was moved to enter a protest from distant Muscovy.

In England, where streams of terrified refugees were pouring into the south coast ports, public opinion was profoundly shocked. La Mothe Fénélon was astonished at the depth of feeling aroused among the islanders who, he reported were expressing 'extreme indignation and a marvellous hatred against the French.' Even after the matter had been explained to them—how a dangerous Huguenot conspiracy had been discovered threatening the lives of the royal family, a conspiracy so far advanced that the King had been obliged to sanction emergency counter-measures which had, no doubt, led to some regrettable excesses—even then the English showed little sign of moderating their opinions 'holding that it was the Pope and the King of Spain who kindled the fire in France . . . and that there is something evil afoot from all three of them against England.'

'These evil times trouble all good men's heads', wrote the Bishop of London early in September, 'and make their hearts ache, fearing that this barbarous treachery will not cease in France but will reach over unto us.' The fear that the events of Bartholomew's Day signalled the beginning of a concerted attack on Protestants everywhere and that the Queen of England would be the next target for assassination, resulted in a renewal of popular agitation against the Queen of Scots. 'All men now cry out against your prisoner' Lord Burghley told the Earl of Shrewsbury.

No one, of course, suggested that Mary had been in any way

directly responsible for the holocaust across the Channel, but it was well known that her Guise relations had headed the killer pack. The Duke of Guise had personally supervised the despatch of Coligny and could now be seen parading about the streets of Paris, wreathed in smiles and fawned on by the mob. Mary could not be held responsible, but the mere fact of her presence within the Protestant state was becoming increasingly unacceptable 'as nothing presently is more necessary than that the realm might be delivered of her.' 'If the sore be not salved' warned Francis Walsingham 'I fear we shall have a Bartholomew breakfast or a Florence banquet.' The Bishop of London had recommended that the Scottish Queen's head should be cut off forthwith and even the humane Matthew Parker, Archbishop of Canterbury, offered much the same advice.

In the excitable aftermath of the massacre top-secret contingency plans were, in fact, being made to send Mary back to Scotland where, it was hoped, the Regent and his party might be 'by some good means wrought . . . so they would without fail proceed with her by way of justice so as neither that realm nor this should be dangered by her hereafter.' The Scots, however, demanded too high a price for doing the Queen of England's dirty work and, no doubt fortunately for Elizabeth's reputation, nothing came of this somewhat sinister plan. That it was seriously considered is, however, an indication of the near-panic created in government circles by events in France, and of the poisoning effect of the passions and prejudices roused by ideological warfare.

X

The Bosom Serpent

By the end of 1573 Elizabeth Tudor had successfully ridden out the crises of the late sixties and early seventies. The French alliance had survived the general outburst of francophobia following the Bartholomew's Day Massacre, and the English Queen was being wooed, both figuratively and literally, by France. The monster which Catherine de Medici had so unwisely let loose in August 1572 had threatened seriously to disturb the precarious balance of power between the House of Valois and the reactionary, pro-Spanish House of Guise—thus making English friendship look still more desirable to the devious Italian matriarch in Paris and leading her to revive the languishing courtship of her youngest son, François Duke of Alençon.

Elizabeth had also suceeded, at least temporarily, in mending her fences with Spain. The intolerable Guerau de Spes had been packed off home in disgrace after the revelations of the Ridolfi affair, but by April 1573 the English government had reached an agreement with the Duke of Alva by which trade with the Netherlands, suspended since the breach of 1568, was restored for an initial period of two years and negotiations had begun to resolve the outstanding claims by both sides for compensation over seizures of property. By the end of the year, therefore, England was technically on friendly terms with all her continental neighbours, despite overt papal hostility and the gloomy conviction, expressed by root-and-branch men such as Francis Walsingham (shortly to be appointed Principal Secretary of State in succession to Lord Burghley) that 'Christ and Belial can hardly agree.'

In 1573 Elizabeth celebrated her fortieth birthday and the fifteenth anniversary of her succession—fifteen years which had seen the transformation of her realm from a factious, impoverished and little-regarded off-shore island into a united and flourishing nation state, while she herself, vigorous, assured and very much in control, had grown immeasurably in international status, her obvious competence as a politician and ruler having earned her the respect, if not always the admiration, of her fellow sovereigns. At home there was no question about her subjects' whole-hearted admiration and affection. The Queen had given them peace, 'and so long a peace as England hath seldom seen'. She had recently succeeded in paying off the debts of her father and brother—a solid achievement which did more to endear her to the business community than any amount of royal affability. She had refused to be intimidated by would-be foreign oppressors and boasted cheerfully of being 'mere English', giving to the ordinary people, the little people going about their toilsome daily lives, a most satisfying focus for their natural patriotism and rising sense of national identity. She was 'their' Elizabeth who had brought them 'a calm and quiet season, a clear and lovely sunshine, a quietus from former broils' and it was about this time that the custom began, quite spontaneously, of keeping her accession day, 'the sacred seventeenth day of November', as a holiday, marked by bell-ringing, sermons, bonfires, feasting and firework displays.

By contrast, the fortunes of Mary Stewart had fallen to their lowest ebb since Carberry Hill. The Duke of Norfolk's execution had deprived her of any respectable, independent power base in England and her public image had suffered disastrously as a result both of the Ridolfi Plot and the massacres in France. She had ceased to be regarded as a rather forlorn figure, a queen torn from her throne, a mother separated from her child, a prisoner to be secretly pitied, and become instead the ungrateful 'bosom serpent' of Francis Walsingham's telling phrase, a papist snake in the grass of the English Eden, irrevocably associated in the popular imagination with subversion, treachery and bloody murder. In Scotland, Elizabeth's latest envoy Henry Killigrew had succeeded in persuading or bribing the Earl of Huntly and the Hamiltons to submit to her old enemy the Earl of Morton, who now held the office of regent, and in May 1573 the English from Berwick had helped Morton to batter down the defences of Edinburgh Castle, where the last outpost of Marian resistance, led by Maitland of Lethington, was entrenched. The Castle fell at the end of the month and Maitland was found dead, some said by his own hand. The French, still embroiled in the aftermath of St Bartholomew's Day and unwilling to offer the Queen of England any further provocation, had not lifted a finger to interfere, although the unilateral English action was certainly contrary to the spirit of the Treaty of Blois. Elizabeth had thus been able once more to secure her vulnerable postern gate and for several years Scotland, under Morton's iron rule, enjoyed an unusual interval of quiet.

Mary had wept bitter tears of disappointment over the Duke of Norfolk's trial and execution but, although Shrewsbury reported that he thought it nipped her very near, she took the news of the ruin of her cause north of the Border with surprising calm. Defeated in Scotland, deserted by England and France—even her Guise relations, who were quietly helping themselves from the income of her French dower lands, did no more than advise patience and dissimulation— and put off with vague promises and expressions of sympathy from Spain, the Queen of Scots had little reason for optimism in the early fifteen-seventies. But while her political future had seldom looked bleaker, the conditions of her captivity were definitely eased during this period of comparative tranquillity. She and her custodians and her miniature court were now installed at Sheffield Castle where, with occasional moves to the nearby Sheffield Lodge or to Chatsworth, she was to be based for nearly fourteen years. Her life remained circumscribed and often no doubt very boring, but it had its small pleasures and compensations.

She was able to see some visitors—the Shrewsburys could not always resist the temptation to show off their glamorous prisoner— and take part in a limited form of social intercourse. She had her famous needlework, her music, her little dogs and the pet birds— turtle doves and Barbary fowls—which she reared in cages. She also continued to take an interest in clothes, ordering patterns of dresses and of silks, 'the handsomest and rarest that are worn at court', from France, and 'new fashions of head-dresses, veils and ribbons' from Italy. For outdoor recreation there were walks in the garden, archery, riding and sometimes even hawking in the park under Shrewsbury's anxious eye. But the highspots of her existence were her visits to the tepid mineral water springs at Buxton, which enjoyed quite a vogue as a spa during the Elizabethan period. These outings, reluctantly permitted for the sake of her health, always did her good she declared, though probably the change of scene and wider opportunities for socialising they afforded were as therapeutic as the baths.

Mary's health, or lack of it, forms a constant topic in her letters and those of her gaolers but exactly what ailed her is still, like so much else concerning the Queen of Scots, a matter of controversy. She had had a serious illness in May 1569, with vomiting, rigors and convulsions which she herself described as being similar to her near fatal attack at Jedburgh two and a half years previously. In November, just before the outbreak of the Northern Rising, Shrewsbury reported that she complained much of grief and pain of her side, her heart and head, adding 'truly her colour and complexion of her face is presently much decayed.'

Early in 1570 she had a fever, 'with pain of her head and swelling of her hand', and was ill again in December of that year, 'troubled with an incessant provocation to vomit', and suffering from insomnia and 'a great inflammation and tension in her left side under her short ribs.' In June 1571 she was sick again for several days and having fainting fits. In the spring of 1572 she was 'unquiet and sickly', 'grieved with her old disease' and saying 'she wanteth strength and use of her left arm.' She told the French ambassador that her head was so full of rheum and her eyes so swollen with continual sickness and fever that she was obliged to keep entirely to her bed, where she had 'but little rest.' The news of Norfolk's execution in June brought on another 'passion of sickness', and Shrewsbury wrote that if she was really as ill as she and her people made out, 'she is like hardly to escape.' Two days later, however, she was apparently on the mend, though weakened by 'over much physic', and her custodian evidently believed that the danger had been exaggerated.

Not the least of the difficulties in the way of trying to reach a fair assessment of the Queen of Scots' physical condition is the need to allow for the natural tendency of any prisoner in her circumstances to maximise her symptoms to gain political advantage. As the Countess of Shrewsbury commented drily in 1581, when Mary once more appeared to be at death's door: 'I have known her worse and recover again.'

It has been suggested that she may have suffered from a gastric ulcer—the occurrence of a haematemesis during her illness at Jedburgh is consistent with this theory—and from rheumatism, a common enough 16th century complaint. But a closely argued case has also been made out to support the presumption that Mary Stewart was a victim of the so-called Royal Malady of porphyria—a hereditary genetic disorder in which the subject is born with an enzyme deficiency causing an abnormality in the biochemical process by which the body makes haem and leading to over-production of the porphyrins—purple-red pigments responsible for the red colour of blood.

Strictly speaking a group of diseases, porphyria can take several forms but the acute type, where the porphyrins, and their precursor substance porphobilinogen, are present to excess in the liver, manifests itself in intermittent attacks of devastating abdominal colicky pain, vomiting, weakness or even paralysis of the limbs, and mental disturbance, including severe depression, hallucinations and delusions. If Mary was a porphyria sufferer, she probably got it from her father and it could explain some at least of her more irrational behaviour as well as her physical afflictions. But there are also contra-indicants and the evidence is by no means conclusive, so that, in the opinion of a leading authority on the porphyrias, the matter must be regarded as 'not proven.'

Whatever the underlying causes of Mary's invalidism, there is no reason to doubt that there were times when she was genuinely ill and in pain. Equally, there are strong reasons for supposing that there were times when it suited her to make the most of her illness, and times too, perhaps, when frustration, disappointment and the 'painful importunate and almost constant workings of her mind' would have been sufficient in themselves to produce actual symptoms. Certainly, there is a recurrent pattern of physical collapse at moments of particular stress—especially during the early years of her captivity—while during the calmer mid-seventies her health showed a marked improvement.

The end of the decade, though, brought the beginning of the end of Queen Elizabeth's peace and the beginning of the end for Mary Stewart. England and Spain were still just about on speaking terms, but few informed observers of the international scene believed that a confrontation could be delayed indefinitely. Harassed by the depredations of English privateers on the commerce of his American colonies and increasingly convinced that he would never crush his Dutch rebels while they continued to receive surreptitious handouts from Elizabeth, even the slow-moving Philip must surely sooner or later be roused to turn on the heretical Queen. In France, where Charles IX had been succeeded by his erratic brother Henri III, the situation remained highly volatile and the ultra-Catholic Guise party was becoming disagreeably strong in Paris and the north. More alarming from England's point of view was the fact that the Guises were once more showing signs of taking an interest in Scotland, where Mary's son James was now beginning to emerge as a factor to be reckoned with.

In September 1579 a dispute over the title and estates of the Lennox earldom brought Esmé Stewart, the seigneur d'Aubigny, an ardent Catholic and client of the Duke of Guise, across from France—ostensibly to stake a claim to the Lennox patrimony, but actually bearing an unadvertised commission from his patron to win the adolescent James's confidence and revitalise the Guise influence in Scotland. Not surprisingly, the thirteen-year-old king, who had been reared according to strict Presbyterian principles, found the companionship of his good-looking, courtly and accomplished kinsman an altogether delightful novelty. Within a matter of months d'Aubigny, or Earl of Lennox as he soon became, and his henchman Captain James Stewart, had established their ascendancy. By 1581 they had engineered the downfall and execution of the unlikeable but reliably pro-English Earl of Morton, and the eclipse of the pro-English faction which had held power in Edinburgh for nearly ten years.

On the domestic front, the Queen's government was becoming increasingly worried by the apparent resurgence of English Catholicism. Elizabeth, to the frequently expressed regret of her more hard-line advisers, had always refused to countenance anything in the nature of a systematic purge of her Catholic subjects, taking the attitude that as long as they 'shall openly continue in the observation of her laws', they could believe what they liked in private. Her Majesty, with her well-known distaste for the practice of making windows into men's souls, would not have loyal Englishmen 'molested by an inquisition or examination of their consciences in causes of religion.' Elizabeth undoubtedly hoped that, given time and patience, the problem of the Catholic minority would wither away of its own accord. The fact that it did not was due in large measure to two people. One was Mary Queen of Scots, who continued to give the Catholic minority a focal point and gleam of hope for the future. The other was William Allen, scholar, teacher and born organiser, whose faith was not of the kind which admitted compromise and who had abandoned a brilliant academic career at Oxford in order to carry on the fight from Catholic Belgium.

As clearly as his sovereign lady, Allen could see that once the old generation of English priests had died out, 'no seed would be left hereafter for the restoration of religion' and in 1568 he rented a house near the theological schools at Douai, in the province of Artois, for the accommodation of a handful of like-minded exiles—a centre where he hoped, the flame of resistance could be kept alight, and from which it might one day be possible to send emissaries to rally the embattled ranks of the faithful at home.

The English College at Douai grew and flourished. A steady stream of students and visitors flowed through its ever open doors, and six years after its foundation the first hopeful contingent of graduates was ready to start on the hazardous task of gathering 'the English harvest.' By the end of the seventies about a hundred Douai-trained priests had slipped unobtrusively across the Channel, and in 1580 they began to be supplemented by Jesuit fathers from the English College in Rome.

The initial impact made by these dedicated crusaders was startling. Many Catholics, who had previously been prepared to attend the Anglican service often enough to satisfy the authorities, while salving their consciences by hearing mass in secret as and when an opportunity occurred, were encouraged to stand up and be counted. Others, who had lapsed altogether, became reconciled to the Church, and there was an especially gratifying response from the younger element, for whom Catholicism had now acquired something of the romantic appeal of forbidden fruit, as well as the attraction of being 'anti-establishment.'

To the English establishment the de-stabilising effects of the missionaries' activities were a source of intense vexation. The priests themselves, no doubt in most cases quite sincerely, insisted that they came only to bring spiritual consolation to those who wished for it and were not concerned with politics; but at a time when the menace of international Catholicism was looming ever larger in Protestant eyes, it is hardly surprising that their unwilling hosts should have responded by regarding them all as traitors and potential spies. Englishmen born, they had chosen to transfer their allegiance to the Queen's avowed enemy the Pope, and were now deliberately exhorting the Queen's subjects to break her laws, with the overthrow of the Protestant state as their ultimate objective. Sneaking into the realm in disguise, they 'privily felt the minds of men, spread abroad that princes excommunicate were to be deposed and whispered in corners that such princes as professed not the Romish religion had forfeited their regal title and authority'.

Annoying though it was, this might have represented no more than nuisance value had it not been for the fact that a prince who *did* profess the Romish religion and who, if such reasoning were taken to its logical conclusion, possessed an undeniable right to the English regal title and authority was actually present in the midst of the Protestant state, waiting only for her prison gates to be thrown open by her friends to claim that title as the heir next in blood.

No one man was more alert to the threat posed by the heir next in blood and her friends than Queen Elizabeth's Principal Secretary of State, Sir Francis Walsingham. As long ago as January 1572 he had made his position clear when he wrote to the Earl of Leicester: 'So long as that devilish woman lives, neither her Majesty must make account to continue in quiet possession of her crown, nor her faithful servants assure themselves of safety of their lives.' Nothing that had happened since had caused Walsingham to change his mind. On the contrary, as he devoted more and more of the resources of his far-reaching intelligence network to building up a dossier on the Queen of Scots and her various intrigues, he became more and more convinced that no honest, God-fearing Englishman would be safe until Queen Elizabeth had been induced to deal with her cousin as 'both reason and justice requireth.'

At the beginning of the eighties the most immediate danger seemed to come from Scotland, where the dominating influence of Esmé Stewart, now Duke of Lennox, had greatly encouraged the Catholic exiles and opened up a whole new range of possibilities. In October 1581, the English Jesuit Robert Parsons wrote to the General of his Order that if contact were made with James 'before he is confirmed in heresy', it could only be beneficial to the cause, and Bernardino de Mendoza, King Philip's ambassador in London, was already considering ways and means of persuading the King of Scots that, if he submitted to the Catholic Church, many of the English nobility and a great part of the population would side with him, have him declared heir to the English throne and release his mother. Another Jesuit, Father Watts, told Mendoza that the best argument to bring about James's conversion—apart, of course, from its being the true road to salvation—was to show him 'that it was the only means by which he could become a powerful King, uniting the crowns of Scotland, England and Ireland', but this, as the ambassador remarked in a dispatch to Philip, could only be achieved 'by his gaining the sympathy of so mighty a monarch as your Majesty.'

Whether or not James would rise to the bait being dangled before him remained in doubt, but throughout the winter of 1581-2 optimistic plans were being laid for a Catholic *coup* in Scotland to be followed by an invasion of England. The threads of this elaborate conspiracy stretched from Mendoza at the Court of St James's to Mary in her prison at Sheffield Castle, from Lennox at Holyrood across the North Sea to the Duke of Guise, Robert Parsons, William Allen and the Spanish and papal representatives in France, while the Jesuit Fathers Holt and Creighton commuted busily between London, Edinburgh and Paris carrying letters and messages, promises and suggestions.

In April 1582 the Duke of Lennox finally agreed to commit himself to the 'design' which the Pope and the King of Spain had in hand 'for the restoration of the Catholic religion and the liberation of the Queen of Scotland'— provided he was guaranteed an army of 20,000 mercenaries paid for eighteen months, plus 20,000 crowns in cash. The Duke of Guise, though he thought six or eight thousand troops would be plenty for Scotland, was full of enthusiasm for the project and proposed making a diversionary landing himself on the coast of Sussex. Father Parsons, who had recently spent a year underground in England, offered confident assurances that the English Catholics were eager to see the design carried out, and that if arms were taken up in Scotland 'with a well grounded prospect of success', they would come flocking to join the invaders. Unfortunately the mercenary army, whether six or twenty thousand strong, as yet existed only on paper and the Duke of Guise, despite his soubriquet of King of Paris, was not King of France. Before any further steps could be taken, the Pope and the King of Spain would have to be prevailed upon to disgorge something more substantial than fair words, and long before this feat could be accomplished there had been regrettable developments in Scotland.

Discreetly prodded by the English government, the elders of the Kirk and the Protestant earls decided that Lennox had had a long enough run for his money, and in August James was kidnapped by a posse of earls in the so-called Raid of Ruthven. Lennox holed up for a time at Dumbarton but was finally obliged to apply to Queen Elizabeth for a safe conduct to return to France by way of England. The Duke was out of the game and by the following spring he was dead.

The Raid of Ruthven came as a bad blow to the hopes of the Guisard-Jesuit alliance, but the plotters were not discouraged for long. In May 1583 the Spanish ambassador in Paris told Philip that

Hercules (code name for the Duke of Guise), seeing matters in Scotland altered, 'has now turned his eyes towards the English Catholics to see whether the affair might not be commenced there.'

For nearly three years Francis Walsingham had been uneasily aware that 'some great and hidden treason not yet discovered' was being hatched, but although there were plenty of rumours and enough clues to confirm the suspicion that an international conspiracy involving the Queen of Scots did indeed exist, hard evidence was disappointingly hard to come by. Meanwhile, Queen Elizabeth, so far from doing justice upon her cousin, had embarked on yet another round of negotiations with her. In this case the initiative appears to have come from Mary. In October 1581 she had written to Elizabeth asking for permission to send an envoy to Scotland and suggesting the possibility of arranging an 'association' between herself and her son.

The idea that Mary and James might rule jointly had been considered in the past and rejected as impracticable, but now that James was reaching years of discretion it seemed worth another look, and Robert Beale (Walsingham's brother-in-law) was sent to try and find out just what Mary had in mind and also, if possible, discover the real state of her relations with her son.

Beale spent nearly three weeks at Sheffield, but could get very little out of the Queen of Scots, who was in the throes of another bout of illness and complaining volubly both about her health and her harsh treatment. She refused to be specific about her plans until she had been allowed to communicate with James, though she was free with promises to do nothing behind Elizabeth's back—'she could not dissemble, but showed in her face what she meant in her heart.' She wanted no revenge, she said, or any alteration in the state of religion or policy in Scotland. On the contrary, she wished only to serve her good sister, to settle affairs peaceably between their two realms to their mutual advantage, and procure more liberty for herself. As for James, she took him to be 'a natural child that would recognise all duties unto his mother', especially seeing she desired nothing but his benefit. She was anxious that he should not be forced to seek other friendships and 'would have him depend wholly upon the Queen of England.'

Beale went back to London not much wiser, and Mary wrote a long letter to Bernardino de Mendoza telling him about the progress of her efforts to secure James's conversion to the Catholic faith and her earnest desire to bind him entirely to the King of Spain.

Little more of any consequence happened for several months. Elizabeth was occupied with extricating herself from her last French courtship and was, as usual, reluctant to become embroiled in Scottish internal affairs or rather, as reluctant as usual to go to the expense of buying Scottish friendship. Then came the Ruthven Raid which, in November 1582, provoked another very long letter from Mary to Elizabeth rehearsing yet again all the wrongs she had suffered ever since her imprisonment at Lochleven and her impetuous resolve to trust to her cousin's solemn promises of support and 'fly unto you in mine adversity as to a sacred anchor', only to find herself seized, guarded by keepers and shut up in more strongholds.

Now she was debarred from all intercourse with her son, was, as a mother, not only unable to advise him but did not even know what condition he was in. She begged Elizabeth, 'by the near kindred that is betwixt us' to have a serious care for James's safety and went on to beseech that 'I may . . . be restored to my liberty upon reasonable conditions, and may for the small remainder of my life refresh my decayed body somewhere out of England, after so long grief and languishing in prison. So shall you oblige me and mine, and especially my son, unto you for ever.'

There is nothing to indicate that Elizabeth was personally touched by this moving appeal from her 'most sorrowful nearest kinswoman and affectionate sister' or that she responded to Mary's plea for a personal reply, but the following spring she did re-open formal talks about terms for her release. In outline, these were the mixture as before: an undertaking 'to attempt nothing which might be prejudicial to Queen Elizabeth or the realm of England', either directly or indirectly, and to resist 'all such as should any ways attempt the same as public enemies', plus a solemn renunciation of any claim to the English throne during Elizabeth's lifetime—all this to be guaranteed by the usual apparatus of oaths, parliamentary ratifications and hostages.

Mary, still in close consultation with Mendoza, was, again as usual, all compliance, but Mendoza advised her not to seek to go to France—it was no part of Spanish diplomatic strategy that the French should 'get their fingers into the matter' or benefit in any way from the Queen of Scotland's freedom—indeed he urged her to offer to remain in England, so as to be on hand when a Catholic invasion fleet arrived on the coast.

Whether Elizabeth was in earnest or, as Mendoza believed simply 'entertaining' Mary (and France) with words while she pursued her own purposes in Scotland, is a matter of considerable doubt. Rather surprisingly, though, the Queen and her Council do seem to have taken at face value the various highly-coloured reports of James's devotion to his mother being spread by Mary and her friends. James, at sixteen, was still very much of an unknown quantity, but his future attitude would obviously be of vital importance. If he were to follow in his grandfather's footsteps, and if his present rather ominous tendency to hobnob with his French Catholic connections were to develop into an attempt to revive the Auld Alliance, then the consequences for England might well prove disastrous. Elizabeth was therefore being scrupulously careful to keep him informed at every stage of her discussions with Mary, and may have been hoping that some way could be found to induce the Queen of Scots to keep her son within the English Protestant orbit. More plausibly she may have been hoping that James, with his own expectations in mind, could be propositioned into taking over responsibility for his volatile parent. But, although James was not showing a particularly friendly face towards England just then, it soon became distressingly apparent that he was by no means such a dutiful son as had been generally assumed, that he had no desire to share his throne with his mother, and that his chief interest in her affairs was that Elizabeth should go on bearing the odium and expense of keeping her safely out of the way.

Talk of a treaty between the two queens was to continue intermittently for another two years—James did not finally repudiate all idea of the 'association' until the spring of 1585—but the last real hope of reaching a negotiated settlement to the problem of Mary Stewart died in November 1583, when the arrest of Francis Throckmorton gave Francis Walsingham the key to the puzzle which had been worrying him for so long.

The confessions of Francis Throckmorton (a young Catholic kinsman of Sir Nicholas) had to be extracted by torture and did not tell the whole story—the capture of Father Creighton the following year filled in some of the gaps—but they did provide much useful information about the Enterprise, the generic term used among Catholics for the forcible re-conversion of England. From Francis Throckmorton the government's interrogators heard about the Duke of Guise's plans for the landing of an invasion force, to be financed by the Pope and the King of Spain, on the south coast, and the subsequent deposition of Elizabeth and release of Mary. As in the case of the Ridolfi Plot, several members of the crypto-Catholic nobility were implicated—notably Lord Henry Howard, brother of the late Duke of Norfolk—and so, of course, was the Queen of Scots. In February 1584 she wrote to the French ambassador asking him to try and get access to Throckmorton and Henry Howard to assure them that she would never forget their affection for her and their great sufferings in her cause.

Throckmorton himself, who had never been much more than a courier, died on the scaffold, Henry Howard spent a few months in prison, and Don Bernardino de Mendoza, who had been revealed as the chief co-ordinator of the English end of the conspiracy, was declared *persona non grata* and left the country at the end of January in a flurry of mutual umbrage. But yet again it appeared that the bosom serpent would go unscathed, even unscotched. Not that Elizabeth was harbouring any illusions. According to the French ambassador, the mere mention of the name of the Queen of Scots seemed to cause her Majesty great vexation and she told him that if Mary 'had had to do with any other, she should long since not have been living', she had held conference in England with her rebels and 'had set on foot intrigues against her throughout Christendom.' When Mary had the gall to complain about the slow progress of the treaty for her release, she got short shrift. 'If her doings had agreed with her protestation', wrote Elizabeth to Shrewsbury, 'the treaty would long ago have taken issue as she desired', but recent events had shown all too clearly that 'her intention was to lull us into security, that we might the less seek to discover practices at home and abroad'.

To Francis Walsingham one of the most disturbing aspects of the Throckmorton affair had been its revelation of the extent of Mary's correspondence, both at home and abroad, and of the ease with which she was able to send and receive uncensored letters in the large, over-permissive Shrewsbury establishments. The Secretary had for some time been urging that the Queen of Scots should be removed from Shrewsbury's custody, while the earl himself was begging to be relieved of an increasingly 'cumbersome' and thankless burden which was wrecking his health, his private life and his marriage and, so he complained piteously, ruining him financially. Mary had now become heavily involved in a more than usually rancorous Shrewsbury family brawl which threatened to create a public scandal, and it certainly seemed high time for a change.

In view of later developments, it is surely at least possible that Walsingham already had a favoured candidate for the post of turnkey at the back of his mind. But, in the spring of 1584, it was decided to call Sir Ralph Sadler out of retirement to take over on a temporary basis. Sadler arrived at Sheffield towards the end of August with instructions to transfer the Queen of Scots to Wingfield Manor about fifteen miles away, and on 4 September was able to report that his charge was 'well and safely placed, and all other things well as far as I can see.'

The integrity of Ralph Sadler was beyond question, and no one doubted that he would guard Mary loyally and efficiently but, looking at the situation in a wider context, few people would have agreed with him that all was well. Three months earlier, with the alarming disclosures of what has become conveniently known as the Throckmorton Plot still fresh in the public mind, news had come in of the death of William of Orange, gunned down on the steps of his house at Delft. William the Dutchman was the second great Protestant leader to have been assassinated in cold blood by Catholic extremists in a little over ten years. Now only Elizabeth was left, and the question most thinking men were asking themselves was—how much longer could she hope to survive?

The previous October a young Catholic gentleman named Somerville, or Somerfield, had set out for London from Warwickshire with the declared intention of shooting the Queen and seeing her head set on a pole, 'for she was a serpent and a viper'. There is no reason to believe that Somerville was part of any larger scheme and no doubt he was more than a little mad, but that did not make him any the less dangerous, as the twentieth century has every reason to know. Indeed, the danger of a single armed madman or fanatic getting within range for the few seconds necessary to perpetrate a single act of violence was probably far greater than that from all the elaborate, leaky conspiracies being hatched in corners during the early eighties.

If Elizabeth had been assassinated as she processed in state to church on Sunday through the press of sightseers thronging the Presence Chamber, or was driven at walking pace in an open chariot through the crowded city streets, the whole structure of English society would have been destroyed literally at a stroke. There would have been no Parliament—it was automatically dissolved by the sovereign's death—no councillors, no Lords Lieutenant, no judges, magistrates or royal officials of any kind—their commissions all expired with the sovereign. There would, in fact, have been no authority anywhere until the heir at law took possession, and that heir was still the Queen of Scotland.

The Privy Council took this threat so seriously and regarded it as so immediate that they were not prepared to wait for Parliament, and in September 1584 embarked on dramatic measures to try and protect the Queen by making it clear in the strongest possible terms that the Catholic heiress would not survive to enjoy an inheritance seized for her by murder. With this aim in view, an association of 'natural-born subjects of this realm of England' was to be formed, dedicated to avenging with their 'whole powers, bodies and lives' any attempt on the life of their most gracious sovereign lady.

The bond which members of this association were to sign, and which was circulated through the towns and shires that autumn, was a straightforward incitement to lynch law. The signatories, and there were tens of thousands of them, solemnly bound themselves 'in the presence of the everlasting God' not merely never to accept any successor 'by whom or for whom any such detestable act shall be attempted or committed', but also 'to prosecute such person or persons unto death.' In other words, in the event of Elizabeth Tudor's untimely end, Mary Stewart was to be killed out of hand—whether she had been an accessory before the fact or not.

The Bond of Association was a naked appeal to the most primitive instincts of its subscribers—a deliberate statement of intent to meet violence with violence—and had the inevitable effect of hardening and canalising national feeling, so that when Parliament met at the end of November its members found some difficulty in containing their loyalty, their patriotism and their rage. Sir Walter Mildmay hardly needed to remind them that 'by the ministry of this our gracious Queen we have enjoyed peace now full twenty-six years, the like whereof, so long together, hath not been seen in any age.' Nor did he need to chill their blood any further by spelling out the consequences of a Guisard 'sacred enterprise', more details of which had just come to light from documents found in the possession of the Jesuit Father Creighton. Quite as clearly as Sir Walter the House of Commons could visualise the 'devastation of whole countries, sacking, spoiling and burning of cities and towns and villages, murdering of all kind of people without respect of person, age or sex, and so the ruin, subversion and conquest of this noble realm.'

Against this looming horror a double line of defence was planned—first to provide for the Queen's safety, and second to extirpate, once and for all, those 'malicious, raging runagates' the Jesuit and other missionary priests. The passage of the Act for the Queen's Safety soon resolved itself into a struggle between a majority of the Commons, who wanted the Bond of Association to be given the force of law, and the Queen herself, who would not consent that anyone should be punished for the fault of another, or that anything should reach the Statute Book 'that should be repugnant to the Law of God or the Law of Nature . . . or that should not abide the view of the world, as well enemies as friends.'

Ethical considerations apart, Elizabeth was determined not to seem to prejudice the ultimate right of Mary's son to the reversion of the English crown, for, as the Bond of Association was worded, any person who might in any way claim by or from a 'pretended successor' would have been included in the wholesale vendetta. James was already beginning to be regarded as the eventual heir apparent—certainly he so regarded himself—and it would obviously have been unwise to pass legislation which might have the effect of driving him into the arms of the Catholic powers. But the House of Commons, whose feelings towards their Queen are probably best summed up in the words of the member who was moved to exclaim: 'It makes my heart leap for joy to think we have such a jewel. It makes all my joints to tremble for fear when I consider the loss of such a jewel.'—were thinking with their hearts and not their heads. They were obsessed with one basic issue—or rather two closely interrelated issues—how best to protect their 'jewel', and how best to protect themselves if they should lose her.

An acceptable compromise still had to be reached when, in February 1585, came further shock horror revelations in the shape of the 'Parry Plot'. William Parry, Doctor at Law and denizen of that strange twilight world of rogues and mountebanks which formed the reverse side of Elizabethan high society, was accused of having planned to collect a party of horsemen 'to set upon the Queen as she rode abroad to take the air and to kill her.' Parry himself insisted that, far from meaning harm to her Majesty, he had been trying to uncover dangerous designs against her life. He had at one time been employed by Lord Burghley as a secret agent and during the course of his duties had made contact with Thomas Morgan, one of Mary Stewart's agents in Paris, who, so he said, had suggested to him that he might undertake the murder of Elizabeth. Parry had returned to England in 1584 and at once made a full report to the Queen, who heard him 'without being daunted' and proceeded to grant him various marks of favour.

In 1585, however, he was no longer in the government service and may have been engaging in a spot of private enterprise in the hope of collecting a reward (he was, like most of his kind, chronically short of cash), or he may have changed sides for the same motive and, as Holinshed's Chronicle grimly suggests, have been practising 'at sundry times to have executed his most devilish purpose and determination; yet covering the same so much as in him lay with a veil and pretence of great loyalty unto her Majesty.' Not the least alarming disclosure of the affair was a letter written to Parry by the Cardinal of Como and produced in evidence at his trial, in which the Papal secretary offered the blessing of Pope Gregory XIII, plenary indulgence and comprehensive good wishes for the success of his 'most holy and honourable purposes.'

Although this most recent scare had still further inflamed public opinion and raised the already feverish temperature of the House of Commons to near delirium, it in no way modified the Queen's refusal to be stampeded into allowing the law of the jungle to become the law of England. Elizabeth had strong feelings about the observance of proper decorum in the public conduct of affairs, and knew that by legalising murder she would achieve nothing except to advertise her insecurity to the world—no Act of Parliament, however draconian, was ever going to deter the kind of mentality set on winning the halo of a tyrannicide.

Neither would she have anything to do with proposals—painstakingly drafted by Lord Burghley—providing for an Interregnum in case of her sudden death and including provision for a sovereign parliament, a revolutionary concept which frankly revolted the Queen. Again, as her coolly sceptical mind would have told her, no such proposals, however painstaking, would have the slightest hope of averting a religious civil war if she died before the Catholic heiress.

The Act for the Queen's Safety, as finally passed, was a much emasculated version of the notorious Bond. In the event of invasion, rebellion or plot against the state, a panel of commissioners, privy councillors and others, was empowered to hold an enquiry into the facts. Then, and only then, might the members of the Association pursue and wreak vengeance upon any person judged by the commissioners to have been privy to such an outrage. In the event of a successful attempt on the Queen's life, the 'pretended successor', unnamed but no prizes offered for guessing her identity, was to be declared disabled. The heirs of such a successor were exempted from the provisions of the Act, unless of course also adjudged 'assenting and privy.' There would be no Interregnum, no Grand Council or sovereign parliament, nothing, in fact, to prevent the country from sliding into anarchy and darkness.

Unquestionably Elizabeth knew the risk she was running, both for herself and for England; that if an assassin's bullet were to find her while Mary Stewart still lived, she would leave behind a reputation for criminal negligence which nothing could ever erase. But, as so often in the past, she preferred to back her own judgement, her own instinctive flair and feminine intuition, against all the sound, logical masculine advice being pressed upon her. Stubbornly she preferred to trust in God, or Providence, to hope to ride out the storm, to gamble on survival. And, as so often in the past, events, or luck, were to prove her judgement, or instinct, a better guide than the best and most logical advice available.

The Act for the Queen's Safety served its purpose. It gave a respectable legal framework for the subsequent proceedings against the Queen of Scots. It did nothing to hinder the eventual, peaceful succession of James and helped to keep him quiet in the meantime. In 1585 it had needed a strong head not to succumb to the prevailing atmosphere of panic and prejudice, but, fortunately for her own and England's reputation among the nations and before posterity, Elizabeth Tudor possessed the necessary courage, self-confidence and common sense to resist the pressure of emotional blackmail. When, many years before, she had told another obstreperous House of Commons: 'I will never by violence be constrained to do anything', she had meant exactly what she said.

XI

If We Were But Two Milkmaids . . .

No one suggested that Mary Stewart had been involved in the dubious activities of Dr William Parry, and she had hastened to denounce him as a detestable wretch and to congratulate the Queen her good sister on having so happily discovered his hateful design. Nevertheless, her general attitude towards Elizabeth was one of increasingly bitter animosity. In the early spring of 1584 this had found expression in the famous 'scandal' letter, in which the Queen of Scots, under the guise of passing on slanderous gossip being retailed by Lady Shrewsbury, accused the Queen of England, among other things, of being a raging nymphomaniac and such a monster of vanity that she did not see when her courtiers were openly laughing at her. This letter was apparently never sent, at least there is nothing to indicate that Elizabeth ever saw it, but when William Waad, one of the Clerks of the Council, visited Sheffield in April of that year, he reported that Mary had broken out into angry complaints of her hard usage, how 'she was grown old in prison, her legs scant able to bear her, her health impaired, her honour defamed, that nobody durst pity her estate.'

Waad was tactless enough to speak of his sovereign's mercy, which provoked another outburst. The Queen of Scots 'entered into extreme choler . . . saying that she was an absolute Prince as well as her majesty, and not her inferior, born from her cradle to be a Queen . . . that there was mercy in her majesty towards her subjects, towards her all extremity, and that she did not maintain the rebels of other Princes against their sovereigns as the Queen my mistress did.'

Mary's bitterness was very understandable, especially at a time when she was having to face the grim truth that her son was preparing to sell her down the river, but it did her no good with Elizabeth and in January 1585 she was taken back to dreaded Tutbury where, she declared, she found herself even worse off than she had ever

previously been—and that was before she had met her new keeper. Sir
Amyas Paulet was no great nobleman, though he was accustomed to
moving in high society, having done a tour of duty as the Queen's
ambassador in France. He was also a close and trusted friend of
Francis Walsingham and well known to share the Secretary of State's
strict Puritanical principles. He treated Mary with scrupulous respect
but, like John Knox before him, was immune to her famous charm and
under his stern regime the last shreds of face-saving pretence that the
Queen of Scots was anything other than a political prisoner rapidly
disappeared.

Paulet took over in April and began as he meant to go on, telling
Mary that he would not be diverted from his duty by 'hope of gain,
fear of loss, or for any other respect whatsoever.' He told Francis
Walsingham that: 'Whereas it hath pleased her Majesty to commit
unto me the charge, as well as the safe keeping of this Queen, I will
never ask pardon if she depart out of my hands by any treacherous
slight or cunning device. . . . My conscience beareth me witness', he
went on, 'and my doing I hope shall testify for me, that as I have been
very careful and curious to perform every syllable contained in my
instructions with all preciseness and severity, so I have done all my
endeavour to make these people and their friends to know that if it
were possible I would not be deceived by them.'

His instructions had been drafted by Walsingham personally and
were extremely detailed. There was to be no communication between
Mary's household (which still numbered over forty) and Paulet's
own, except in his presence; none of Mary's servants were to leave the
house without a guard; no strangers were to be admitted on any
pretext whatever, and special attention was to be paid to the comings
and goings of 'laundresses, coachmen and the like.' The laundresses,
three in number, lodged in a little house in the park, caused Sir Amyas
a certain amount of concern. He could hardly prevent them from
going to Mary's chamber to collect her washing, and it was true, as he
admitted delicately, that such intimate feminine matters might
sometimes require 'conference as were not meet to be uttered in the
presence of soldiers.' It was all very tiresome, for who could tell what
a laundress might be concealing about her ample person, and 'to make
narrow search of these clothes at the gate, as it cannot be comely, so it
will be as little profitable, unless the women be also stripped to their
smocks.' All the same, he had reformed a number of abuses of
possibly dangerous consequences and, he wrote, 'experience doth

inform me daily of other such new faults as might carry great peril, which I omit not to redress by little and little as I may.'

Throughout the spring and summer of 1585 Walsingham and Paulet were engaged in methodically stopping the earths. Mary's official correspondence with the French ambassador was now quite openly read by Paulet before it was delivered, and in September she was informed that in future any packets she wished to send to France must be given to her gaolers, instead of being forwarded direct to the French embassy. By this time, the Secretary of State felt pretty confident that he had achieved his objective of isolating the Queen of Scots from her undesirable friends. In December, Mary, at her own urgent and repeated request had been moved from the cold dreariness of Tutbury and installed at the nearby Chartley Manor where, to Paulet's relief, the washerwomen could be accommodated inside the house itself. Now, he reported happily, it was impossible for a piece of paper as big as his finger to be conveyed without his knowledge. Stage one of the plan had been successfully completed and it was time to put stage two into operation.

In December 1585 a Catholic exile named Gilbert Gifford travelled over from France, entrusted by Thomas Morgan with the task of trying to find a way of evading Paulet's unsleeping vigilance and reopening a secret channel of communication with the Queen of Scots. Gifford was arrested on his arrival at the port of Rye and at once sent up to Walsingham in London. He may or may not have already been in Walsingham's employment—certainly his appearance on the scene at that particular moment looks rather too convenient to have been entirely coincidental. At any rate, he spent some time in conference with the Secretary and, so far as is known, raised no objections when it was suggested that he might care to undertake a mission for the English secret service.

Francis Walsingham, it appeared, was as interested as Thomas Morgan in setting up Mary's private post office again. This time, though, it was to be a supervised private post office. The arrangements discussed between Gifford, Walsingham and Walsingham's confidential assistant, Thomas Phelippes, were ingenious but essentially quite simple. Beer for the household at Chartley was delivered once a week from the town of Burton. With the connivance of the brewer, letters could be carried in and out in a watertight container, a leather bag or box small enough to be inserted into the bung-hole of a beer barrel. Gifford's role was to make himself known to the French ambassador and, having gained his confidence, to collect Mary's personal mail from the embassy, where it arrived by diplomatic bag. He would then pass it over to Thomas Phelippes, an expert linguist and genius with codes. While Phelippes translated and deciphered the letters, Gifford would travel up to Chartley by leisurely stages and wait until the originals were returned to him by Paulet. He would then hand them on to the brewer and the brewer, unknown to Gifford, would take them back to Paulet, who could thus check that nothing had been added to the package, which was then sent in by beer barrel as arranged. The outgoing post would work in reverse order. Gifford came well recommended by Mary's friends abroad. The trap looked foolproof and Walsingham undoubtedly hoped it would prove a death trap.

The first trial delivery was made on 16 January 1586 and went without a hitch. Mary, overjoyed to have made contact once more with the world of intrigue which was her lifeline, and fatally unsuspicious, gave orders that the backlog of clandestine correspondence piling up at the French embassy should be sent on to her as soon as possible. Eighteen years before Francis Knollys had written of the Queen of Scotland, 'she hath courage enough to hold out as long as any foot of hope may be left unto her.' She had not changed.

To start with, the person who did best out this unusual postal service was the brewer from Burton, code-named 'the honest man'. He was, of course, being handsomely paid for his trouble by both parties to the transaction but, as a man of sound business instints, it soon occurred to him to raise the price of his invaluable beer. Paulet considered his demands both unreasonable and peremptory, but was forced to give in to them 'or lose his service.'

Meanwhile, an exceptional amount of overtime was being worked in Walsingham's office as letters, twenty-one packets of them 'great and small', some of which had been waiting nearly two years for delivery, began to emerge from the French ambassador's private coffers. There were letters from the Queen of Scots' agents in the Low Countries, from Thomas Morgan and the Archbishop of Glasgow in Paris, from Charles Paget and Sir Francis Englefield, both prominent figures in the exiled community, from Robert Parsons, now in Spain, from the Duke of Guise and the Duke of Parma, King Philip's commander-in-chief at Brussels. They provided a complete picture of everything Mary's partisans in Europe had been doing and saying on her behalf since the time of the discovery of the

Throckmorton Plot, and for Walsingham were the sort of windfall of which every intelligence chief dreams. But although they filled many gaps in his knowledge and gave him a great deal of interesting information to be filed away for future use, they did not, in general terms, tell him anything that he had not known or guessed already.

By the middle of May, Mary's replies were coming back. In them she made it perfectly clear that she was fully in sympathy with the aims of Queen Elizabeth's enemies and would welcome a Spanish invasion. She asked Charles Paget if he could find out whether the King of Spain did indeed intend 'to set on England', and offered advice about certain preliminary steps which might with advantage be taken in Scotland. To her old friend and fellow conspirator Bernardino de Mendoza, now *en poste* at the Spanish embassy in Paris, she wrote that, considering the lamentable obstinacy of her son in heresy, and foreseeing the irreparable harm which might be done to the Catholic cause if he were to succeed Elizabeth, she had resolved, for the discharge of her conscience, to disinherit him if he did not submit to the Catholic religion before her death and to bequeath her rights in the English succession to the King of Spain, 'praying him on this account to take henceforth into his entire protection both the state and the affairs of this country. . . . Let this be kept secret', she went on, 'foreasmuch as if it came to be revealed, it would mean in France the loss of my dower, in Scotland a complete rupture with my son, and in this country my total ruin and destruction.'

No doubt Walsingham noted these interesting plans for England's future, which provided helpful corroborative evidence about Mary's relations with Spain, but again, in general terms, her letters had not so far told him anything very much that he did not already know or guess. From long experience of his sovereign lady, the Secretary of State knew that the only hope of getting Elizabeth to proceed 'to extremity' against Mary would be by presenting her with incontrovertible proof that the Queen of Scots had brought herself within the scope of the 1585 Act. From long experience of the Queen of Scots, he had little doubt that sooner or later such proof would be forthcoming. Meanwhile, the beer-barrels were providing him with a first-rate listening post at a time when it was more than ever crucial that he should be in a position to know what certain foreign powers were thinking and planning.

During the eighteen months or so in which Mary Stewart had been in quarantine, several significant developments had taken place in the world outside. James of Scotland had finally made up his mind on which side his bread was buttered and signed a treaty of friendship with England, at the same time accepting a pension of £4,000 a year—the most he had been able to wring out of his thrifty cousin. Also on the credit side, though this was not so immediately obvious, Elizabeth's arch-enemy Pope Gregory XIII had died, to be replaced by Sixtus V, who was privately sceptical about the chances of the Holy Enterprise and who disapproved of assassination as a political weapon. In France, too, things had changed. Elizabeth's Frog, the last of her suitors and the last of the Valois princes, was dead and, as Henri III was, for conspicuous reasons, never likely to father a son, the Huguenot leader Henri of Navarre had become heir to the French throne. This was too much for the Duke of Guise, and in January 1585 he had concluded a secret treaty with the King of Spain which ensured that Philip now had nothing to fear from French interference in whatever foreign adventures he might be contemplating. It meant, in fact, that France and Spain had reached the sort of understanding England had most reason to fear—more especially as by the end of the year England and Spain were, to all intents and purposes, at war.

In May, Philip had seized all English shipping in Spanish ports. In August, Elizabeth had at last stepped over the brink, taking the Dutch under her protection and despatching an expeditionary force to the Netherlands. In September, that enthusiastic private entrepreneur Francis Drake was unleashed with instructions to 'annoy the King of Spain' on his own coast as only Drake knew how, before going off to pay another of his unwelcome visits to the Caribbean. By the winter, the King of Spain had become sufficiently annoyed to begin giving serious consideration to a final solution of the English problem, and had instructed his veteran naval commander, the Marquis of Santa Cruz, to draw up detailed estimates of the forces that would be required for such an undertaking.

By the spring of 1586, therefore, the international prospect, as viewed from London, could hardly have looked much bleaker. With the King of France apparently helpless in the hands of the King of Spain's hired bullies, with the King of Spain's army in the Netherlands currently sweeping all before it, England stood alone with nothing but the hard-pressed Dutch and the equally hard-pressed French Huguenots between her and an inexorably advancing Spanish tide, which would soon be lapping the shores of Western

Europe from Gibraltar to the Elbe. It was against this menacing backcloth that the last act of the tragedy of Mary Queen of Scots was to be played out.

At first glance the Babington Plot seemed to bear a close family resemblance to any one of half a dozen other hare-brained schemes cooked up by conspirators more noted for their over-heated imaginations than their grip on reality, and followed the usual pattern—a rising of English Catholics aided and abetted by a foreign invasion force, the release of Mary, removal of Elizabeth and the 'restoration of religion.' Two things, however, gave this particular affair its distinctive character. One was the fact that the assassination as well as the deposition of Elizabeth—'the despatch of the usurping competitor'—was an integral part of the plan from the beginning. (Some conspirators had been less explicit on this point, though, of course, the death of Elizabeth had always been an essential pre-condition for the success of any plot to raise Mary to her throne.) The other fact was that on this occasion, thanks to the increasing efficiency of its secret service, the English government was able to monitor developments from a very early stage.

Mendoza, Thomas Morgan and Charles Paget were all involved to some extent in the scenario, plus the usual supporting cast of exiled malcontents, spies, counter-spies and double agents, but in England the two principals were a priest named John Ballard and Anthony Babington. Both Ballard and Babington were already known to Walsingham, who had begun to keep an eye on their movements before the end of May. Ballard was in the habit of associating with a group of ardent young Catholic gentlemen who hung about the outer fringes of the Court under the leadership of Anthony Babington—a young man of good family with a great deal more money than sense, handsome, charming, conceited and cowardly. He had first made the acquaintance of the Queen of Scots in the days when he had been a page in the Earl of Shrewsbury's household and had since acquired the reputation among her friends in France of being one of her staunchest adherents. He therefore seemed the obvious person to organise the actual rescue operation and act as her liaison officer.

Towards the end of June 1586 Mary received a letter from Thomas Morgan through the beer-barrel post advising her to write a friendly letter to Babington. This she did, and Babington's reply, addressed to his 'dread sovereign lady and Queen', contained a lengthy exposition of the plans currently afoot for her liberation. From Francis

Walsingham's point of view, the most interesting paragraph came
towards the end. 'For the despatch of the usurper', wrote Babington,
'from the obedience of whom we are by the excommunication of her
made free, there be six noble gentlemen all my private friends, who
for the zeal they bear unto the Catholic cause and your majesty's
service will undertake that tragical execution. It resteth that
according to their good deserts and your majesty's bounty their
heroical attempt may be honourably rewarded in them if they escape
with life, or in their posterity and that so much I may be able by your
majesty's authority to assure them.'

This was what Walsingham had been waiting for. Everything now
depended on Mary's reply and Thomas Phelippes was sent up to
Chartley to be on hand to decipher it the moment it emerged from
the beer-barrels. First came a brief acknowledgement with the
promise of more to follow. 'We attend her very heart at the next',
reported Phelippes and on 17 July it came.

It was a very long letter. After warmly commending Babington's
zeal in general terms, the Queen of Scots proceeded to offer the
conspirators some sound practical advice on how 'to ground
substantially this enterprise and bring it to good success.' For
example, they must consider carefully 'what forces as well on foot as
on horse you may raise amongst you all and what captains you shall
appoint for them in every shire . . . what place you esteem fittest to
assemble the principal company of your forces . . . what foreign
forces, as well on horse as foot you require, for how long paid and
munitioned and what ports are fittest for their landing in this realm
. . . by what means do the six gentlemen deliberate to proceed . . .
also the manner of my getting forth of this hold.'

Having worked out their plans in detail, her advice was to make
contact with Bernardino de Mendoza who would 'employ himself
therein most willingly', but Mary was very anxious that there should
be 'no stirring on this side before you be well assured of sufficient
foreign forces' and, above all, that the strictest security should be
observed. 'Take heed of spies and false brethren that are amongst
you, and in any wise keep never any paper about you that in any sort
may do harm.' Failure to take such elementary precautions had been
the downfall of many who had 'heretofore travailed in like occasions'
and Mary, knowing that if anything went wrong this time the
consequences were likely to be disastrous, not only for Babington and
his friends but for herself, was understandably emphatic that there

should be no leaks, that no detail of the preliminary staffwork should be overlooked.

'Affairs being thus prepared', she wrote, 'and forces in readiness both without and within the realm, then shall it be time to set the six gentlemen to work, taking order, upon the accomplishing of their design, I may be suddenly transported out of this place, and that all your forces in the same time be on the field to meet me in tarrying for the arrival of the foreign aid, which then must be hastened with all diligence.'

If this did not sign the 'bosom serpent's' death warrant then nothing would, but Walsingham, in his natural anxiety to make a clean sweep of the conspirators, either instructed or allowed Thomas Phelippes—who included the art of forgery among his other talents—to add a postscript asking for 'the names and qualities of the six gentlemen that are to accomplish the designment' before the letter was sent on to its destination. He thus provided useful ammunition for all those partisans of Mary who were later to insist that she had been framed.

As it happened, it was a waste of effort, for Babington never replied. Already events were slipping out of his precarious control and he contemplated flight. On 2 August Walsingham decided it would be dangerous to wait any longer and warrants were issued for the arrest of Babington and his accomplices. On that same day, Mary, who had been corresponding freely with Mendoza, with Charles Paget, Francis Englefield and Thomas Morgan about the 'designment', wrote again to Mendoza congratulating herself that 'this way [the beer-barrels] thank God, begins to be so safely established that henceforward you will be able, if you please, to write to me on all occasions that you may have.'

A fortnight later the trap was sprung. The Queen of Scots, whose health had improved again in recent months, received an unexpected but welcome invitation to attend a stag hunt in Sir Walter Aston's park at neighbouring Tixall and set out, poor woman, 'hoping to meet some pleasant company' escorted by the omnipresent Amyas Paulet and a retinue which included her secretaries, Claude Nau and Gilbert Curle. On the road, the party was met by a troop of horsemen, the two secretaries were arrested and Mary herself, protesting bitterly, was taken on to Tixall where she remained incommunicado while her rooms at Chartley were searched and her papers confiscated.

The gloves were off at last. 'This lady', reported Paulet, 'finding that her papers were taken away, said in great choler, that two things could not be taken away from her, her English blood and her Catholic religion, which both she would keep until her death, adding further these words, "Some of you will be sorry for it", meaning the taking away of her papers.'

Mary's indignation as, on this occasion, more than equalled by Elizabeth's. 'Let your wicked murderess know', she wrote energetically to Paulet, 'how with hearty sorrow her vile deserts compelleth these orders and bid her from me ask God forgiveness for her treacherous dealings towards her saver of her life many a year, to the intolerable peril of her own.'

The interrogations of Babington and the others were now proceeding. According to William Camden, 'many days were spent in examining of them, who cut one another's throats by their confessions, and discovered the whole truth of the business.' Certainly Babington seemed determined to make a clean breast of it, freely admitting everything, including the murder plot and his correspondence with Mary. The secretaries Nau and Curle also had no hesitation in betraying their mistress. When confronted with a copy of Mary's fatal letter to Babington, they both attested that it was substantially correct. Nau deposed that he had made a fair copy in French from a draft drawn up by Mary, and Curle that he had made an English translation and put it into cipher. And not only the Babington letter. As Curle subsequently explained: 'They did show me her Majesty's letters to my lord Paget, Mr Charles Paget, Sir Francis Englefield and the Spanish ambassador, all penned in my own hand which I could not deny.'

Preparations were now in hand for the trials of the conspirators and, more important, for the next step to be taken against the Queen of Scots. Elizabeth's first outburst of rage had subsided and she was being difficult about a suitable venue. On 8 September Lord Burghley wrote to Walsingham, who was temporarily out of action with a bad leg, 'yesterday the Tower was flatly refused, and instead of Fotheringay, which we thought too far off, Hertford was named . . . and so for a time both liked and misliked for nearness to London. . . . We stick upon Parliament, which her Majesty mislikes to have, but we all persist, to make the burden better borne and the world abroad better satisfied.'

Her Majesty was only too well aware of the mood her faithful

Lords and Commons would be in, and the pressure they would combine to exert upon her. Already she was trying to gain time and look for possible lines of retreat. She made an unsuccessful last minute attempt to have any mention of the Queen of Scots removed from Babington's indictment and insisted there should be no enlargement of Mary's crime and no sharp speeches used against her at the trial. She may have been hoping that public opinion would be satisfied with the execution of the conspirators, who suffered all the horrors of a traitor's death before the end of September, but although the citizens of London celebrated with bonfires, bell-ringing and feasting in the streets, they were not appeased. They knew the wretched Babington was only a side-show, and this time they meant to have the blood of the 'monstrous and huge dragon' herself.

The Queen continued to vacillate over the choice of setting for the final act, but her preference for Fotheringay Castle in Northampton-shire remained. 'How long this determination will last I know not', wrote the much-tried Burghley, 'but I have set it forward.' The determination did last though and Amyas Paulet hastened to instal his prisoner at Fotheringay before Elizabeth, whom Burghley described as being 'as variable as the weather', could change her mind again.

Obsessive care was taken over the wording of the commission and the appointing of the panel of commissioners who were 'to hear the cause', but Elizabeth continued to interfere over details, driving her harassed councillors to near distraction. 'I would to God', snapped Francis Walsingham, 'her Majesty could be content to refer these things to them that can best judge of them, as other Princes do.' Eventually all was ready and the commissioners—thirty-six peers (including Lords Lumley and Montague, both Catholics and known to be sympathetic to Mary), Privy Councillors and judges—assembled at Fotheringay on 11 October. They brought with them the Queen's formal commission and a personal letter from the Queen to her cousin. 'You have in various ways and manners attempted to take my life and to bring my kingdom to destruction by bloodshed' wrote Elizabeth. 'I have never proceeded so harshly against you, but have, on the contrary, protected and maintained you like myself. These treasons will be proved to you and all made manifest. Yet it is my will that you answer the nobles and peers of the kingdom as if I were myself present. I therefore require, charge, and command that you make answer, for I have been well informed of your arrogance. Act plainly without reserve, and you will sooner be able to obtain favour of me.'

In spite of this implied promise, Mary began expectably by refusing to recognise the jurisdiction of the court. She was a sovereign princess. She was not the Queen of England's subject and therefore not bound by English law. It was a nice legal point, but the time for nice legal points had passed. All the same, the commissioners spent the best part of two days patiently trying to induce the Queen of Scots to appear before them, until at last Lord Burghley told her bluntly that if she persisted in her refusal they both could and would proceed without her. It was a curious reversal of the situation of 1568 when Mary had clamoured in vain to be heard. In the end, it seems to have been Christopher Hatton who persuaded her to lay aside the privilege of royal dignity, appear in judgement and show her innocency, lest by avoiding a trial she should draw suspicion upon herself and lay an eternal blot upon her reputation.

The actual trial occupied another two days and was neither more nor less inequitable than any other 16th century treason trial. All the evidence—the letters, the confessions and the sworn statements—were painstakingly rehearsed and Mary defended herself with eloquent dignity, answering 'with a stout courage, "That she knew not Babington; that she never received any letters from him, nor wrote any to him: that she never plotted the destruction of the Queen; and that to prove any such thing, her subscription under her own hand was to be produced."' It would, after all, she pointed out, have been only too easy for someone to have counterfeited her ciphers.

It was perfectly true that, to Walsingham's disappointment, the Queen of Scots' original draft of the letter to Babington had not been found among her papers at Chartley; nor had the original letter itself, forwarded by Phelippes, ever been recovered—the Casket Letters all over again. This time, though, the circumstantial evidence was overwhelming and Mary's cry that she would never 'make shipwreck' of her soul by conspiring the hurt of her dearest sister rang hollow in the ears of the commissioners.

The issue was not in doubt—or was it? Certainly the court would have proceeded to judgement without further ado had its members not been suddenly called back to London by royal command. Francis Walsingham feared the worst. 'I see this wicked creature ordained of

God to punish us for our sins and unthankfulness' he lamented in a letter to the Earl of Leicester.

On 25 October the commissioners re-assembled in the Star Chamber to hear the evidence once more passed solemnly in review, while Nau and Curle were produced to repeat in person the statements previously made in writing. The panel then unanimously pronounced its verdict, finding the Queen of Scotland 'not only accessory and privy to the conspiracy but also an imaginer and compasser of her Majesty's destruction.'

Four days later Parliament met at Westminster. It was an extraordinary session. All normal business went by the board as the Lords and Commons, united as seldom before or since, concentrated their energies on what had become the issue uppermost in everyone's mind—ensuring that the Scottish Queen should 'suffer the due execution of justice, according to her deserts.' Elizabeth had won some notable battles of will with Parliament in the past and could no doubt have won again—when she had made up her mind on a matter of principle she was immovable—but on this occasion her battle was with herself, and that her indecision and distress were both genuine and agonising there can be no question.

She felt no personal malice against Mary, she told a deputation of twenty peers and forty MPs on 12 November. Although her life had been 'full dangerously sought', her strongest feeling was grief that another woman, another Queen and her near kin should have fallen into so great a crime. Even now, if 'we were but two milkmaids with pails upon our arms', with no more depending on the matter but her own life and not the safety and welfare of the nation, she would 'most willingly pardon and remit this offence.'

Two days later she sent a message to the Commons asking if they could suggest any alternative to execution. Again the question was debated and again the decision was unanimous—Mary must die. Still Elizabeth hesitated. What would the world say 'when it shall be spread abroad that for the safety of her life a maiden queen could be content to spill the blood even of her own kinswoman?' And yet, as she told another deputation which had made the journey to Richmond, where she had withdrawn in a deliberate gesture of dissociation from the proceedings at Westminster, and yet—'I am not so void of judgement as not to see mine own peril, nor yet so ignorant as not to know it were in nature a foolish course to cherish a sword to cut mine own throat.'

It was an awesome, unprecedented dilemma, but even now, at this eleventh hour, if Elizabeth could have found a way of keeping Mary alive, she would undoubtedly have done so. For one thing, although the Scottish Queen had come to represent such an intolerable threat to internal security, she also, paradoxically enough, remained England's best protection against attack from abroad. While she lived, Philip of Spain was likely to go on hesitating about launching the much discussed Holy Enterprise against the Protestant island and its anathematized Queen. The success of such an endeavour might well store up treasure in heaven for the Most Catholic King, but he would still be lavishing earthly treasure (always in painfully short supply) on elevating the half-French, half-Guise Mary to the English throne. Once that had been achieved, it was not to be supposed that either she or the Duke of Guise would remain so devoted to Spanish interests and the end result would be the close Anglo-French alliance which the Hapsburg family had laboured for generations to prevent. Once Mary was dead, the situation would look quite different to a King who could, after all, trace his own remote descent from John of Gaunt.

There was French reaction to be considered, too, and, nearer home and more crucial, Scottish reaction. James was making, at least in public, what appeared to be a genuine effort to save his mother's life. In private, though, it was pretty plain that anxiety lest her execution should in any way affect his own title to the succession far outweighed considerations of filial piety, and William Camden records that his special envoy, the Master of Gray, 'many times buzzed into the Queen's ear that saying *Mortua non mordet . . .* a dead Woman biteth not.' But James was still only twenty years old and under considerable pressure from a chauvinistic nobility and people who, although they had once only with difficulty been restrained from executing Mary themselves, were now showing every sign of outrage that the English should presume to usurp their privilege.

Meanwhile time was running out. It was more than a month since sentence had been passed on Mary and still it had not even been published, as required by the 1585 Act. The second parliamentary delegation to Richmond had been dismissed with a classic 'answer-answerless' and Elizabeth was talking of a prorogation until March. It looked very much as if she meant to do nothing after all—to try and defuse the situation by a series of endless delays and postponements.

Then, in a sudden flurry of behind-the-scenes activity during the last week of November, the Queen changed her mind again. She agreed to shorten the recess to mid-February and on 4 December, two days after Parliament had risen, finally authorised a proclamation of the sentence under the Great Seal—possibly as a result of persuasion by the Earl of Leicester, who had just returned briefly from the Low Countries.

The news was taken to Fotheringay, and on 19 December Mary sat down to write her last letter to Elizabeth. After affirming her 'constant resolution to suffer death for the maintenance of the Apostolic Roman Catholic Church', she asked to be buried in holy ground in France, near 'the late Queen my mother', begging that her cousin would permit 'free sepulture to this body when the soul is separated, which when united could never obtain liberty to live in peace.' And, she went on, 'because I fear the secret tyranny of those into whose power you have abandoned me, I beg you not to allow me to be executed without your knowledge—not from fear of pain, which I am ready to suffer, but on account of the rumours which would be spread concerning my death if it were not seen by reliable witnesses. It is for this reason that I require that my attendants remain to be spectators of my end in the faith of my Saviour and in the obedience of His Church. . . . In conclusion, I pray the God of Mercy that He will deign to enlighten you by His Holy Spirit and that He will give me grace to die in perfect charity. . . . Do not accuse me of presumption if, on the eve of leaving this world, I remind you that one day you will have to answer for your charge as well as those who are sent before. Your sister and cousin wrongfully imprisoned, Marie, Queen.'

Mary, naturally enough, was now in daily expectation of her death, but Christmas came and went, the New Year came in, the days began to lengthen and still there was no word from London. Towards the end of January a sudden spate of rumours that the Scottish Queen had escaped began to sweep the country, together with other frightening stories that a Spanish fleet had been seen off Milford Haven; that the Scots were over the Border and the northern parts up in rebellion; that the Duke of Guise had landed in Sussex with a strong army; that there was a new conspiracy on foot to kill the Queen and set London on fire—even that the Queen was dead. On 3 February, the Mayor of Exeter, much perplexed by an outbreak of panic in his area, applied to Lord Burghley for guidance, but by this time Elizabeth had at long last signed Mary's death warrant.

Walsingham was ill again and William Davison, the second Secretary, in attendance. As he was about to leave her presence, with the precious document in his hands, the Queen 'fell into some complaint of Sir Amyas Paulet and others that might have eased her of this burden' and gave orders that Walsingham and Davison should write 'to sound his disposition in that behalf.' Her meaning was plain enough. There were other ways for a Queen to die than at the hands of the public executioner.

Meanwhile, Elizabeth's councillors were taking no chances. The warrent had passed the Great Seal with scarcely an hour's delay and two days later was despatched to Fotheringay by the hand of Robert Beale without further reference to her Majesty who, it was agreed, had now done 'as much as in law or reason' could be expected of her.

On 4 February, the Queen called William Davison to her again and told him, smiling, how she had been troubled in the night by a dream that the Scottish Queen was executed, which had put her in such a passion against him that she could have done she knew not what. Davison, uneasily conscious of Mr Beale already on the road, asked her what she meant, and whether 'she had not a resolute meaning to go through with the said execution according to her warrant.' Her reply, as he later recalled it, was yes, confirmed with a vehement oath, but she wanted to know if there had been any word from Paulet.

His letter arrived that night. He would do anything for the Queen, he would die for her any time she liked to say the word, but he would not shed blood without law or warrant. This episode has scandalised many latter day historians, but at the time Elizabeth had good reasons for wanting, if at all possible, to avoid scandalising her fellow monarchs, to whom the idea that one of God's anointed should suffer judicial execution was not only sacrilegious—it set a grimly dangerous precedent. Unfortunately, though, Paulet was a practical man of the world, who knew the rules of this particular game quite as well as did his sovereign lady. Morally, no doubt, he was in the right, but he had signed the Bond of Association as readily as anyone and the Queen had a good deal of justification for her complaints about the 'daintiness' and, as she called it, perjury of all those devoted subjects who, contrary to their Oath of Association, persisted in casting the burden upon herself. Precise fellows, she grumbled, who in words would do great things for her surety, but in deed perform nothing. Probably, though, she had never expected anything else. Like Amyas Paulet, she knew the ways of the world too well.

So, on the morning of Wednesday, 8 February 1587, Mary Stewart went to keep the appointment which had been waiting for her ever since she had sailed from Calais just over a quarter of a century before. She was forty-four now and the glowing, graceful beauty of the young Queen of Scotland had long since vanished. She had put on weight, become round-shouldered, double-chinned and 'lame of her limbs', but that scarcely mattered. All the evidence indicates that the officials in charge at Fotheringay that day were in a state of acute nervous tension, while Mary's serene self-command was total. As Mr Beale, in his capacity of Clerk to the Privy Council, read out Queen Elizabeth's warrant, she seemed calm, even cheerful, and, says one eye-witness, 'listened with so careless a regard as if it had not concerned her at all.' She was ready to play her last scene, secure in the knowledge that every eye in the crowded Great Hall was fixed upon her, aware that to many in the carefully selected audience of some two hundred knights and gentlemen she represented a figure of romance, almost of legend, the Princess in Dolorous Guard for whose sake so many men had died, that some at least of those present in their secret hearts thought of her as rightful Queen of England.

Throughout her life Mary had failed and failed again, but she might yet triumph over the last enemy—by martyrdom she might yet be revenged on the woman who had won every round of their long struggle—her death might rally Catholic Christendom to bring about the destruction of Elizabeth Tudor. If she played her last scene well, then the enigmatic motto she had used in her captivity might yet prove a true prophecy—in her end there might indeed be a beginning. She had been denied the comfort of her own chaplain and scornfully refused the Protestant ministrations of the Dean of Peterborough—the days when she had been prepared to flirt with Anglicanism were long past. 'Trouble not yourself, Mr Dean nor me', she told him, 'for know that I am settled in the ancient Catholic and Roman religion and in defence thereof, by God's grace, I mean to spend my blood.' Her faith had become a weapon now, as, crucifix held high, Mary flung the Latin prayers—familiar from childhood to everyone in her audience over the age of forty—in a kind of defiance at the world which, though it had rejected and imprisoned her and was about to kill her body, had never been able to defeat her restless, indomitable spirit. But her last public prayers were in English, for the peace and unity of Christendom, for the conversion of England, for her son, for the soul of her cousin Elizabeth.

It took two strokes of the axe to kill her, and there was one further ceremony to be performed. But when the executioner stooped for the head to display it to the company, an elaborate auburn wig came away in his hands, and the head itself appeared 'as grey as if she had been three-score and ten years old', the hair cropped close to the skull, the face so altered that none could recognise it.

When the news that the Queen of Scots was dead at last reached London, the citizens rejoiced and gave heart-felt thanks for the lifting of what had grown into an intolerable burden of dread. To them it seemed 'as if a new era had begun in which all men would live in peace.'

Their Queen was less optimistic. At Greenwich the court was plunged into mourning, and it was more than anyone's place was worth to have been seen to rejoice. Despite the pleadings of his colleagues, the unlucky William Davison was committed to the Tower for the crime of having allowed Mary's death warrant to leave his possession and, to the alarm of her friends, Elizabeth was even threatening to hang him out of hand. To King James she wrote: 'I would you knew, though not felt, the extreme dolour which overwhelmeth my mind for that miserable accident which far contrary to my meaning hath befallen.'

Although James's most honest emotion was undoubtedly relief, it is embarrassing for any reigning monarch to see his mother beheaded in a neighbouring realm, and the King of Scots was going to need all the help his good sister and cousin could give him if he was to avoid the unwelcome obligations of family honour. She certainly did her best, and detailed descriptions of her confusion, her rage and her sorrow were hastily circulated to the courts of Europe.

Elizabeth had always been a consummate actress—'a princess who can play any part she pleases'—and there may well have been an element of playacting in the performance which was currently dazzling the public. But it went deeper than that, for it is clear that in the weeks which followed Mary's execution the Queen of England came close to a complete nervous breakdown. Her violent reaction cannot be explained by political considerations alone, any more than it can by personal regrets for the Queen of Scots—theirs had been a duel to the death and both had known it. But while Elizabeth Tudor had no cause to mourn the passing of that daughter of debate who had sown discord in her realm for the past eighteen years and been a nuisance and source of anxiety for longer than that, to one of her background and training there was something inherently atrocious in the very idea of subjecting an anointed queen to the process of earthly trial, and Elizabeth was suffering now in part from the superstitious revulsion of one who had violated a sacred tabu.

And there was something else. Ever since the day when she had first come to her throne to try the unprecedented experiment of a single woman ruling a notoriously turbulent and intransigent nation, all her energies, all the resources of her formidable intellect and subtle, analytical mind had been necessarily devoted to one end—to staying on top in a world dominated by the ambitious, thrustful, impatient male, to preserving her independent judgement and freedom of action, to never allowing herself to be manoeuvred into a position where any man or group of men would be able to say to her 'you must.' So far always she had succeeded by using her own special brand of magic—that artful mixture of authoritarianism, 'I will have here but one mistress and no master', and feminine blandishment, fishing for men's souls with so sweet a bait that no poor fool could escape her network.

But in the matter of the Queen of Scots the magic had not worked. Step by inexorable step Elizabeth had been driven back to the point from which there was no retreat. The trial of the Babington conspirators had made Mary's trial inevitable, and once Mary had been tried and convicted there was no way by which the men who formed the inner circle of power could have let her live. Always in the past this inner circle—Burghley, Leicester, Hatton, even the dour Francis Walsingham—had contrived to keep a toehold in Mary's camp, to find ways of assuring her privately of the reversion of their loyalty were she to succeed Elizabeth in the course of nature. But once they had sat in judgement on her at Fotheringay that road was closed. The Queen of Scots had to die.

Elizabeth knew this—hence her last minute efforts to prevent any mention of Mary at Babington's trial. She also knew that once the warrant had been signed there would be no question that it would at once be executed. But she still realised she had been trapped and seems to have been overcome by an irrational, near hysterical panic—the worst of her wrath being reserved, as is so often the way, for her best friend, good, faithful old Burghley, who remained in black disgrace for several months. Walsingham, too, though he had been fortunate enough—or wise enough—to be off sick during the most critical period, felt the icy wind of royal displeasure. 'If her Majesty could be otherwise served, I know I should not be used' he wrote to Leicester in March.

It was not a comfortable time to be at court—'I think your lordship happy to be absent from these broils', remarked another of Leicester's correspondents. But, as it became apparent that there would be no thunderbolts from Scotland or France, that the skies were not about to fall, that the Queen's authority had not really been impaired, the storm began slowly to abate. William Davison, the official, necessary scapegoat, remained in the Tower until other events had diverted attention from him and was then quietly released. By June, Elizabeth had recovered from her devastating emotional *crise* and made it up with Lord Burghley and at the end of July the coffin containing the mortal remains of the Queen of Scots was at last taken from Fotheringay to be given Christian (Protestant) burial in Peterborough Cathedral near the tomb of Catherine of Aragon, that other tragic queen who, had she been able to bear a living son, might have saved Mary from her deadly inheritance.

The rights and wrongs of the case of the Queen of Scotland have been exhaustively rehearsed over the centuries. But, in truth, Elizabeth Tudor and Mary Stewart were trapped by history in a life and death struggle over which they had very little control—cousins foredoomed to enmity by their blood and birth. The image of Mary as a helpless, hapless victim persistently and wickedly traduced, which she herself promoted enthusiastically during the years of her captivity, dies very hard, but it surely does her less than justice. The Queen of Scots was a 'bonnie fechter' and a lioness of the royal breed. Unhappily, though, her grasp of reality was often as tenuous as that of so many of her partisans, and she was handicapped by a fatal lack of judgement which led her so often to fight the wrong enemies with the wrong weapons at the wrong time. 'The circumstances of her suffering 'tis not my business to relate', observed a 17th century Master of Balliol, 'but the event gives way to this note upon it, viz: How dangerous a thing it is, first to lay claim to a crown and afterwards to fly for succour to the head that wears it.'

That Mary had coveted Elizabeth's crown ever since the days when, as Queen of France, she had quartered the English royal arms on her shield, is not really in question. Just how deeply she was involved in the plots to seize that crown by violence will probably always remain a matter of debate. But by 1587 her 'guilt' or 'innocence' had long ceased to have any relevance. The mere fact of her existence had become insupportable and England, feeling itself threatened by aggression from without and subversion from within, quite simply could no longer contain the rival queen.

After her death the fear of the enemy within the gates began to lose its urgency, for, while the English Catholics could have welcomed the peaceful succession of Mary Stewart with clear consciences, only the lunatic fringe would ever have accepted Philip of Spain as their king, and when the dreaded Armada actually appeared in the English Channel the nation, Catholic and Protestant alike, could unite against a common enemy.

The problem of the succession, too, which had dominated the English political scene for a generation, now at least ceased to be an issue. Although James, like his mother before him, nagged for recognition and like her failed to get it, his claims were never seriously challenged—especially after he married a Protestant princess and began to raise a family. The brutal truth is that the Queen of Scots had served her historical purpose on the June day in 1566 when she gave birth to her son at Edinburgh Castle, and from then on that brilliant, fascinating, dangerous woman was destined to become a mere supernumerary to be discarded or used as it suited the purposes of others. That, perhaps, was the real tragedy of Mary Stewart.

Henry VII = Elizabeth of York
1485–1509

Margaret
= 1. James IV
of Scotland
1488–1513

2. Archibald
Douglas
Earl of Angus

Henry VIII
1509–1547
2. Anne Boleyn

3. Jane Seymour

Mary
= Charles
Brandon
Duke of Suffolk

Frances
= Henry Grey
Duke of Suffolk

= 1. Catherine
of Aragon

James V
of Scotland
1513–1542
= Mary of
Guise

Margaret Douglas
= Matthew Stewart
Earl of Lennox

Mary I
(b. 1516)
1553–1558

Elizabeth I
(b. 1533)
1558–1603

Edward VI
(b. 1537)
1547–1553

Jane Grey
ex. 1554

Katherine Grey
d. 1568

Mary
d. 1578

Mary Queen = Henry Stewart
of Scots   Lord Darnley
1542–1567   d. 1567
ex. 1587

James VI and I
(b. 1566)

English Royal Line

A Note on Sources

There is an enormous and controversial literature both contemporary and modern, covering every aspect of the career of Mary Queen of Scots. *The Enigma of Mary Queen of Scots*, Ian B. Cowan, 1971, provides an illuminating short survey. An almost equally large, if somewhat less controversial, amount of print has been devoted to Elizabeth I and her times.

These notes mention only those works which I have found most useful in writing this book and are not intended to be more than a general guide. For fuller details the interested reader is referred, in the first instance, to the *Bibliography of British History, Tudor Period, 1485-1603* edited by Conyers Read, 1959, but the two most recent full length biographies of the Queens—*Mary Queen of Scots*, Antonia Fraser, 1969, and *Elizabeth I, A Study of Power and Intellect*, Paul Johnson, 1974, also contain detailed notes and bibliographies. For older lives, see *Mary Queen of Scots*, T.F. Henderson, 2 vols., 1905, and *Queen Elizabeth I*, J.E. Neale, 1934. Mary's voluminous correspondence is printed in *Lettres, Instructions et Memoires de Marie Stuart*, Alexandre Labanoff, 7 vols., Paris, 1844; *Lettres de Marie Stuart*, Alexandre Teulet, Paris, 1859 and *Letters of Mary Queen of Scots*, Agnes Strickland, 2 vols., 1843. (A new and definitive edition of Mary's letters would be of great value to students of the period.) Some, though by no means all, of Elizabeth's letters are printed in *The Letters of Queen Elizabeth I*, G.B. Harrison, 1935.

My principal source throughout for this study of the relationship between the cousins has been the *Calendar of State Papers Relating to Scotland and Mary, Queen of Scots*, 1547-1603, 12 vols., ed. J. Bain Edinburgh and Glasgow, 1898-1952 (hereinafter referred to as *C.S.P. Scot.*), supplemented by other calendars and collections of State Papers.

Prologue

There is a full description of Elizabeth's funeral in Vol. 3 of *The Progresses and Public Processions of Queen Elizabeth*, John Nichols, 3 vols., 1823, but see also the *Chronicle* of John Stow, 1605 edition. The reference to the removal of Mary's remains from Peterborough to Westminster is in the 1631 edition of Stow.

Chapter One

The 'fiancels', journey to Scotland and marriage festivities of Margaret Tudor are described in loving detail by John Young, Somerset Herald and his account is printed in Vol. 5 of John Leland's *De Rebus Britannicis Collectanea*, ed. Thomas Hearne, 6 vols., Oxford, 1715. For the description of James IV by Pedro de Ayala, see *Calendar of State Papers, Spanish*, Vol. I, but it is also printed in *Early Travellers in Scotland*, P.H. Brown, 1891. There are dated, but still interesting biographies of Margaret and of her daughter, the Countess of Lennox in Vols. 1 and 2 of Agnes Strickland's *Lives of the Queens of Scotland*, 8 vols., 1850-59. For a modern life, see *The Sisters of Henry VIII*, Hester Chapman, 1969.

Modern biographies of Mary Stewart's parents are—*James V*, Caroline Bingham, 1971 and Rosalind K. Marshall's excellent *Mary of Guise*, 1977. See also vols. 1 and 2 of *Lives of the Queens of Scotland*, Strickland.

A recent survey of Scottish history for this period is *Scotland: James V-James VII*, Gordon Donaldson, Edinburgh, 1965. For two near contemporary views, see *The History of Scotland* by Robert Lindsay of Pitscottie, ed. A.J.G. Mackay 3 vols., Scottish Text Society, 1899-1911, and *The History of Scotland from the Death of James I* . . . by John Leslie, ed. T. Thomson, Bannatyne Club, Edinburgh, 1830.

The detailed course of Anglo-Scottish relations up to 1547 can be followed in the relevant volumes of the monumental *Letters and Papers, Foreign and Domestic, of the Reign of Henry VIII*, ed. Brewer, Gairdner and Brodie, 21 vols., 1862-1932. See especially vols. 16 and 17 for the abortive 'summit meeting' at York and its aftermath, and vols. 18 and 19 for Solway Moss and its immediate aftermath.

For Ralph Sadler's missions of 1540 and 1543 see Vol. 1 of the *State Papers and Letters of Sir Ralph Sadler*, ed. A. Clifford, Edinburgh, 1809.

Chapter II

For the 'Rough Wooing' see Vol. 20 of the *Letters and Papers of Henry VIII*, the Sadler Papers, John Leslie, Lindsay of Pitscottie and *Fragments of Scottish History*, ed. J.G. Dalyell, Edinburgh, 1798.

For two discussions of Henry VIII's much discussed will, see *The Last Will and Testament of Henry VIII*, Lacey Baldwin Smith, Journal of British Studies, 1962 and *The Last Will and Testament of Henry VIII*, Mortimer Levine, 1964.

For Mary Stewart's life in France there is *The Girlhood of Mary Queen of Scots*, Jane T. Stoddart, 1908 and *Mary Queen of Scots from her birth to her flight into England*, D. Hay Fleming, 1897, which provides a valuable guide to and commentary on the sources.

The Girlhood of Queen Elizabeth, F. Mumby, 1909, prints much useful material on Elizabeth as princess in handy form. The Seymour episode is documented in *State Papers of William Cecil, Lord Burghley*, ed. S. Haynes, 1740, and Elizabeth's troubles during her sister's reign can be followed in Vol. 8 of John Foxe's *Acts and Monuments* (commonly known as The Book of Martyrs), ed. Cattley and Townsend, 1837 and the *Papers of Henry Bedingfield*, ed. C.R. Manning, Norfolk and Norwich Archaeologial Society, 1855. See also *Rival Ambassadors at the Court of Queen Mary*, E.H. Harbison, Princeton, N.J., 1940 Vols. 11, 12 and 13 of the *Calendar of State Papers, Spanish*, ed. Gayangos, Hume and Tyler, 1862-1954, and Vols. 6 and 7 of the *Calendar of State Papers, Venetian*, ed. Rawdon Brown, 1864. For Elizabeth's accession, Vol. 4 of Holinshed's *Chronicle*, 1807 edition and the *Diary of Henry Machyn*, ed. J.G. Nichols, Camden Society, 1848.

Chapter III

For Elizabeth's first Parliament and a lucid account of the religious settlement of 1559, see Vol. I of J.E. Neale's classic *Elizabeth I and Her Parliaments*, 1953, also Vol. I of *Calendar of State Papers, Spanish, Elizabeth*, ed. M.A.S. Hume, 4 vols., 1892-9.

Anglo-French relations during the first few years of the reign are documented in *A Full View of the Public Transactions in the Reign of Elizabeth*, Patrick Forbes, 2 vols., 1740 and the *Calendar of State Papers, Foreign, Elizabeth*, ed. J. Stevenson, (1558-65), 1863, but see also *C.S.P. Spanish*.

For Anglo Scottish relations, the *C.S.P. Scot.*, *C.S.P. Foreign* and the Sadler Papers, supplemented by Conyers Read's *Mr Secretary Cecil and Queen Elizabeth*, 1955.

The best general account of the Amy Robsart affair is in *Amye Robsart and the Earl of Leycester*, George Adlard, 1870, but see also *The Death of Amy Robsart*, Ian Aird, English Historical Review, 1956. For foreign reaction to the scandal see *C.S.P. Spanish*, *C.S.P. Foreign* and *Queen Elizabeth and Some Foreigners*, ed. Victor von Klarwill, trans. T.H. Nash, 1928. Two modern studies of the relationship between Elizabeth and Robert Dudley are *Elizabeth and Leicester*, Milton Waldman, 1944 and *Elizabeth and Leicester*, Elizabeth Jenkins, 1961.

Chapter IV

For Mary's first widowhood and her return to Scotland see Nicholas Throckmorton's dispatches printed in *C.S.P. Foreign*, Vols. 3 and 4, the *C.S.P. Scot.* and Fleming's *Mary Queen of Scots*. Much useful material relating to this period is also printed in *Elizabeth and Mary Stuart–the Beginning of the Feud*, F. Mumby, Boston, 1914.

For a short modern account of the unhappy Katherine Grey, see *Two Tudor Portraits*, Hester Chapman, 1960, and William Maitland's account of his first interview with Elizabeth is printed in *A Letter from Mary Queen of Scots to the Duke of Guise*, J.H. Pollen, Scottish Historical Society, 1904.

Chapter V

The uproar following Elizabeth's attack of smallpox is described in *C.S.P. Spanish*, *Elizabeth*, and the Parliament of 1563 in Neale, *Queen Elizabeth and her Parliaments*.

For the Leicester proposal see *C.S.P. Scot.* and James Melville's mission of 1564 is fully described in his own *Memoirs*, ed. Frances Steuart, 1929.

For the Darnley marriage, see *C.S.P. Scot.*, Fleming and Melville.

Chapter VI

For the dramatic events in Scotland during the years 1565/6 the principal source is Vol. 2 of the *C.S.P. Scot.* supplemented by Fleming, James Melville's *Memoirs*, *Memorials of Mary Stewart*, Claude Nau, ed. J. Stevenson, Edinburgh, 1883, Vol. 8 of the *C.S.P.*

Foreign and *The Fall of Mary Stuart*, F. Mumby, 1921, which prints many of the documents.

For the proceedings at Westminster in 1566, see Neale, *Elizabeth I and her Parliaments* and *C.S.P. Spanish, Elizabeth.*

Chapter VII

Controversy over the Darnley murder is still very much alive. To mention two general accounts only—*The Tragedy of Kirk o'Field*, R.H. Mahon, Cambridge, 1930 is pro-Marian, *The Crime of Mary Stuart*, George Malcolm Thomson, 1967 is not.

Many of the documents are printed in *The History of the affairs of Church and State in Scotland*, Robert Keith, ed. J.P. Lawson and J.C. Lyon, 3 vols., Spottiswoode Society, 1844-50 and see also Fleming and Nau *Memorials.*

For Throckmorton's mission see *C.S.P. Scot.* and further comment in *C.S.P. Foreign, C.S.P. Spanish* and Vol. 7 of *C.S.P. Venetian. Maitland of Lethington*, E. Russell, 1912 is also valuable.

Chapter VIII

Mary's own recollections of her flight into England are preserved in Nau's *Memorials*. For the English government's reactions see William Camden's *History of the Renowned and Virtuous Princess Elizabeth*, Selected Chapters ed. W.T. MacCaffrey, Chicago, 1970, *C.S.P. Scot.* and Vol. 2 of *C.S.P. Spanish.*

The First Trial of Mary Queen of Scots, Gordon Donaldson, 1969 provides an invaluable guide to the proceedings at York and Westminster in 1568 as well as a scholarly discussion of the evidence for and against Mary and of the Casket Letters. For the documents see *C.S.P. Scot.* and the *Burghley Papers*, Haynes.

Mary Queen of Scots in Captivity, J.D. Leader, 1880 gives a detailed account of Mary's years in the Earl of Shrewsbury's custody and many of that much-tried nobleman's letters are printed in *Illustrations of British History*, E. Lodge, 3 vols., 1838.

Chapter IX

For the negotiations with Mary in 1569-70 see *C.S.P. Scot.* The machinations of Guerau de Spes can be followed in *C.S.P. Spanish* and the Rising in the North is dealt with in detail in *Memorials of the Rebellion of 1569*, Cuthbert Sharpe, 1840. A modern, Catholic study of the Norfolk-Ridolfi affair is *The Dangerous Queen*, Francis Edwards, 1964, and see also *The Marvellous Chance*, Francis Edwards, 1968. Documents—letters, depositions and confessions are printed in the *Hardwicke State Papers*, 2 vols., 1778, in the *Burghley State Papers*, ed. Haynes and Vol. 2 ed. William Murdin, also in Lodge, *Illustrations*.

The papal bull *Regnans in Excelsis* is printed in *The English Catholics in the Reign of Elizabeth*, J.H. Pollen, 1920. See also *Papists and Puritans*, Patrick McGrath, 1967 and Conyers Read's *Lord Burghley and Queen Elizabeth*, 1960. For foreign policy and the French marriage projects, see *The Complete Ambassador*, ed. Dudley Digges, 1655 and *Mr Secretary Walsingham*, Conyers Read, 3 vols., 1925. For an account of contemporary reaction to the Bartholomew's Day massacre, see John Strype's *Annals of the Reformation*, Oxford, 1824 and Murdin for the plan to send Mary back to Scotland.

Chapter X

For the visits to Buxton, about which there was much anxious correspondence between Shrewsbury and Lord Burghley, see Lodge, Leader and the *C.S.P. Scot.*

Mary's health is discussed in *Mary Queen of Scots: the Daughter of Debate*, Sir A.S. MacNalty, 1960 and in *Porphyria: A Royal Disease*, I. Macalpine and R. Hunter, B.M.A. Publication, 1968.

For the Catholic resurgence in England and the activities of the missionary priests, see *England the Catholic Church under Queen Elizabeth*, A.O. Meyer, trans. J.R. McKee, 1967, also Pollen and McGrath.

For Beale's visit to Sheffield and the negotiations for a 'treaty' with Mary, see Leader and the C.S.P. Scot.

The Lennox-Guise-Throckmorton affair can be followed in Vol. 6 of the *C.S.P. Scot.*, Mendoza's despatches, printed in Vol. 3 of the *C.S.P. Spanish, Elizabeth* and Read's *Mr Secretary Walsingham*. The official account of the Throckmorton Plot is printed in Vol. 3 of the *Harleian Miscellany*.

For the Bond of Association and the Parliament of 1584-5, see Neale's *Elizabeth I and her Parliaments*, Vol. 2. For the Parry Plot, Holinshed's *Chronicle*, Camden's *History* and Read's *Walsingham*.

Chapter XI

The 'scandal' letter is printed in Labanoff and see *C.S.P. Scot.* and Leader for William Waad's visit to Sheffield. For the period immediately following Mary's removal from Shrewsbury's custody, the *Sadler Papers* and *C.S.P. Scot. The Letter Books of Sir Amyas Paulet*, ed. John Morris, 1874, gives a full account of Paulet's stewardship and for the Babington affair see J.H. Pollen's *Mary Queen of Scots and the Babington Plot*, Scottish Hist. Society, 1922, C.S.P. Spanish and Read's *Walsingham*.

For Mary's trial, see the *Hardwicke State Papers*, Vol. 1, *The Bardon Papers*, ed. Conyers Read, Camden Society, 1909 and *C.S.P. Scot.*

For the Parliament of 1586, see Neale, Vol. 2, Read *Lord Burghley* and Camden, plus, of course, the *C.S.P. Scot.*

James's attitude towards his mother's trial and execution is covered in *King James's Secret*, R.S. Rait and A. Cameron, 1927, and for the sad story of William Davison see *Life of William Davison*, N.H. Nicholas, 1823.

Index